The
Fall of
the House of
Borgia

Cesare Borgia. Woodcut from Paolo Giovio, Gli Elogi
*(Basle, 1577), said to be one of the more authentic
of the many, mostly posthumous, representations of Cesare.*

The Fall of the House of Borgia

E. R. Chamberlin

TEMPLE SMITH·LONDON

First published in Great Britain 1974
by Maurice Temple Smith Ltd
37 Great Russell Street, London WC1
Copyright © 1974 E. R. Chamberlin
ISBN 08511 7065 X
Printed in Great Britain by offset lithography by
Billing & Sons Limited, Guildford and London

Contents

Illustrations follow page 132

PROLOGUE	The Princes and the Powers	ix
	The Coming of the Borgia	xvi
1	The Cardinal from Spain	3
2	The Path to the Throne	22
3	The Papal Monarch	48
4	The Court of Rome	69
5	The Dynast	92
6	The French Invasion	119
7	The Rise of Cesare Borgia	142
8	At the Court of France	162
9	Conquest of the Romagna	186
10	Lucrezia	205
11	The Prince	226
12	Lucrezia in Ferrara	247
13	The Duke of Romagna	265
14	The Fall of Cesare Borgia	297
BIBLIOGRAPHY		333
NOTES		339
INDEX		341

THE DESCENDANTS OF ALEXANDER VI (born during his lifetime)

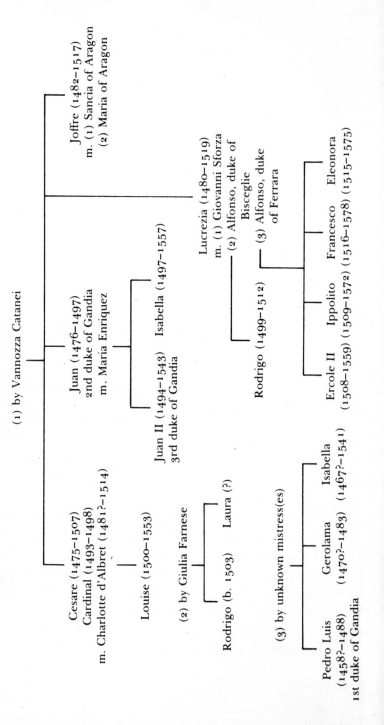

(1) by Vannozza Catanei

Cesare (1475–1507)
Cardinal (1493–1498)
m. Charlotte d'Albret (1481?–1514)

Louise (1500–1553)

Juan (1476–1497)
2nd duke of Gandia
m. Maria Enriquez

Juan II (1494–1543)   Isabella (1497–1557)
3rd duke of Gandia

Joffre (1482–1517)
m. (1) Sancia of Aragon
    (2) Maria of Aragon

Lucrezia (1480–1519)
m. (1) Giovanni Sforza
    (2) Alfonso, duke of
        Bisceglie
    (3) Alfonso, duke
        of Ferrara

Rodrigo (1499–1512)

Ercole II   Ippolito   Francesco   Eleonora
(1508–1559) (1509–1572) (1516–1578) (1515–1575)

(2) by Giulia Farnese

Rodrigo (b. 1503)   Laura (?)

(3) by unknown mistress(es)

Pedro Luis   Gerolama   Isabella
(1458?–1488)   (1470?–1483) (1467?–1541)
1st duke of Gandia

Prologue

THE PRINCES AND THE POWERS

Five powers dominated the land.

In the North, in the heart of the great Lombard plain, lay Milan, a city curiously regular in shape and color, a polygon of rosy brick whose enormous walls protected in the mid-fifteenth century nearly a quarter of a million people—a hardworking, rather dour, rather unimaginative people, physically somewhat taller and fairer than the average Italian. Beyond the walls, another 800,000 people or so looked toward the city as the nucleus of their State. Once, these extramural citizens had belonged to communities as ancient and as fiercely independent as Milan—to Verona and Brescia, to Bergamo, Piacenza, Pavia, Lodi and occasionally some malcontent or scholarly crank would raise the cry of "Freedom" and try to lead a breakaway movement.

But only the young or the foolish paid any

attention. The mature and the sensible—the manufacturers and farmers and merchants who were making their fortunes in a boom period—were perfectly content to exchange a purely notional freedom for stability, to rid themselves of the clangor of partisan violence and settle down to make money under the strong arm of the prince. They no longer even cared that the prince was a usurper, that the line of the gorgeous Sforza dukes of Milan had been founded by a semi-bandit who had had the temerity to seize an empty throne. The Lombards were an eminently practical race, preferring to leave theory to the effervescent Tuscans.

Four days' journey eastward from Milan, beyond the fertile plain, another power, Venice, reared itself improbably from the Adriatic, born of the sea in a blaze of mosaic and gold and marble. Its citizens referred to their republic as the *Serenissima* and it was, indeed, the most serene of all Italian states for it turned its back upon the turbulent peninsula while building up its astonishing maritime empire. But now the Venetians were no longer able to ignore their restless fellow-Italians: new pressures were building up, new goals disclosing themselves, new perils becoming evident in an exciting, heady, dangerous new world. In the East, Islam was rising; behind them, in the West, the rapidly expanding state of Milan posed a sudden threat. Reluctantly and then relentlessly, the Serenissima carved itself a bridgehead on the mainland until, by the 1450s, it was a power on land as well as sea. Venice shared a frontier with Milan—the Lombard plain—which was productive of much future tragedy. The Venetians were well equipped to survive in the dazzling, lethal world of the Renaissance: Trade and warfare with half the known world had not only crammed the treasury of the state, it had also made the citizens tough, subtle, wholly unscrupulous and almost fanatically patriotic. Highly intelligent, highly sophisticated though they were, this short, stocky people speaking their curious, clicking dialect created a society whose members seemed instinctively capable of reacting as a single body, no matter how complex and diverse the problem.

The population of Venice proper was not much more than 100,000, less than half the size of its major rival, Milan, but in times of peril that population moved like a single weapon against the lumbering uncertainty of Milan.

Beyond the Apennines, deep in the heart of Italy among the vineyards and silver glitter of the olive groves of Tuscany, the brown walls of Florence protected about 95,000 people, a fantastically growing wealth, and an uncomfortable ideal. The people were attractive, articulate, the most volatile of a highly volatile race, forever experimenting with ideas, forever coming up with some new political theory that would make an earthly paradise and turning everything upside down to accommodate it. The wealth was symbolized by the florin, the tiny coin of purest gold that was virtually an international currency, so absolute was the faith that all Europe held in the integrity of Florentine merchants. Increasingly, the Florentines were using money to make money, acting as bankers to the world—little enough of the new wealth came from the Florentine "empire." In theory, some 300,000 Tuscans acknowledged Florentine hegemony: in practice, the resentfully subject cities of Pisa, Arezzo, Prato and others cost far more to police than they yielded in tribute. And their possession, too, troubled the more thoughtful Florentines for such subjugation clashed with that disturbing, uncomfortable

but ineradicable Florentine ideal—that each man had the
right to order his own life within the rule of law. Already
there was a prince, a ruler in fact if not in law, but the
Medici rode with a very gentle touch, partly through prudence but partly, too, because they were also Florentines
and "Liberty" was therefore something a little more than
a political catchword.

At the other end of Italy, eighteen days' journey from
Florence, Naples lay in another world. Italian was spoken
here, but an Italian of such inflection and with so curious
a vocabulary that it was scarcely less alien than other European languages to the Italians of the North—even as the
habits and customs of the Neapolitans were foreign to their
fellow countrymen. Like the people who thronged its dark,
tunnel-like streets, the physical heart of the city was an
amalgam of many races. Greek, Roman, Lombard, Saracen,
Norman, Angevin, Aragonese—each had had a hand in
shaping the granite and the basalt and the marble that
made of it the largest city in Western Europe, and each race
supplanted the preceding one by conquest, imposing upon
this city of nearly a million people a wholly alien dynasty so
that, over the centuries, the gap between the native population and the foreign overlords grew ever wider. In consequence, the city lacked any sense of unified identity. It was
unlike the cities of the North where every citizen was aware
of belonging to a single body no matter how bitter and
fratricidal the struggle for power. In Naples, there was no
upward social movement to revivify the stale upper strata,
for there was no means of crossing that gulf between the
vast mass of Neapolitans and a more or less powerful, more
or less sympathetic but always foreign ruling dynasty. An
archaic feudalism still flourished, for in this wild, southern

part of Italy, there were no great cities to challenge the king of Naples. As long as that king was powerful, the pyramidal structure of feudalism bound together the manifold aspects of the South. Of the scores of "kings" which Italy had known since the fall of the Roman Empire, the King of Naples alone survived as both a power and an idea, and for all Italians, the huge tract of land stretching almost from Rome to the southernmost shores of Italy was known simply as *il Regno*—the Kingdom.

The fifth power was Rome.

Rome in the middle of the fifteenth century was a city awakening from a long nightmare. For nearly a century there had been no effective government, for at first the popes had been absent, then they were too deeply embroiled in the Schism to worry about anything except personal survival. As a result, Rome had fallen apart both socially and physically. The city, which had sheltered up to a million people during the days of Augustus, had shrunk to perhaps 25,000 in the 1370s. The great walls remained to mark the extent of its former grandeur, but within them the tiny population pursued a life in what resembled a rural slum. Cattle grazed in the once-sacred Forum and wandered at will down the triumphal avenues; pigs rooted for sustenance where they would; the beautiful gardens became small, inefficient farms while street after street of empty houses decayed, forming breeding grounds for plague or lairs for bandits. Construction ceased, except for the constant patching up of private forts.

During the preceding century, violence had become a casual, accepted fact of everyday life—the macabre Brotherhood of Prayer and Death made its pious rounds at dawn to collect the bodies of men slain in the streets at night. On the political level, too, there was violence. Each great Roman family, headed by a baron, battled for dominance in the leaderless city, and the only check upon the power of a baron was the envy and hatred of his equals. The Roman barons were a species of living fossil, for elsewhere in Italy they had been rendered extinct—in all but name. In the flourishing cities of the North, the nobles had been expelled by a middle class of merchants who had made common cause with the plebs and, with intellect sharpened by commerce, had evolved a system to limit chaos and promote brisk trade. In Florence the nobility was so impotent that it became the standard practice to ennoble a man who made a nuisance of himself, thereby in one stroke disfranchising him.

Pride of ancestry was a dominant Roman characteristic: When young Lorenzo de' Medici married Clarice Orsini both families agreed that he had stepped up in the world even though the Medici were probably Europe's wealthiest family. Some of the clans, such as the Doria from Genoa, were Romans by adoption only; others, like the Colonna, affected to regard even Romans as upstarts and traced their lineage back to the near-mythical Etruscans. Whatever their origins, the families, once established, adopted the rigorous Roman family discipline which had survived for two millennia. The head of the clan was lord absolute with powers of life and death over his sons, his servants, his slaves. The typical family derived its economic power from its great estates in the countryside but its true home was in one of the dark, comfortless, immensely powerful palace-fortresses in Rome where, protected by mercenaries, it created an independent universe of its own. The barons were as much prisoners of their system of violence as the common people were its victims. Food came into the palaces from the family's estates, the corn and wine and oil brought in under heavy guard. The women lived in a kind of harem for fear of their own hired soldiers, while the men ate communally with those same mercenaries in the great hall. The family worshiped as an exclusive group in the chapel attached to the palace; their prisoners were taken down into the extensive private dungeons and the family cardinal—the vital link with the source of all power and wealth—either lodged in the palace or erected his own adjoining it.

Technically, Rome possessed a civil government headed by an officer who bore the ancient and noble title of Prefect. But in 1420, how much the true power had passed into the hands of the pope was made clear when a unified papacy again established itself in its traditional seat and, almost immediately, order began to return to the distracted city. Violence was not eradicated—that would have been an impossible task in any Italian city—but its more motiveless, senseless outbreaks were curbed. The pope was no longer forced to rely upon the dubious loyalty of the Romans to support him in his struggle against Avignon, and he could now afford the luxury of suppressing the more blatantly criminal nobles. Despite his theoretically absolute power he would be at the mercy of the barons if they chose to rise in unison; but like most Italians, they were incapable of unified action and a skillful man could maintain relative peace by threatening one with the other. The city that had once hovered on the edge of extinction again picked up the rhythm of life. Haltingly, painfully at first, but with increasing confidence, the population slowly moved up to about fifty thousand. It was still a small city by Italian standards, but it had recovered.

Milan, Venice, Florence, Naples, Rome—already they were anachronisms in a period when giant nation-states were edging tribalism from the stage. In the South and East a great sultan seemed to be welding Islam into one great pincer around Christendom; to the West, Spain, having crushed its alien Moor, was groping painfully toward unity; to the North, the King of France counted his income and his subjects by the millions; and even England, though temporarily distracted by the Wars of the Roses, was secure behind its bastion of fog and water. Yet all Europe continued to court or oppose these Italian city-states, dazzled —hypnotized—by their glittering past. In Italy itself the power of the five was sufficient only to maintain their position in an embattled and fragmented society, and was based far less on natural wealth or military power than on a complex of intangibles. Many of the lesser states possessed rulers of equal or even greater ability than the rulers of the five, enjoyed incomes as great, matrimonial alliances as brilliant, geographical settings as secure. Nevertheless, all other pretenders to autonomy in Italy survived as best they could by allying themselves with one or another of the five, behaving for all the world like fat sheep engaged in mock battles while the wolves gathered outside.

In 1455 one of the wolves slipped in.

THE COMING OF THE BORGIA

His Excellency Don Alonso y Borja, Archbishop of Valencia, Cardinal of Quattro Coronati, did not appear to be the typical wolf. An aged, pedantic, ailing lawyer, unknown except by a tiny handful of specialists who looked upon him as a sound but highly conservative man, he had reached the time of life when most men contemplate their ultimate end rather than consider embarking on a new career. In 1455, at the age of seventy-seven, his fellow Cardinals in conclave elected him Pope—much to his sour surprise and to the amazement and then the delight of his Spanish kinsman. No matter that it was a purely stopgap election, that his major qualifications were his age and illness: In a single bewildering moment he had, theoretically, been transformed into the most powerful person in the physical universe, holder of the keys of heaven and hell, arbiter of eternity and, rather more important, Lord of Rome.

Borgia—for so the Italians had softened his harsh Spanish name—had come to Italy nearly twenty years earlier, summoned by his master Alfonso, King of Aragon, who was intent upon the conquest of Naples. Organizing conquests of Naples was very much a European tradition and an activity in which lawyers were, on the whole, rather more valuable than soldiers. The key to Naples lay in Rome with a Papacy which claimed to be the suzerain—the ultimate feudal lord—of Naples and for nearly ten years after his arrival in Italy, Borgia trod the rounds of Chancery chambers in quest of that key while his master fought in the open field. Borgia's task was twofold: he had to persuade the Pope that an Aragonese dynasty in Naples would be a more loyal supporter than the French whom the Papacy had always favored; and he had to persuade Alfonso to recognize the rights of the ruling Pope and to ignore the Councils—last echoes of the Schism—which tried to limit the powers of that Pope. Rather remarkably, he succeeded in both apparently contradictory tasks: Alfonso gave him a palace and the Pope gave him a hat, the broad, tasselled, dull crimson hat of the Cardinal, an ugly, ungainly head-piece symbolic of greater power than the beautiful jeweled crown of many a monarch.

The newly made Cardinal took up permanent residence in Rome in 1445. The city was then being prodded out of its squalid sleep by the energetic, scholarly little Pope Nicholas V, a virtuous priest who believed that the human values of the Renaissance could pump fresh life into Christianity. Book-learning was Nicholas's true delight—it was he who founded the Vatican Library and under his influence, genuine scholars edged out the Latin pedants who had ruled dustily in the Vatican Chancery for genera-tions. But it was the physical body of Rome itself—the battered, filthy, time-wearied city—that he intended to turn into a monument to the glory of God and His Vicar on earth. The streets were cleaned, the viler slums demol-ished, the aqueducts cleared of the filth that had choked them for centuries, and foundations were laid for an enor-mous new Palace of the Popes on Vatican Hill.

Cardinal Borgia took little part in all this activity. The passion for antiquity that was the driving impulse of the Renaissance was for him either meaningless or thoroughly suspect. The law was his only interest—the crabbed Latin of the canonists was his music, his literature and his art. Politics, too, passed him by. Alliances and rivalries in Rome were based on family, not national, interests and he, the sole representative of the foreign house of Borgia, had nothing to offer, no part to play in the tightly knit baronial network. He was neither a happy nor a popular man and would, in fact, have thought it a weakness to wish to be either. All his life he had followed an arid path of duty, expecting nothing, hoping for nothing but the satisfaction of duty done. The elegant literary gossips and socialites of Rome ignored him, for there were no pickings to be had in his frugal palace, no patronage to be obtained from an austere Spaniard whose only delight was the study of dreary law. The fact that he unobtrusively devoted a good part of his income to charity was uninteresting both to those who sought purple scandals for the pages of their diaries and those who were genuine scholars and believed that high-ranking prelates should give the lead in learning. Cardinal Alonso Borgia was simply an elderly man of poor health who had climbed high through the skilled exercise of commonplace talents. He was very unlikely to go any higher. He was twenty years older than the reigning Pope, and his colleagues in the College included men of international reputation for learning and sanctity. The laws of probability consigned him to permanent obscurity as one of the thousands of men who had, indeed, moved into the high circles of the Church but who would remain, for posterity, simply a name occurring on a handful of documents.

Yet, when Nicholas V died at the early age of fifty-seven it was the unglamourous Cardinal Borgia who emerged from the ranks of his glittering equals as unique Pope and Supreme Pontiff. It was a common enough phenomenon. The Conclave had merely arrived at a deadlock, fragmented into small parties none of which could hope to dominate, none of which would compromise with the others. By electing an elderly and ailing man, the Cardinals were gambling on the chance that he would live long enough to allow a dominant party to emerge, but die soon enough to allow a member of the Conclave who had elected him to be elected as his successor.

But though Alonso Borgia as Cardinal Borgia had been a sick and retiring old man, Alonso Borgia as Pope Calixtus III seemed to be rejuvenated by the sudden infusion of power—another common result that the conclave ought to have borne in mind. His health was still bad—affairs of state moved from the elegant new audience chambers of the Vatican to the Pope's hushed and shuttered private bedroom—but from that unlikely base the old man not only continued to administer the Church in a manner at least as efficient as his predecessor's, he also attempted to deploy its forces in a wholly new direction. In 1453, just two years before his unexpected election, Constantinople had at last fallen to the Turks. The capture of that city had long been inevitable, but now it demonstrated in the most drastic manner a fact of life that every Spaniard drew in with his mother's milk, that looming behind the squabbling nations of Europe had been a resourceful, courageous, merciless enemy who needed only the right leader to pose a terrible threat to Christendom. Now, under the great Sultan Mahomet II—the sultan who had grieved at the end of Constantinople but who promptly sent his war galleys probing deep into Christian waters, his vanguard deep into Christian lands—Islam at last had the leader that Christianity lacked so gravely.

Until now. For it was as war leader that Calixtus III saw himself.

The task might have intimidated even a young man with skill in arms and experience in European diplomacy. The squabbling nations had to be prodded, cajoled, threatened and bribed until they formed a united front. The massive inertia of the Papacy had to be heaved almost bodily off its comfortably established lines. It seemed to many nothing less than miraculous—or lunatic—that a sick old lawyer could even contemplate such a task. But under the spur of his titanic ideal, this man who had spent all his life in lawyer's chambers, who had handled nothing more lethal than parchment documents, now emerged as the would-be leader of men, the supreme organizing general of an immense military undertaking. The fastidious lawyer still remained, demanding written record for every trans-action. The chief monument of his reign was an immense collection of material documenting this, the last of the Cru-sades. Transcripts of impassioned speeches and sermons, prosaic lists of chandlers' stores, reports from Papal legates abroad, his own official Acts—all these were carefully filed away, bearing testimony to the passion that filled his frail body and enabled him to ignore its pathetic limitations so long as his Crusade triumphed.

It failed. In part, the failure was the result of his own deep-seated coldness, his ingrained austerity which kept the world at arm's length. But in the main, his failure was simply the result of trying to reverse the tide of history. The unity of Christendom was now nothing more than a scho-lar's dream, for Europe was composed of sovereign states each perfectly prepared to make common cause with the Moslem if politics or commerce demanded. Envoy after envoy returned to the Vatican with dismal tales of the in-difference, vaccilation or downright hostility of France, of England, of Spain, Portugal, Germany. And with each rebuff, each disappointment, Calixtus became more sour, less tolerant. His attempt had been noble, his failure hon-orable, but he stirred no sense of admiration, no compassion. Men did not see an aged and lonely figure battling against time, but a nagging, pedantic bureaucrat endlessly demanding the submission of petty accounts, endlessly expecting the impossible and raging when it was not performed.

It was his misfortune that his pontificate should follow the glowing reign of Nicholas V. Suspicious of the new learning with its pagan overtones, frugal by nature, employing every available resource to combat Islam, Calixtus looked on the secular work of his predecessor as frivolous at best. The new buildings of the Vatican Palace remained unfinished, the hunt for classical manuscripts ceased, and the writers took their revenge, laying the foundations of the Borgia legend. Vespasiano da Bisticci, the Florentine bookseller whose gossiping biographies made or broke many a man's reputation, contributed the story of how Calixtus was supposed to have broken up the Vatican Library in a combination of ignorance and avarice:

> When Pope Calixtus began his reign and beheld so many excellent books—five hundred of them resplendent in bindings of crimson velvet with clasps of silver—he wondered greatly, for the old lawyer was used only to books written on linen and stitched together. Instead of praising the wisdom of his predecessor he cried out as he entered the Library, "See now where the treasure of God's Church has gone." Then he began to disperse the books and that which had cost golden florins was sold for a few pence.[1]

So eager was Vespasiano to pillory his victim that he overlooked the inherent contradiction in his narrative: a man like Calixtus was unlikely to accept pence for books

that were worth golden florins. Even though Calixtus undoubtedly did strip many of the books of their gold and
silver bindings in order to finance the Crusade, most of
them remained to form the nucleus of the Vatican Library.
The twisting of his motives was a natural product of the
dislike he was beginning to arouse. It was only a short step
from the accusation that he destroyed the Church's treasure in ignorance to the accusation that he adorned his
relatives with that treasure in prideful and contemptuous
arrogance.

The origins of Calixtus's nepotism were innocent
enough, being nothing more than the natural desire of a
foreigner to surround himself with familiar faces and to
relax in a familiar tongue. Nepotism was, in any case, more
or less forced upon every Pope. His oath of acceptance
bound him not only to maintain the Christian religion but
also to defend the Church's temporal possessions—and
these included the rich Papal States which stretched in a
broad belt diagonally across Italy. An hereditary monarch
faced with such a task would automatically have the support
of his brothers, his sons, his uncles. Not only was a Pope
alone, but the majority of his Cardinals and counselors
were themselves blood relations of the potential despoilers
of the Papal States, their loyalty to family only slightly
modified by the knowledge that they might themselves become Pope one day and be charged with the defense of the
glittering burden. The Pope had to have allies, and the only
allies whose steady loyalty could be counted upon were
those who knew that their power would vanish with that of
their great relative. In his defense, Calixtus could have
pleaded that his Spanish relatives and their retainers were
conspicuous only by being Spanish—Rome had long since

become accustomed to papal court dominated by great Roman or Italian families, with a sprinkling of Frenchmen. Although jealousy of another race initiated the protests, during Calixtus's reign the endemic nepotism became epidemic.

Among the relatives whom Calixtus had left behind in Spain was a favorite, his widowed sister, Isabella, whom he had installed with her children in his archbishop's palace in Valencia when he became Pope. Despite his preoccupations in Italy, despite the fact that he returned to Spain only for the most fleeting of official visits, he acted like a father to her family. In particular, he arranged for the education of Isabella's two sons, Pedro and Rodrigo. Pedro, the elder by a year, would some day inherit his father's small estates and so the only education he needed was the smattering of Latin grammar that a country gentleman ought to have. But Rodrigo was intended to follow his uncle into the Church, and he therefore began that long, drawn-out study of the law which could eventually provide a key to the highest offices.

Isabella hastened to profit from her brother's sudden elevation. In addition to her two sons, both now strapping young men in their early twenties, she had a flock of daughters, each of whom needed dowries on a scale with the family's new importance. Her long residence in the bishop's palace seems to have convinced her that she had a natural right to the treasury of St. Peter—her Spanish piety did nothing to abate her opportunism. Even Calixtus grew irritated by her continual importunities, bursting out that he heard nothing from Spain except requests for money. Nevertheless, dowries were provided and his nieces moved up a notch or two on the social scale in Valencia.

But it was not the gaggle of lovesick girls in which the

Pope was really interested. It was their brothers—the two strong young men who could be a support in his rapidly failing years, whose courage and loyalty could be his shield against a throng of devious enemies—it was toward these that his mind turned, these whom he wanted in person. Pedro and Rodrigo Borgia accordingly took the sea road that led from Valencia to Rome.

Pedro Borgia's career was like that of a rocket—soaring very quickly and flashily to a great height and plunging back, spent, as swiftly. He left behind him only an evanescent memory of cruelty, of arrogance and, what was far more self-destructive in Italy, of stupidity. No one bothered to record any detail of his character or his appearance; posterity knows him only by the disturbances he caused and by the fact that he was Rodrigo's brother.

Rodrigo not only survived, he prospered and in so doing, attracted the attention of the literary gossips. Later, when he strode gorgeously to stage center, there would be a super-abundance of portraits but even in these early years there was an air about the young man which ensured at least passing attention. His tutor in Italy, Gaspare da Veroba, provided an vivid assessment of the young Spaniard:

> He is handsome with a most cheerful countenance and genial bearing. He is gifted with a honeyed and choice eloquence. Beautiful women are attracted to him and are excited by him in an extraordinary manner, more powerfully than iron is attracted by a magnet.

Even without his uncle's backing such a man would go far in Rome; with his backing he picked up effortlessly what other men spent a lifetime working for. At the age of twenty-five he became a Cardinal. A few months later he was made Vice-Chancellor of the Roman Church, responsible for the day-to-day administration of the enormous and venerable institution.

By calling his nephews to Rome Calixtus had acted in an expected and, indeed, approved manner. The Papacy was a dual organization, spiritual and temporal, and it was therefore natural that he should wish to ensure support from both sides. Pedro, the layman, was made Prefect of Rome, Captain-General of the Papal armies and given the lordship of a string of cities in the Papal States, while Rodrigo was given incomes and sinecures to match his high office. All this was to be expected, but from then on, Calixtus seems to have lost control of the situation. His uncritical adulation of his family and compatriots transformed the mild dislike the Romans had held for him at first into a vicious hatred that encompassed him and all his followers.

Xenophobia was not an Italian or even a Roman characteristic. Italians tolerated the naive, uncouth Germans, the more subtle French, the condescending Greeks; Jews found Rome the safest home in Europe. But from the first, a fierce and lasting hatred smoldered between the two related races. To Spaniards, the Italian was the soft, rich predestined victim of a fighting Spanish race; to Italians the Spaniard combined ignorance and arrogance to the ultimate degree. Two centuries earlier Dante Alighieri had dismissed the entire Spanish race in a single, cutting phrase —"the greedy poverty of Catalonia"—and the phrase now received fresh currency, for all who came to Rome in the train of Calixtus III and his nephews were styled Catalans whether they came from Aragon or Castile, from Sicily or Naples. Roman families were shouldered aside as the newcomers grasped the plum jobs in the city and the Curia. Although the total number of Spaniards in Rome was never very great, they were so utterly alien that they would have been conspicuous even if they had acted with restraint. The nobles, with their thin veneer of culture, were barely tolerable: their followers were offensive even to the noses of the Romans: Because the Spaniard associated the taking of baths with Moors and therefore with heresy, uncleanliness became an active virtue, and it was said that if the wind lay in the right quarter, an advancing Spanish force could be detected before it was visible. They ate like animals, bolting their food as though an enemy was just on the horizon. They slept with an indifference to comfort and hygiene that disgusted a people whose wealth had allowed them to develop rules of conduct.

But Romans had learned to tolerate even wilder, even more unpleasant barbarians than these: it was the Spaniards themselves who erected a permanent barrier between the races. Transported from the most austere to the most voluptuous of European countries they reacted at first with pride and contempt for their effete hosts. But when they gave way they crumbled totally: their natural indifference to suffering became a devilish cruelty, their natural vigor became unrestrained lust, their natural pride became unbounded arrogance. The hatred they aroused was kept in check only by a complex balance of forces deriving from the presence of a Spaniard on the papal throne. But as soon as that Pope was dead. . . .

Despite the fact that Rodrigo was showered with fat Church appointments, including his uncle's old archbishopric of Valencia, it was Pedro who received the full force of Roman hatred, partly through his insolent, arrogant manner, partly because he was thrust into the thick of a Roman feud when his uncle made him Prefect. The great family of Orsini had always provided the Prefects of the city and they had come to look upon the office as private property. Now, not only were they thrust aside in favor of a young upstart, they found themselves despoiled and plundered by that same upstart, ostensibly on behalf of the Papacy. They fought back and found that they were not simply fighting a greedy young Spaniard but the Church itself, for Calixtus merely assented to whatever measure Pedro claimed was necessary. It is probable that the old man never intended —and perhaps was never aware of—the degree of power which Pedro exercised. He was, after all, an old and sick man who, in addition to the normal heavy burdens of a Pope, was preoccupied to the point of obsession with his Crusade. He simply dismissed the complaints about Pedro as the expression of jealousy and envy.

Rodrigo proved remarkably level-headed, frequently exercising restraint on his unstable brother. But Pedro completely misjudged the situation in which he found himself. Lacking his brother's insight into the Italian nature, dazzled by the visions of splendor which he believed lay in store for him, he mistook the Italian pliancy for cowardice, the automatic flattery for recognition of his inherent superiority. The flimsy foundations of his position became obvious when Calixtus's health abruptly worsened in July of 1458 and he became so ill that rumor sped around that he was dead. Immediately the Catalans were hunted down in the streets of Rome, an ominous herald of their fate when the old man should at last die. He rallied and the city quieted again; but there were bitter protests when it became known that in his last clarity of mind he had invested

Pedro with Neapolitan cities that had fallen to the Papacy on the death of King Alfonso of Naples.

Calixtus sank again and this time it was clear that he would not recover. The uncertain quiet of Rome was broken and broken with it was the power of Pedro Borgia. Immediately the Sacred College, so obsequious until now, demanded the keys of the fortress of Sant' Angelo. Pedro never lacked courage and he was prepared to hold the castle against all Rome if necessary; but Rodrigo argued him out of an idea that would have been suicidal, advising him to get what he could out of the situation and to leave Rome as swiftly as possible. Deprived of a military base, Pedro's position in the city was hopeless. The Orsini rose, intent on vengeance against the man who had robbed and humiliated them; his official bodyguard, composed mainly of Italians, hated him as cordially as the other Romans did and they abandoned him. On August 6 Pedro and his brother slipped out, disguised, on the road to Ostia where they were supposed to meet a galley laden with treasure. The galley-master, too, had abandoned the fallen Prefect— no galley was there. As best he could Pedro made his way to Civitavecchia where, three weeks later, he was dead of a common fever.

Rodrigo had turned back to Rome a few miles outside the city in the belief that his brother was safe on the way to their native land. In all the turbulent years that lay ahead of him no single act required such cold courage as this return to a city whose mobs were howling for the blood of his kinsmen. He personally was popular; but he was also a Catalan, and the Orsini would have seen no valid distinction between the popular cardinal and the hated Prefect. Still in disguise, he made his way safely through the city to

the Vatican where Calixtus lay in his death agonies, alone
in the shuttered room where he had directed the affairs of
the Roman Church. And there Rodrigo waited until the old
man died.

The Borgia dynasty, it seemed, was at an end scarcely
two years after it had been transplanted on Italian soil.

*The
Fall of
the House of
Borgia*

The
Cardinal
from Spain

1

Late on the evening of August 17, 1458, a group of eighteen men were gathered together, talking desultorily, on the first floor of one of the new buildings of the Vatican Palace. Despite the stifling heat of a Roman summer the windows were boarded over, as they had been for the past twenty-four hours. Through all that period the only light had come from candles—made of pure wax as befitted the station of these men but nevertheless still giving off an odor so that the air was dead.

Arranged around the sides of the low-ceilinged hall were eighteen wooden huts or cells, each furnished with a table, a bed and a stool. These cells, with their meager furnishings, offered each man the only possibility of privacy for a period that might conceivably extend into weeks. For this was a conclave—the cardinals of the Sacred College meeting together to elect a successor to the dead Pope Calixtus and cut off from the world until they did so. Their only connection with that outside world was a heavily guarded wicket gate through which food was passed and empty utensils removed, twice daily. They could, however, hear the outside world—or at least one aspect of it. Below the blind window facing the great basilica of St. Peter was a courtyard and this now echoed to the tramp and metallic clatter of armed men, one of the detachments of the papal guard which patrolled inside and outside the Palace to make sure the sacred deliberations were not disturbed by riot.

The hall with its wooden cells formed the living and recreational area for the conclavists. Leading off it was another, smaller chamber furnished with eighteen cardinal's stalls, each with its high-backed wooden chair and its canopy bearing the arms of its occupant. The vital business of lobbying was pursued in the larger chamber where ever-changing groups formed in this or that corner as now one, now another man won the temporary support of the uncommitted. In the smaller room the effect of the lobbying was put to the supreme test—here a slip of paper bearing a scrawled name would join seventeen other slips of paper in the chalice on the altar facing the stalls.

Among the eighteen men in the large chamber was Aeneas Silvius Piccolomini, Bishop of Siena and one of the candidates for the tiara. He looked like a peasant for he was a thickset man with a heavy, fleshy face which could appear sullen or even stupid. But appearances belied reality: his family, though poor, was one of the noblest in Siena, and behind the commonplace façade was a unique mind, darting, questioning, enlivening all it touched upon. There was, too, a colossal vanity, but a vanity so open, so childish that it was difficult to be offended by it. Traveler, scholar, gossip, diplomat, Piccolomini was essentially a man of his day, even down to the classic names that his parents had bestowed upon him. Curiosity was perhaps his most obvious characteristic and Man, in all his fascinating, exasperating aspects was for him the only study really worthwhile.

Even now, while one half of his mind was engaged in the vital but tedious business of drumming up votes, the other half was engaged in observing, speculating, recording. No one in a position to know had ever before troubled to write an account of a papal election. True, each election had produced a crop of rumors and even written reports, but their authors' audacity and imagination had been equaled only by their ignorance. Never before had a conclavist left a first-hand account of the tortuous negotations, the sudden tantrums, the unpredictable, irrational currents that could suddenly sweep a man toward the supreme goal. He, Aeneas Silvius, intended to write such an account and leave for posterity at least one true record of a conclave and of the men who had made the decisions.

Dominating the group physically was Bessarion the Greek, burly, remote, immensely dignified with the great patriarchal sweep of beard that set him apart as the alien he was. His natural ally was the Russian, Isidore; they spoke in Greek, Aeneas noted, virtually a secret language even among this gathering of learned men. There was no danger from this quarter, he considered; Isidore was unknown and Bessarion, though an honorable man and possessed of great prestige, was fatally hampered by his nationality. The same consideration applied to that other group of men who were speaking a language that had been heard only too much in Rome recently: that harsh Catalan which sounded, to Piccolomini's Tuscan ears, like the barking of dogs.

There were four in this group: young Rodrigo Borgia, plump, affable, watchful with his cousin Luis in his shadow as usual; and two quieter, older men whose names Piccolomini could never quite remember. Not one of them represented a challenge to him but each had a vote. Would they support foreigners, or Italians?

The Italians outnumbered all other nationalities but were split up in little, bitterly opposed groups. Pietro Barbo, the Venetian, had a couple of supporters: He had been a merchant and it was said that he had precipitately abandoned his career for the Church when his uncle became pope a few years back—a typically Venetian move and a prosperous one. There was Calandrini of Bologna, a quiet, modest man with considerable influence, for he had been the half-brother of the brilliant Pope Nicholas V and the dead man's mantle was still upon him. There were, of course, cardinals from the Orsini and Colonna families, pointedly ignoring each other. It was inconceivable that a papal election could take place without representatives from these two families appearing to complicate an already complex business with their tribal hatreds. And the French. Alain of Avignon was a windbag, but Estouteville of Rouen represented the greatest challenge of all, Piccolomini considered. A hatchet-faced man with thin lips that seemed set in a permanent sneer, an aristocrat from the tips of his slender bejeweled fingers to the exquisite set of the robe around his neck. Fabulously wealthy, totally unscrupulous, he had already made a scathing personal attack upon Piccolomini, mocking his poverty, his scholarship, even his physical disability. "What is Aeneas to you that you think him fit for the pontificate? Will you give us a pope lame in both feet and poor? How will he who is sick cure our sickness? Shall we put a poet in Peter's place?" The cruelty of the attack was equaled only by the crudeness, the unblushing appeal to the basest instincts, with which he had put forward his own claim to the tiara. "I am the senior cardinal. Royal blood flows in my veins. I am rich in friends and money. I have many benefices which, when I resign them, I will divide among you and others."[2] The defeat of this arrogant man would give Piccolomini intense pleasure even if he himself should fail to win the tiara.

But such a defeat seemed increasingly unlikely. On this, the second day of the conclave, matters had proceeded to their almost inevitable deadlock with each of the tiny groups pulling its different way. Shortly after midnight, however, support seemed to gather for Estouteville. "A number of cardinals, seeking a private place," Piccolomini wrote, "met in the latrines and agreed together that they should elect Estouteville pope and bound themselves with signatures and oaths. Relying on them, he straightaway began promising priesthoods, magistracies and offices and divided his provinces among them. A worthy setting for the choice of such a pope!"

One more vote was needed and Calandrini tried to persuade Piccolomini to vote for the favorite, pointing out how dangerous it would be to have the new pope as an enemy. Piccolomini declined and, after an argument, went off in search of Rodrigo Borgia. He found the young man sitting pensive in his cell. Borgia was less than half Piccolomini's age and had been a cardinal for scarcely two years; nevertheless, as vice-chancellor, he held the highest office among the eighteen men. He had excellent reason to be pensive, however, for even his limited experience of affairs told him how easily the favorite of one reign could be stripped of all he possessed in the next. He shrugged when Piccolomini demanded to know whether he had sold himself to Estouteville. "What would you have me do? The thing is settled. Many of the cardinals have met in the latrines and decided to elect him. It is not to my advantage to remain with a small minority out of favor with the new pope. I am joining the majority and I have looked out for my own interests. I shall not lose the chancellorship—I have a note from Estouteville assuring me of that. If I do not vote for him the others will elect him anyway and I shall be stripped of my office."

Piccolomini exploded. "You young fool! Will you then put an enemy of your nation in the Apostle's chair? And will you put your faith in the note of a man who is faithless? You will have the note, and Alain of Avignon will have the chancellorship. Will a Frenchman be more friendly to a Frenchman or a Catalan? Take care, you inexperienced boy! Take care, you fool."

Piccolomini's vigorous argument seemed to have some effect, at least enough for Borgia to promise his support during the next ballot. This took place in the morning, after the conclavists had had a few hours' sleep. Estouteville, who was acting as teller, attempted trickery and announced that Piccolomini had only eight votes. "The rest said nothing about another man's loss," as Piccolomini remarked drily in his lively record and he insisted on a recount. He had, in fact, received nine votes, the highest that morning but still not sufficient to break the deadlock, so the conclave decided on "accession," the spontaneous announcing of the candidate favored by each person present. Nothing happened. Each man sat in a heavy silence, waiting for the other to make the first move. "It was a strange silence and a strange sight, men sitting there like their own statues. No sound was to be heard, no movement seen. Then Rodrigo, the vice-chancellor, rose and said 'I accede to the cardinal of Siena,' an utterance which was like a dagger in Estouteville's heart, so pale did he turn." Others followed, if reluctantly. Some withdrew from the conclave on the pretense of physical needs, hoping either to bring this session to a close or waiting to see which way the majority would move. But by mid-morning Piccolomini's election was assured, very largely through Rodrigo Borgia's ability to assess a trend and act swiftly upon his judgment. It was an impressive debut for a young man of twenty-seven; more important, it ensured his political survival, for gratitude was one of Aeneas Silvius Piccolomini's outstanding virtues.

That first conclave was very nearly the most important of Borgia's long career, for it marked the moment when he ceased to be the favored nephew of a reigning pope and was thrown entirely on his own resources. He had survived. He had turned the potential destroyer into a grateful patron. The new pope—who took the name Pius II—confirmed him in the office of vice-chancellor. The gesture was partly one of friendship, for a curious intimacy, almost that of father and son, had sprung up between the two dissimilar men, the one grizzled in the ways of the world, deeply pious, much traveled, the other with the buoyant confidence of youth, from a world limited to provincial Spain and the brown walls of Rome, with a piety satisfied by the gorgeous outer forms of religion. In part, the granting of the office was a natural reward for the young man's timely support. But it was also a public demonstration of Pius's belief that "Rodrigo was an extraordinarily able man." Pius was plagued by the usual swarms of place-hunting relatives and he had every personal reason to follow precedent and distribute high office among them—including that of vice-chancellor. The fact that he did not do so was clear evidence that the young man could maintain by his own merits what he had gained by good fortune.

Pius had an eye for everyone and everything within his orbit and, with his itch to record what he saw and felt, he snatched time from the endless pressure of affairs to keep that voluminous, lively diary of his. It is only through this diary that posterity is able to catch a glimpse of the young Spanish cardinal, as cautiously, discreetly, he worked himself into Roman society. The gossiping writers of Rome saw no particular reason to refer to him—his conduct was demonstrably normal (if it had not been they would have regaled the world with accounts of his doings); he held an important position but he was still young and there was no guarantee that he would continue to hold that position in the whirligig of Rome; and his family was obscure. So they ignored him. But fortunately Pius's bright, speculative eyes frequently fell on his young colleague and his pen contributed to the slowly emerging picture of a most unusual man.

Pius saw Borgia as a hardworking, good-humored man who made friends easily, enjoyed life enormously but usually took care to conform to the relatively puritanical standards established by the pope. He seemed, like his uncle before him, to have little interest in the speculative ferment of his day. Highly intelligent, he was essentially a pragmatist, using his intellectual abilities for strictly practical ends.

But he delighted in display and possessed a talent for organizing those flamboyant religious spectacles, such as the Corpus Christi pageants, that were becoming increasingly part of social life.

Wherever Pius went, Borgia went with him, and that was no simple matter, for the pope crossed and recrossed Italy in his ultimately futile attempt to stir Italians to Crusade. Borgia's loyalty, whether calculated or spontaneous, involved much hard riding, many uncomfortable quarters and peasant meals taken by roadside. Pius genuinely preferred simple meals—bread and cheese, fruit and wine—to an elaborate banquet in some nobleman's palace. Unlike most cardinals, Rodrigo shared the pope's indifference to food and physical comfort. It was one of the last traces, perhaps, of his Spanish origin and it proved very useful now.

Sometimes he made a tactical mistake. One night during a violent storm at Ostia he, with other senior members of the Curia, had been lodged comfortably in the bishop's palace while the servants had been obliged to camp out. During the night a hurricane arose and destroyed their tents. They fled, "but in the dark they could not see their way," Pius recorded compassionately.

> The force of the rain drove them naked among the thistles which grew thick in that place and they were wounded by the sharp spikes. Covered with blood, stiff and almost stupefied by the cold they at last reached Cardinal Borgia who was lying in the palace terrified by the storm. And when he saw that his people had abandoned the tents and arrived naked, he inquired not whether they were safe but where they had put his money.[3]

Pius's affection for his protégé did not blind him to certain obvious flaws in the young man's character and when it came to his ears that Borgia and Estouteville—of all people—had taken part in an orgy in Siena he fired off a blistering letter that must have left Borgia a very thoughtful man. As Pius heard the story, Borgia and Estouteville, "whose age alone ought to have recalled him to his duty," had locked themselves up for several hours with a number of noble but lighthearted ladies of Siena. "Shame forbids mention of all that took place—not only the acts themselves but their very names are unworthy of your position. In order that your lusts might be given free rein the husbands, brothers and kinsmen of the young women were not admitted. All Siena is talking about this orgy. Our displeasure is beyond words."[4] Pius was relying on hearsay and certainly there were sufficient ambiguities about the report—in particular why the touchy noblemen of Siena should tamely stand by while two foreigners debauched their womenfolk —so that Pius could accept Borgia's protestations that the whole thing had been exaggerated, together with his promises of good behavior in the future.

Borgia never made quite that mistake again during his patron's pontificate and Pius continued to regard him not merely with approval but with active admiration.

Pius recorded a description of Borgia's new palace, probably the first description of a Renaissance palace in Rome. Borgia's motive in building was not merely a desire for the grandiose; he had set out to make himself a Roman and the first essential was a base. Native Roman cardinals had an immense advantage over their non-Roman colleagues for they could retire to the family fortress in the frequent moments of crisis and defy the world for as long as need be. In the past there had been little incentive for "foreign" cardinals to go to the trouble and expense of building, for the popes were very rarely in Rome, preferring to travel on an endless circuit through the safer, pleasanter, healthier cities of the Papal States. But as normality returned and the court settled at last in its ancient home the non-Romans realized the need for a permanent home. Pietro Barbo had already begun his own palace, selecting a site below the mournfully deserted Capitoline Hill. There he laid the foundations of that enormous Palazzo Venezia which, in the twentieth century, was to provide an appropriately grandiloquent headquarters for Mussolini. Borgia preferred a site closer to hand, in the fast growing region just across the river from the Vatican. He built to a smaller scale, but just as well as Barbo did, for his palace also survived into the twentieth century.

On Palm Sunday 1462 Pius headed a great procession past that palace when the head of St. Andrew was brought to Rome. Emotionally he described the scenes of penitence and religious fervor as the priceless relic was carried through the streets of Rome—but he had an eye, too, for the splendors of the decorations on the processional way.

All the cardinals who lived along the route had decorated their houses magnificently . . . but all were outstripped in expense and effort and ingenuity by Rodrigo, the vice-chancellor. His huge, towering house, which he had built on the site of the old mint, was covered with rich and wonderful tapestries, and besides this he had raised a lofty canopy from which were suspended many and various marvels. He had decorated not only his own house but those nearby, so that the square all about them seemed a kind of park full of sweet songs and sounds, or a great palace gleaming with gold such as they say Nero's palace was.[5]

Borgia had bought the site from his uncle only a few months before the old man's death in 1458. The site lay deep in Orsini territory, almost under the shadow of the main Orsini stronghold on Monte Giordano and, considering that the Orsini were hunting his brother to death while the palace's foundation was being laid, Rodrigo's decision to build there might have seemed foolhardy, to say that least. But it was an expression of his immense confidence in his ability to flourish no matter what vicissitudes the Borgia family encountered, and this confidence was well-founded, for the great building was complete when Pius noticed it on that Palm Sunday only four years later.

The style of the building was transitional, reflecting the style of Rome itself as it passed reluctantly from medieval squalor to Renaissance splendor. It was as much castle as palace, a massive structure designed to withstand siege as well as provide a home, but the interior was most splendidly furnished. Cardinal Ascanio Sforza visited it in October 1484 and sent a description of it to his brother Ludovico, the magnificent lord of Milan who was ever eager to hear of any magnificences that might rival his own. Ascanio was impressed by the priceless tapestries and carpets —particularly the latter. They were still rare in Rome and yet here they were not only scattered in abundance but actually matched the furniture and decorations. In a small room leading off the great central hall Ascanio noticed "a couch with a canopy all upholstered in crimson satin, and a beautifully carved cupboard full of vases of gold and silver as well as an enormous quantity of plate all very beautiful to see."[6] Exploring further he found two more rooms, even more ornately decorated with satin hangings. Each had its own great couch or divan for ceremonial audiences, one upholstered in velvet, the other in a richly decorated cloth of gold.

The overall impression conveyed by Sforza's description is of a desire to display wealth rather than taste. If there had been anything worthy of note Ascanio would have remarked it. The other new palaces in Rome were already bearing the imprint of the Renaissance intellect as expressed through the work of its artists. In the new Borgia palace there seemed to be nothing but a profusion of objects—precious plate, expensive but gaudy hangings and upholsteries—thrown together without underlying plan. The palace did indeed seem to express the personality of its owner—rich, gaudy, durable.

That was precisely what impressed the Romans: They liked life the way they liked their food—highly spiced, rich, unsubtle—and the foreign Rodrigo Borgia more clearly divined, more faithfully reflected, the nature of that anonymous Roman populace than many a native Roman. At every major public festival the exterior of his house was decorated like a theater; free wine was in abundance and the square outside became a major attraction for the idle, the curious and the thirsty. At one time or another one could see splendid, if obscure, allegories performed here with kings and angels and demons jostling and weaving amid a rain of fireworks. Here were jousts and fights with animals —even, on one occasion, a lion. When Granada fell to his compatriots, the cardinal from Spain proudly put on a peculiarly Spanish performance—a bullfight. The beast killed two members of the crowd and badly injured others before it was despatched, but that, in the eyes of the Romans merely added to the excitement. On special occasions vast, immensely heavy tubes of bronze, richly chased and decorated, were set up in that square for the Romans to wonder at. Tubes like these had yet to be turned against the walls of Rome. Cannon were a delightful novelty, and when the cardinal's Spanish gunners touched off the blank charges the Romans merely shivered deliciously at the appalling bellow, regarding it as just another larger and noisier firework. They had yet to experience the helpless terror as giant stone cannonballs crashed from a hostile heaven.

All together, the square before Cardinal Borgia's palace took over in miniature the role which the ruined Colosseum had once performed, providing ever-changing entertainment for people who seemed incapable of making their own. These inhabitants of the filthy warrens of the city had no vote in the Sacred College, possessed no overt political right of any value whatever—but in their mass they were the Roman people, and he who had the sympathy of the people, even a purchased sympathy, had added significantly to those imponderable values which might, eventually, place the tiara on his head.

Pius died; Barbo ascended the throne; Borgia was confirmed for the second time in his high office. Pietro Barbo was a personal friend of Borgia's but he was no man's fool and certainly would not have allowed friendship to overcome judgment in a matter which vitally affected his well-being as Pope Paul II. He, like Calixtus and Pius before him, like Sixtus and Innocent after him, discerned the core of solid competence behind Borgia's jovial front.

Over a period of thirty-seven years, five popes in turn provided a solid rung for his advancement, five men whose characters covered almost the whole spectrum of human personality but who shared a dominant characteristic. Each was a veteran fighter in the political battles of Italy who very rapidly would have discarded a useless political tool, particularly an inherited one. Each automatically adopted the Spanish cardinal, the sincerest testimony to his abilities. Years later, when he at last broke through the barrier and emerged as pope his secretary summed up the cause and effect of that long apprenticeship.

> It is now thirty-seven years since his uncle Calixtus III made him a cardinal and during that time he never once missed a Consistory except when prevented by illness, and that was most rare. Throughout the reigns of Pius II, Paul II, Sixtus IV and Innocent VIII he was at the center of affairs so that few understood etiquette as he did. He knew how to dominate, how to shine in conversation, how to appear dignified for, majestic in stature, he had the advantage of other men.[7]

His foreignness, his isolated position in Rome sufficiently accounted for the fact that he was passed over for the supreme office when his youth no longer disqualified him, but that very isolation rendered him simultaneously tough and supple. He survived, and advanced, without the dynastic or even the civic support that his Italian colleagues enjoyed.

It was under Sixtus, who had small personal liking for him, that he undertook a major mission that both brought him to a wider audience and allowed him to strengthen his own distant base. The mission was to Spain and its ostensible purpose was to persuade the Spaniards to turn from their private war and join a major Crusade in the East. In reality, he was ordered to take part in some very delicate negotiations between the kingdoms of Aragon and Castile, whose outcome would immediately affect all Spain and ultimately all Europe. The Castilians had been engaged in a lengthy and unsavory debate regarding the legitimacy of their monarch's daughter and heiress. The fact that King Enriquez of Castile bore the opprobious nickname of "the Impotent" gave substance to his subjects' suspicions and increased his resentment of his sister Isabella, who was not only legitimate but attractive, highly intelligent, and popular. In addition, she had had the audacity to marry Ferdinand, the eighteen-year-old heir to the throne of Aragon, in direct opposition to her brother's wishes. The marriage had taken place under utmost difficulties, in circumstances charged with a romance that writers of ballads would exploit for decades—the handsome young man gallantly making his way in disguise through hostile country, in danger of arrest by the king's men; his bride's astonishment and unfeigned joy at his arrival; their poverty, which forced them to borrow money for the ceremony—all this was common knowledge. But what long remained a secret was that the papal bull of dispensation, which enabled them to marry though they were cousins, was a forgery—almost certainly Isabella didn't know it.

Rodrigo Borgia carried with him a genuine bull of dispensation, but it was left entirely to his discretion whether it should be published—or quietly destroyed. If destroyed, the young couple would stand convicted of technical incest, their marriage automatically under the ban of the Church. If published, it would not merely give the papal blessing to a couple who were, as it happened, much in love, but it would also prepare the ground for the union of the kingdoms of Aragon and Castile, making in effect one great kingdom of Spain with all the incalculable effects upon the balance of Europe such a union involved. And finally, it would implicitly brand King Enrique's heiress as bastard. All together, the immense discretionary power thus given to the vice-chancellor was evidence enough of his standing among the diplomats of the Curia.

Rodrigo Borgia left Rome as the vice-chancellor of the Roman Church, bound on a mission of great political importance. But he was also a member of a minor Spanish nobility, returning now to his native land for the first time since he had left it as an inexperienced youth. Happily, personal vanity coincided with diplomatic protocol, and he dipped heavily into his accumulated wealth to furnish his Spanish mission with a magnificence almost vulgar, creating another species of theatrical show that Spain remembered for a long time afterward. He was not disappointed in his reception. There were those who recorded privately their contempt of the softened, italianate Spaniard, but in public he was feted as visiting royalty. Valencia, the titular city of his bishopric, exerted itself to honor its splendid son who could now do so much for it: Crimson draperies were hung over the great city gates; a royal canopy was borne over him to shield him from the rays of the June sun; and, splendid on his great white horse he rode into the city of his youth to receive the plaudits of the crowds and the speeches of the welcoming committee of nobles. He remained in Valencia for more than a month, returning lavish entertainment with lavish entertainment, surpassing the expectations of even those who had heard from a distance of the Borgia fortune. So impressive was the show that crowds of young Valencian nobles determined to attach themselves to his train when it returned to Italy.

He left the beautiful sea-cooled city in the gasping heat of a Spanish August, riding inland to begin the work for which he had come—and succeeding to a degree greater than perhaps even he had expected. His first task was to assess the potentials of Ferdinand and Isabella. The gap between the young prince and the prelate was great: Rodrigo was in his forty-second year, a portly, impressive figure exuding the self-confidence born both of his worldly experience and the power of his great office. Ferdinand was just twenty, a fair-haired lively youth, quick of intelligence but with a certain shallowness. Isabella, a year older than Ferdinand, seemed considerably more mature, physically attractive enough to be accounted beautiful without obvious flattery but possessed, too, of a genuine intellect that, despite her youth, enabled her to judge the man who was judging her. Out of that brief contact the couple who were to be known as Their Catholic Majesties and the later Pope Alexander VI cemented a political and personal bond that was to endure until Alexander's son shattered it. Isabella never wholly trusted Rodrigo, but mindful of that careful balance she had established with her husband, she followed his lead in this matter.

They received their dispensation, but there still remained the matter of ensuring that Isabella's brother, in rage or pique, would not ally himself with the thronging enemies of the Holy See. And here Cardinal Borgia's prime talent was employed with brilliant effect. The bitterest of enemies could not help conceding that his eloquence was extraordinary. The very fact that it was devoid of fashionable literary qualities enhanced its value even though it earned him the contempt of humanist scholars in Italy. Speaking in the Spanish that even in Italy, was never far from his lips, he urged the young couple's case so forcefully to the king's advisers that Enrique agreed to a formal reconciliation. Isabella traveled to her brother's court at Segovia and there, at a great public banquet, Borgia was able to witness the consummation of his Spanish mission.

He left Spain in September 1474, having spent some fourteen months in the country. Much of that time seems to have been spent in solid political work as the representative of a supranational power in a country on the brink of momentous change. His mission earned goodwill for the papacy, even while it enabled Rodrigo to lay the foundations for the development of the Borgia power and wealth in his native country—foundations which were to act as buttress for the far more important task of establishing the Borgia in Italy.

The Path
to the Throne

2

Rome had changed during the short time Borgia had
been absent. It seemed, indeed, as though it were trying
to repair in a decade the neglect of centuries, so
ruthless, so frantic was the speed with which it was
renewing its physical and social parts. The energy of the
papacy, so long diffused, was now singlemindedly
directed toward the enormous task of reconstruction,
channeled through the iron will of Sixtus IV, a man who
had fought his way unaided to the top. Edict after edict
poured from him, affecting every aspect of the city's life.
It was he who gave Rome its most precious gift, one
almost unique in Italian cities—an abundant supply of
cold, clear water. There had been more than a thousand
fountains in the days of the Caesars and, choked by
neglect though they were, their elaborate conduits were
still in existence awaiting only a water supply and an
army of men to clean them. Both were provided and
even in the most squalid courts, water flowed again,

splashing joyously from ancient conduits into modern basins. A much-needed new bridge was thrown across the Tiber; the Cloaca Maxima and its complex sewage system was restored; wide and handsome new roads pierced the tangled squalor of centuries. Its lungs and arteries cleared, Rome began to stir from its centuries-long sleep.

The monuments of the imperial city formed somber islands of haunted decay, diminishing in size as their brick and marble and tile were removed for the new buildings; but they seemed indestructible, on so titanic a scale had they been built. In between the shattered baths and temples of the Caesars, between the collapsing porticoes and weed-grown forums new life sprouted urgently upward. Money was pouring into the city: the cautious bankers of Venice and Genoa and Florence first settled in rented accommodations and then confidently built their own palaces on the handsome new Via Papalis, sure evidence of social stability. Sixtus granted outright ownership to those who built, and houses now pressed close to Cardinal Borgia's palace, where before there had been only trampled earth. That palace was now only one of many and no longer particularly conspicuous in its size, for his fellow cardinals, taking courage from the pope's own confidence and energy, threw themselves into the frenzy of building. They even crossed to the unfashionable right bank in their search for sites. Domenico della Rovere, one of the pope's nephews, tore down a mass of squalid buildings in front of St. Peter's and erected an enormous palace in a fantastically short space of time; another nephew, Piero Riario, migrated to the Janiculum and built himself a beautiful villa where Nero once had a pleasure garden sweeping down to the river. But it was in the triangular plain on the left bank

immediately opposite the Vatican where building was concentrated. Here arose the palaces of the new princes of
Rome. Stafano Nardini was the last to build in the old,
massive fortress style—barely a stone's throw from Borgia's own palace-fort. Piero Riario, trusting in the power of
his uncle the pope, opted for a more elegant building, a
house rather than a castle, complete with beautiful gardens
closer to the river. Estouteville took over an existing palace
not far from the Piazza Navona, the ancient stadium that
was now Rome's principal marketplace, and used his enormous wealth to make of it a showplace to challenge any
other in Europe.

Against this background of splendid new buildings the
people themselves were changing in habits and appearance. In the lowest stratum of society there was little to
mark a new age. They lived as they had always lived—in
windowless burrows scraped out of the ancient ruins or
formed by heaping stones together. They ate what they had
always eaten—pasta, two or three varieties of vegetables
flavored with strong herbs, washed down with harsh wine.
Their diet was, if anything, reduced by the new health
regulations which drastically limited the number of pigs
and chickens that once roamed the city. Their clothes remained the same coarse, sack-like garments; their morality,
based on a widespread but close-knit family grouping, remained unchanged; religious faith was still a dominant fac-
tor in their lives. But in the strata above them, among the
new rich and the ancient nobility, the quality and appearance of life altered.

The old still clung to the sober robes that marked both
class and profession; the young strutted forth in a peacock
blaze of color. Velvet and brocade, silk and damask became

everyday materials, with emeralds and rubies, pearls, sapphires, and diamonds worked into the fabric to proclaim a man's status in a gaudy show of wealth. In their palaces, the old rough-and-ready service tendered by loyal but unsophisticated servants began to give way to specialization and then to a more precise division of labor with a corresponding increase in the number of servants.

Even a private household would reckon on providing wages and meals for at least a hundred people and probably some two hundred men wore Borgia's livery of yellow and red. These were just his household servants, totally distinct from his ecclesiastical staff. Borgia remained indifferent to food throughout his life; even as pope his meals were so frugal that people disliked dining privately with him. But he nevertheless had a position to uphold and there was accordingly a large staff to carry out the complex ritual of a Renaissance meal—a master of the table, with assistants, a chief carver with more assistants, some fifteen waiting men, a butler of the pantry with an assistant, and a butler of the wines. Behind the scenes there were yet more servants exclusively devoted to the table, each with his specialization and many with assistants—marketer, store-keeper, cellarer, water carrier, as well as the cooks themselves. Throughout the great palace were other, virtually autonomous departments, the master of each jealously guarding his prerogatives, enjoying greater power and prestige the closer his duties brought him to the person of the cardinal.

Each department had its quota of slaves, male and female, adult and juvenile, engaged for the most part on dirty rough work, although an alert and attractive youth could hope to work his way up even as far as the great audience chamber. Slavery, which had almost disappeared from Italy, had returned on the wave of prosperity: twenty thousand men, women and children passed through the slave market in Venice alone each year. So plentiful was the supply that even small merchants could buy a human animal to help out in the home while the nobility came more and more to rely upon them in place of expensive and arrogant servants. Prices varied immensely so that the lady of the house could expect to pay only six ducats for a hard-working but ill-favored woman while the pretty young girl who would probably grace her husband's bed would cost anything up to a hundred. The purchaser had the choice of a half dozen races, white as well as black, Christian as well as pagan or Moslem. "Tartars are hardiest and best for work. Russians are built on finer lines but, in my opinion, Tartars are best. Circassians are a superior breed wherefore everybody seeks them,"[8] a Roman lady noted. They were, on the whole, well treated. In some cities, notably Florence, the children of slaves automatically became free citizens. Romans declined such an expensive sop to conscience but a slave in a household such as Cardinal Borgia's could expect a life far more attractive than that of the average peasant farmer.

In most princely houses there would have been virtually a separate establishment for the *Letterati*, the learned men who, while living at their patron's expense, could "converse in the four principal languages of the world, namely Hebrew, Greek, Latin and Italian" and as a by-product earn fame for that patron. Borgia had little personal interest in such garnishes; nevertheless he was sufficiently a man of his time to realize the propaganda value of humanist scholars. The head of his household was a

German, Lorenz Behaim, one of the leading members of
the new Roman academy. His secretary was a Cypriot,
Ludovico Podocatharo, who brought to the household the
glamor of Greek learning and the skills of Greek intrigue.
His legal adviser and notary was a Roman, Camillo Beneimbene, who probably knew more secrets of the great families
of Rome than the entire Curia put together. There was
good employment for many lesser men—secretaries, lawyers, accountants—who could turn Borgia's letters into elegant prose and keep track of his ever-growing possessions,
but none of them were of sufficient stature to attract scholars and so transform Borgia's chancery into an academy.

Housed in a separate part of the palace were the men
who organized his transport—a master of horse with a
small army of grooms and stablemen, wheelwrights, car-
penters. The master's task was no easy one: at a moment's
notice he could be called upon to provide transport to
move the entire household hundreds of miles distant and
furnish an efficient escort for it. Admittedly, Cardinal
Borgia rarely left Rome if he could help it and, when he did,
he was usually bound no further than one of the villas in
the Alban Hills. But if His Holiness decided to go on a tour,
then those cardinals who valued their careers prepared to
go with him and there would be a scurrying in Rome as a
score of masters of horse feverishly set about hiring the
necessary equipment, vehicles and animals for a journey
which could last weeks.

The hiring of an escort was the responsibility of the
cardinal's chamberlain. If a cardinal was traveling with the
pope, then a papal guard would provide a more than adequate escort, but if he was bound on a private journey, then
it was necessary to find his own soldiers as guard. There

was never any difficulty in raising a force even at a moment's notice: it was even possible to indulge a preference for nationality if a great man felt safer under the protection of Swiss pikemen than that of Spanish swordsmen or Burgundian halberdiers.

Those with an eye for change could detect another new element in the city, a sinister counterpart to the new gaiety of jeweled clothes, the new dignity of palaces and churches, and that was the increasing number of bands of armed men. For over a century, the endless wars between the city-states of Italy had been conducted by bands of mercenaries, each under its condottiere who would bargain on behalf of his followers, plan tactics on behalf of his employer, and hope to win fame and fortune for himself. The reign of the condottieri was now, in fact, just past its noonday splendor. No longer would it be possible for such a man as Sforza in Milan, or Malatesta in Rimini or Montefeltro in Urbino to found a state of legal banditry. But the tens of thousands of men who had followed the condottieri and made fortunes for them remained still at large, not yet aware that their sun was declining, seeking employment among the rich and the envious and the ambitious. Until now, the trade of mercenary had been bloodless enough, but the changed nature of warfare was made evident by the ubiquity of those bronze tubes with which Cardinal Borgia had entertained his adopted fellow-citizens. Cannon now ringed the great upper platform of Sant' Angelo, poking their snouts forward and downward, indifferently prepared to hurl their stone balls into an attacking army or into the roofs of Rome. Cannon commanded the bridges and guarded the Vatican: they appeared in a dozen unexpected places throughout the city—beside the Mint, in embrasure on the ancient Torre delle Milizie from whose height, men said, Nero had regarded the burning city, and in private palaces. Young bravos still swaggered with sword and dagger, but one or two of them carried, for strictly professional purposes, those long slender tubes set in a stock of wood which were the terrible children of the great bronze cannon. There was peace for the moment, but when war came again it would come in a new and most terrible form.

And at the heart of the political machine itself—in the cramped lobbies of the Vatican offices, in the gorgeous throne rooms of the cardinals' palaces, in whatever place the handful of men who ran the Curia met—occurred the most profound and far-reaching change of all. "I remember the time when the Sacred College was full of learned and virtuous men," Lorenzo de' Medici wrote sadly to his young son Giovanni, who was about to take his place in the College. "Theirs is the example for you to follow. The less your conduct resembles that of those who now compose it the more beloved and respected you will be."[9] Gone was the pure love of learning which had enabled Nicholas to dedicate the infant Renaissance to Christ; gone the fierce loyalty that had led Calixtus to challenge the apathy of Europe; gone the gentle Christianity of Pius. In its place was a struggle for power that not merely ignored the sacred nature of the organization but used it as an instrument. In part, the change in the College was a product of the Renaissance itself, for that bubbling ferment, in bursting apart the constricting intellectual ties of the old order, burst too the moral bonds which held society together. It seemed that the purely pagan element had triumphed as old Calixtus had feared it would. Scholars drew mocking parallels between Christ and Apollo and were applauded for their skills; the courtesan flaunted her pride and her beauty on the very steps of St. Peter's; even the merchant had his concubine and was less disposed to hold up his hands in horror at a cardinal's mistress. The College was a symptom of change, but under Pope Sixtus IV, it was also a cause of change, beginning a cycle of corruption that would be almost impossible to break.

Sixtus had fought his way to the top almost unaided. His father was commonly reputed to have been a boatman in Genoa harbor and the future pope's career was a classic example of the manner in which an able man could ascend the heights via the path of church preferment. He entered the Franciscan order, studied law and obtained a solid reputation for learning and, indeed, piety which probably contributed toward his election, for the College was still mainly composed of men who had been under the influence of Pius. The election wholly changed his character, as it had changed Pius's, but whereas Piccolomini had passed from worldliness to an almost ascetic austerity, in Sixtus's case ambitions long suppressed under a monk's habit burst forth like some monstrous flower under the influence of the tiara. Displaying the same energy with which he had tackled the task of restoring Rome, he set about promoting his family, in particular two nephews, Girolamo and Piero Riario.

Five months after his election he poured out the papal cornucopia before Piero in so blatant and doting a manner as to give substance to the belief that the young man was in fact, his son. Bishoprics, archbishoprics, and finally a cardinal's hat were rapidly bestowed upon a youth who a few months earlier had been hard-pressed for the necessities of life. The result was predictable. "Although of very ow origin and mean rearing, no sooner had he obtained he scarlet hat than he displayed a pride and ambition so ast that the pontificate seemed too small for him—he gave a feast in Rome which would have seemed extraordinary for a king, the expense exceeding twenty thousand florins.''[10] Sixtus did refuse Piero one small request—he declined to abdicate in his favor—but there was nothing else he would not grant.

Piero enjoyed his new splendor for barely two years before he died at the age of twenty-eight—probably the victim of his own excesses. Upon his death, his brother Girolamo became the object of the pope's love. That young man was provided with a beautiful and influential bride—Caterina Sforza, the illegitimate daughter of the duke of Milan. Girolamo was installed as lord of the papal cities of Imola and Forli and the temporal and spiritual arms of the Church were activated for his advantage.

The Medici of Florence presented a threat, so their assassination was arranged. The young and handsome Giuliano was hewed down in the cathedral but Lorenzo escaped, the Florentines rallied round him and central Italy was plunged into war.

Borgia took care to avoid commitment to either side in the ensuing lineup. It was not too difficult: He had no family ties to drag him into the Italian whirlpool and so could afford the luxury of choosing friends and allies according to purely personal advantage, collecting good opinions as efficiently and as assiduously as he collected rich offices. The Roman diarists, ever prepared like some pack of hunting dogs to drag down whoever emerged from the herd, were as beguiled as the rest, speaking warmly of his intellectual abilities, noting admiringly, not censoriously, his steady accumulation of wealth. "Intellectually he is capable of everything," the emigré Jacopo of Volterra noted.

> He is a fluent speaker, writes well—though not in a literary style—is extremely astute and very energetic and skillful in business matters. He is enormously wealthy, and through his connection with kings and princes, commands great influence. He has built a beautiful and comfortable palace for himself between the Bridge of Sant' Angelo and the Campo di Fiori. His revenues from his papal offices, his abbeys in Italy and Spain, his three bishoprics of Valencia, Portus and Cartagena, are vast. His office of vice-chancellor alone yields him eight thousand gold ducats annually. His plate, his pearls, his stuffs embroidered with gold and silk, his books are all of such quality as would befit a king or pope. I need hardly mention the sumptuous bed-hangings, trappings for his horses and similar things of gold, silver and silk, nor the vast quantity of gold coin which he possesses. Altogether, it is believed that he possessed more gold and riches of every sort than all the cardinals put together, excepting only Estouteville.[11]

It occurred to no one to wonder how a cardinal who was possessed of no great family estates was able to live "as would befit a king or a pope." There was an ineradicable streak of vulgarity in the Roman consciousness and a recital of Cardinal Borgia's wealth was, for long, considered the equivalent of a catalogue of virtues. Rome and the cardinal were eminently suited to each other.

Camillo Beneimbene had performed many a discreet little service for Cardinal Borgia during the seven years that

Beneimbene had been his notary. But undoubtedly the oddest was the wedding ceremony he was called upon to supervise in the cardinal's palace in the autumn of 1474. Externally, there was nothing particularly remarkable about it. The cardinal himself was present, affable and jovial as ever, his robes of princely purple lending a portentous air to an otherwise simple occasion. The bride, a darkly handsome girl in her early twenties, was a little old for a first marriage, but in these days of soaring dowries a girl's family had to be very rich or noble to marry her off in her teens. And Vannozza Catanei's family, Beneimbene knew, was certainly neither rich nor noble. The bridegroom's family was even less exalted and Beneimbene had been forced to describe Messer Domenico d'Arignano, the bridegroom, simply as an "officer of the Church" on the marriage contract. All together, the occasion might have been the wedding of a poor but favored relative of the cardinal, taking place in such exalted surroundings only through his generosity.

But Beneimbene knew better. This solemn wedding ceremony was simply a front, the marriage contract the first of a complex series of devices with which Borgia sought to provide legal protection for the children he would have by this woman. The first of them, Cesare, was born just a year after the ceremony. D'Arignano died not long afterward and Vannozza remained a widow for four years during which she had two children, a boy, Juan, and a girl, Lucrezia. Over the following four years she married twice more and gave birth to two more children, both boys. One of them was given the Spanish name Joffre and the other the resounding Roman name of Ottaviano. All three husbands were chosen by Borgia: each accepted the position because of strong financial inducements and presumably each gave Borgia certain undertakings regarding the more intimate side of the relationship. How he ensured that none of the three took advantage of their curious position was a matter of some mystery to his contemporaries. The system seems to have broken down toward the end because Vannozza's fifth child, Ottaviano, was publicly acknowledged to be the son of her legal husband, and Borgia himself declared in moments of anger that the fourth child—Joffre—was no child of his. Why Borgia should have gone to such extraordinary length, creating a situation which bristled with future complexities, was equally unknown. His was a legalistic mind, careful always to observe the letter if not the substance of the law, perhaps even convincing himself that, by granting his mistress the protection of marriage, he removed in some degree the stigma of illegitimacy from his children by her.

In later years, the charge was to be made that Vannozza Catanei came from the glittering class of courtesan that the wealth and corruption of Rome had produced over the preceding few decades. The few certain facts about her origin indicate that her family was probably from the lowest ranks of the nobility. And she was, in addition, ineradicably middle-class in her approach to life. The dominant characteristics of the courtesan were generosity and improvidence. Few died wealthy, most died in utter want, justifying the belief and hope of the respectable that "Venus reduces her worshipers to her own nudity." Vannozza, on the contrary, kept a wary eye on the future. Presumably she received the usual gifts of jewels and perfumes and precious stuffs for garments, for Borgia was both generous and fond of gaudy show. But she put her faith in humdrum, unglamorous property. After d'Arignano died, Borgia established her in a large house near his own palace, and all its furnishings were in her name. Later, she acquired another house and that, too, was in her name, although she had by then married her second husband, Giorgio di Croce. She bought a vineyard near the baths of Diocletian and build a villa upon it. She acquired a controlling interest in three important inns, including the great Lion which stood near the bridge of Sant' Angelo and so had first choice of all travelers entering Rome. Vannozza also made gains indirectly through her husbands, for each benefited financially from Borgia's patronage. Carlo Canale, her third husband, was made jailer of Rome's civil prison, the Torre Nona. The job was more than merely an honorary position, for a prisoner's comfort was in exact proportion to the bribe he was prepared to pay his jailer, and many wealthy prisoners passed through the Torre Nona. She even obtained for herself and Canale the grant of the Borgia arms and with it the nobleman's exemption from certain classes of tax.

In return Vannozza gave Borgia—what? A sense of stability, probably: a home in a land that was and would remain essentially alien to him. He had had his share, and more, of the glittering creatures whose generosity toward casual lovers was equaled only by their rapacity toward their protectors. Vannozza never demanded, always acquiesced—even in the last and most bitter acquiescence of all when Borgia took her only daughter Lucrezia and placed her in the keeping of another woman. Vannozza's and Borgia's relationship was the sober affection of the married couple rather than the passion between lovers. Toward her, Borgia never showed the almost frantic jealousy which he displayed for her successor, yet he was remarkably faithful to Vannozza during the ten years of their active association. There may have been other women, but if so they were transient affairs unknown to or ignored by Rome and certainly there were no other children born to him during Vannozza's reign. Despite the unsympathetic picture she presents posterity, Vannozza Catanei must have possessed very unusual qualities that enabled her to bind this most volatile lover to herself when he had the pick of Rome; to retain his affection and protection even after she had been supplanted by a younger and more glamorous rival; and above all, to direct his interest almost exclusively upon the four children she had borne him and not upon the children of his previous liaison.

For, at that time when he installed Vannozza as his official mistress, Borgia already had a family consisting of two little girls, Isabella and Gerolama, and a boy Pedro, approaching manhood. No one outside the tiny circle of his intimates knew the name of their mother. She, whoever she was, had given birth to her firstborn during the reign of Pius, and Pope Pius had held the inconvenient belief that he was responsible for the spiritual as well as the financial well-being of his subordinates. To maintain Pius's favor, Cardinal Borgia had to keep both her and her children well in the background. Even when the necessity for secrecy disappeared, the existence of these children caused scarcely a ripple compared with the storm of notoriety that would swirl round the cardinal's four children by Vannozza. This was largely because they posed no threat to the great Italian families. Borgia used his influence in Spain to obtain for his eldest son, Pedro, the Dukedom of Gandia and it was entirely in Spain that the young man pursued an active and honorable career as soldier until his death, in 1488, at the early age of thirty. Pedro's sisters, Isabella and

Gerolama, were quietly married off into the minor Roman nobility. Gerolama, too, died young, but Isabella lived well into the next century, outliving all the children of Vannozza. Their names became legendary even in their lifetime, but Isabella ignored them and was ignored by them.

The reason why Cardinal Borgia concentrated his love and interest upon his second family, instead of his first, is almost beyond conjecture. The fact that Pedro and Gerolama died before he became pope necessarily limited the scope of his ambition for them; nevertheless, even as cardinal he possessed wealth and influence enough to make of them more than he did. It is possible that he remembered the almost disastrous results of his uncle's too blatant nepotism and bided his time until his position was unassailable. It is possible that he fell genuinely in love with Vannozza and, in consequence, turned aside from his first children after having done his duty by them. Almost any explanation is possible, for Borgia, behind his open, affable front, could be as close and secretive as a peasant. There were certain matters about his family that he did not want the world to learn of, and the world never did learn of them, despite the endless probings first of enemies and then of generations of scholars. The greatest mystery stemmed from precisely this ability of the Borgia family to keep its secrets to itself. Few families in Italy—or for that matter in all Europe—attracted such wide, sustained and detailed attention as did the four children of Rodrigo Borgia by Vannozza Catanei. Cesare, Juan, Lucrezia, Joffre —each in turn came under a scrutiny that ranged from the bitterly hostile to the coldly legal, expressed not only in the ferocious satire of political enemies but also in the precise statements of lawyers. The ambitious matrimonial plans that their father prepared for them over a decade ensured that, again and again, some aspect of their antecedents would come under close inspection. Politically, the motives and the interrelationships between the members of the family—in particular between the father and his son Cesare —provided the key to the tumultuous events in Italy during the closing years of the fifteenth century. Nevertheless, despite this enduring interest, despite the swarms of courtiers and ambassadors who surrounded the family for some twenty years and who were paid to ferret out every last detail about its members, despite the profuse legal documentation, the relationship of these Borgias one with another remains rooted in obscurity.

Even during the youth of Vannozza's four children there was considerable doubt as to who was the eldest, doubt as to whether all were siblings. Their father himself deliberately compounded the doubt and obscurity as, foxlike, he doubled and redoubled upon his tracks to protect his young. The most extraordinary example of this occurred when Borgia, as pope, sought to legitimize Cesare in order to give him a cardinal's hat. Two statements were prepared regarding the boy's paternity: one was secret, the other was published, and they contradicted each other at every vital point. Cesare himself very clearly harbored a bitter grievance about his place in the family, but what exactly that grievance was, none outside Borgia family councils ever knew.

Cesare, the eldest, was barely eight years old and the youngest, Joffre, was still a baby when their father added yet another inexplicable twist to the family mystery. He took the four children away from their mother Vannozza and placed them under the guardianship of his cousin,

Adriana da Mila. His relationship with Vannozza remained friendly; she continued to flourish financially under his protection; she was permitted frequent contact with her children. But from January 1483 she ceased, for all practical purposes, to be their mother. That role was now filled by Madonna Adriana, that most shadowy, most enigmatic of the Borgia figures—unimportant in herself, devoted to her cousin, and yet the person who brushed in the first lurid colors of the infamy that would cling to Rodrigo's name. It was through Adriana that his love life, deplorable but commonplace enough, was transformed into a tale that might have been told by Ovid or Boccaccio.

Adriana was born in Rome—her father had come to Italy in the first wave of Catalans under old Calixtus—and had married a minor member of the Orsini clan by whom she had a single child, a son, before being widowed. She was some ten years younger than the magnificent cousin whom she hero-worshiped, and she and her son Orsino Orsini came under Rodrigo's protection after she was widowed—an anomaly in itself, for custom dictated that her natural protector should be the head of her husband's clan. There occurred, however, an even more anomalous, a final and inextricable tangling of the bizarre Borgia family relationship. In May 1489 Orsino Orsini was married, in the Star Chamber of the Borgia palace, to the sixteen-year-old Giulia Farnese, a girl of astonishing beauty but small dowry, from an unimportant family. Before or shortly after the marriage ceremony, her new husband slipped into the marital background and the fifty-eight-year-old Cardinal Borgia took his place.

There were many and growing indications of Borgia's power in Rome but none were so unequivocal as this. Under normal circumstances the debauchment of a young noblewoman would have been followed swiftly by the avenging daggers of her own or her husband's kin. But now those concerned kept quiet—the Orsini because they feared, the Farnese because they hoped. The Farnese certainly received their reward in due course. Borgia's first act on ascending the papal throne was to make a cardinal of Giulia's brother, starting him on the path to the throne itself and making the family's fortunes. To Adriana the act itself was its own reward for her cousin Rodrigo was her universe. No one knew for certain whether she acted the part of conscious bawd, organizing the marriage as a means of putting the teen-aged girl into her aging cousin's bed, or whether Adriana merely acquiesced in the grotesque arrangement. But her role as Giulia's mother-in-law provided the cloak of legality and respectability which Borgia always insisted on throwing over his actions. Giulia shared the same house with Adriana and the children of Vannozza, while her young husband Orsino withdrew wanly to his family's country estate.

In exchanging the mature love of thirty-eight for the fresh love of sixteen, Borgia entered upon a second youngmanhood. He was extravagantly happy, doting upon the voluptuous, beautiful child like a youth in his first love affair, restless and querulous should she be absent from Rome even overnight, bubbling with joy when she returned. It speaks much for Giulia's generous if somewhat shallow nature that she made little attempt to profit financially from Borgia's infatuation. Her family used her unshingly, and her lover acceded to everything demanded him. But Giulia, personally, was content to accept the ial trappings due a great man's mistress: the delight in taking precedence over those who had been her equals or even her superiors; the heady pleasure of granting or refusing patronage; the casual, endless gifts of jewels and rich dress. Meanwhile, Borgia paid for his new lease on life with bitter sexual jealousy.

It was not so much that Giulia delighted in testing her power over a man who wielded power over others. Admittedly, she was quite different from Vannozza and in a manner that was not simply due to the great difference in their ages. Where Vannozza had been dedicated both to her own financial interest and her lover's well-being, Giulia was lighthearted and featherbrained, never looking beyond the delights of today. And where Vannozza sought to tie her lover to her by submission and acquiescence, Giulia displayed an independence of spirit which kept Borgia's interest at fever pitch even while such spirit could enrage him.

But after all, it was her very difference from Vannozza which had attracted him in the first place. There was, indeed, only one real flaw in Giulia's and Borgia's relationship and that was the existence of her husband. Unexpectedly, Orsino Orsini declined to stay discreetly in the background, as Vannozza's husbands had done. His protests were feeble enough, for he was a weak, spiritless man, and when at last he was goaded to action, his cuckolder had succeeded to the papal throne, thus adding the crushing power of the Keys to Borgia's already immense advantages. But the ever-generous Giulia seems to have become disturbed by her husband's pitiful pipings from the family estate at Bassanello and would defy Borgia from time to time, journeying to Bassanello to spend a few uneasy days with Orsino. She continued to do so even after Borgia became pope, earning now full papal thunders against her impious conduct. "Thankless and teacherous Giulia," Borgia spluttered in the autumn of 1494,

> We have heard that you have again refused to return to us without Orsino's consent. We know the evil of your soul and of the man who guides you but we would not for one moment have thought it possible for you to break your solemn oath not to go near Orsino. But you have done so, risking your very life in order to go to Bassanello so that you could surrender yourself once more to that stallion. We herewith ordain, under pain of excommunication and eternal damnation, that you shall not go to Bassanello.[12]

Even the faithful Adriana was upbraided and reproached for her supposed part in Giulia's obstinacy. Where the affair might have ended, with a raging lover seemingly prepared to excommunicate and damn eternally all who stood between him and his desire, was anybody's guess. But the intriguing question as to whether a wife could be excommunicated even by a pope for obeying her marriage vows remained speculative. Orsino Orsini backed away from the storm and returned his wife to her lover. Nevertheless, Giulia's warmth of heart enabled her to add yet another puzzle to the growing Borgia legend. The calumnious whispered that her only child, Laura, was in fact the perfectly legitimate offspring of the Orsini marriage.

In the opinion of most Romans, Cardinal Borgia's tangled domestic life was strictly his own affair. Far greater interest was displayed in the relatives of Pope Sixtus himself, for so greatly had the papal court changed in these last few years that the Riario clan appeared like some royal family to be studied minutely and assiduously courted by those with a decent care for their ambitions. Piero Riario's death had altered the direction, not the force, of Sixtus's anxious love so that it was now Piero's brother Girolamo who had first call on that love and the treasury behind it. But there was a third nephew, Giuliano della Rovere, who profited from Piero's death, though indirectly.

Sixtus had made Giuliano della Rovere a cardinal. That was the least any pope could do for a nephew, but thereafter, despite the fact that he bore the same family name as the pope, della Rovere remained in the background while his far less talented cousins were dizzily elevated. The gossips nodded knowingly: did this not give substance to the rumors that the Riario brothers were rather closer relatives of the pope than was publicly acknowledged? A massive, handsome, taciturn man, della Rovere seemed, to those who knew him, to be clamping down on an explosive energy. Bitterly jealous though he must have been of his cousin, Cardinal Piero Riario, yet he bided his time. Piero's death was his opportunity, for Giuliano, too, was a cardinal and so the only one of the family to fill the vacant place. Reluctantly, Sixtus brought him into the foreground. But he still remained in a subordinate position in the papal as well as the family councils. Compared with him, Rodrigo Borgia was a dazzling figure, moving effortlessly in the upper circles of power. Nevertheless, when Sixtus died suddenly in 1484 it was as though the long-suppressed energies of Giuliano della Rovere now served to propel him forward irresistibly toward the highest levels of power. It was he who now delivered the first real check to Rodrigo Borgia's advance, sounding the challenge notes of a feud that would continue for the rest of Borgia's life and end only when della Rovere, mounting the throne as Pope Julius II, utterly destroyed all that Borgia had created.

An outbreak of violence was as much a part of a pope's obsequies in Rome as was the chanting of the Mass for the Dead. Sixtus was probably still alive clinically when his body, clad in nothing but a threadbare shift, was pushed to one side and virtually forgotten during the following forty-eight hours while the Romans went about the traditional business of attacking the papal favorites. Rodrigo Borgia's fine new palace now became wholly a fortress, with its great door stoutly barricaded and cannon poking out of the embrasures to threaten the square and street below. Others followed his prudent example, for although it was the Riario family which was the prime target for the popular rage, a Roman mob rarely troubled to differentiate between victims. The Riario palace had already fallen to that mob. "We saw a great throng of people around the Count's house," the Florentine ambassador Vespucci wrote to his principals, giving a vivid eyewitness account of the rapacity of a Roman sacking. "The doors and windows were carried off and a large part of the window railings. The trees and plants in the garden were uprooted and a marble fountain in the garden, the lead in the conduit, the partition in the stable and the racks and mangers taken away. Chimneys were cut down and thrown from the windows, even a piece of the gilded rose in the ceiling was hacked out and still they did not cease to destroy and take away until they came to the hinges and nails of the house."[13] Girolamo Riario was away fighting in the North, but his wife Caterina—

despite her seven months' pregnancy—mounted on horseback and with only a small bodyguard, tempestuously galloped through Rome to seize Castel Sant'Angelo, military key to the city.

On the following day, August 14, the Florentine ambassador wrote privately to Lorenzo de' Medici saying that Riario had arrived in Rome. "His Excellency is very bold and says that he will remain until the new pontiff is elected. His boldness is founded upon the papal army and the Orsini faction and upon having Castel Sant' Angelo and, he imagines, having some of the cardinals in his favor—among them the Vice-Chancellor, but I do not know how it will turn out." Writing to the Signoria, the Florentine government itself, he emphasized that Riario depended upon Borgia's support, "But I do not know how much trust can be put in the latter except insofar as his cause is the Count's. There are two leaders here at present, the Vice-Chancellor and della Rovere."[14]

Vespucci was correct in saying that Borgia's support of Girolamo Riario was merely incidental: he had no intention of advancing any other candidacy but his own at this, the fourth conclave of his career. He was still comparatively young, at the age of fifty-four, for an office whose holder usually entered upon it in his late sixties. Nevertheless, Borgia was approaching a critical age, for another pontificate as long as the last would see him an old man at the close. He was prepared now as he had never been before, the accumulated experience and wealth and influence of nearly thirty years of high office were directed, at this moment, to one supreme end. Most observers rated his chances high, agreeing among themselves that he possessed fully the intangible qualities which made a man *papa-*

bile. The ambassador from Ferrara was in a minority with his colder appraisal. "The Vice-Chancellor is exerting himself to the utmost, but at the moment it is not possible to give a firm opinion of his chances. One must also remember that proverb that he who enters a conclave a pope, leaves it a cardinal."[15]

The proverb proved correct. Despite Borgia's standing, despite the energy he derived from the knowledge of time's passing, he could not yet withstand the crosscurrents of Italian peninsula politics that swept through the College of Cardinals. Again, he paid the penalty for the fact that he was isolated in Italy, without natural allies. He abandoned his own candidacy in an attempt to place an aging fellow-countryman, Cardinal Moles, upon the throne. That, too, failed and at last he was forced to compromise with Giuliano della Rovere and support della Rovere's own candidate, the Genoese Battista Cibo. For once, Borgia miscalculated, ignoring or underestimating the fact that Cibo was wholly under the control of his fellow citizen della Rovere. "Cibo has not much experience in state affairs, nor much learning, though he is by no means illiterate," Vespucci informed Lorenzo de' Medici. "He was altogether in the hands of della Rovere, and it was he who secured him the cardinal's hat. Della Rovere may now be said to be pope, and will have more power than he had with Pope Sixtus if he knows how to hold his ground."[16]

Giuliano della Rovere was perfectly capable of holding his ground and from then onward he loomed ever larger on Borgia's horizon. Nevertheless, the nature of the new pontificate was such that only a very weak or very scrupulous man could have failed to profit from a collapsing system. The papal court was now, for all practical purposes, indistinguishable from an ordinary monarchy, for Innocent VIII, as Cibo styled himself, broke with the discreet tradition of the papal "nephew" and openly acknowledged his children, a son and a daughter. They were sumptuously installed in the Vatican and there flattered and treated in the manner of royalty. Previous pontiffs might have been as besotted with their relatives, but each had been, in addition, preoccupied with some major enterprise, whether it was crusade in the East or dynastic war in Italy. In consequence some form of discipline had been imposed by necessity upon the Curia. Innocent, a sick man who spent days in a semi-torpor, virtually abdicated responsibility, apart from a disastrous interference in the Kingdom of Naples. The unguarded riches of the Church, whether riches of specie or of office, fell to those who had a nerve to plunder. During the eight-year pontificate Rodrigo Borgia took his share and more, thrusting forward neck and neck with della Rovere toward the penultimate position. In the last few months of the pontificate della Rovere miscalculated in his turn, displaying naked ambition to a suddenly frightened College, so that when Innocent exchanged his normal lassitude for death, Borgia took the final step with ease.

The
Papal
Monarch

3

In the early hours of the morning of August 11, 1492, a window on the first floor of the Vatican Palace was opened and a figure, indistinguishable in the dusk, emerged and peered out at the handful of people below. There was an anticipatory stir and then, in the hush of dawn, the figure raised his voice in the haunting chant which marked the end of yet another conclave. "Habemus papam," the chant rose and fell, dying away, to be echoed by the response in the same key, "Deo gratias." The response was thin for there were few people in the square so early in the morning. The conclave had already lasted four days and nights, and there had been no indication that it would so suddenly be brought to an end. The watchers awaited the name of the new successor of St. Peter; it came, but not only in the traditional chanted form. Another figure appeared at the window and hurled something into the air—a bundle of small slips of paper which separated and fell softly, slowly through the windless darkness. Those nearest picked them up, peering at the hastily scribbled, barely visible writing. "We have for pope Alexander VI, Rodrigo Borgia of Valencia."

Inside the palace the author of the message was struggling into the largest of the three sizes of papal robes which, by custom, had been prepared in readiness for this moment. After thirty-seven years the apprentice had emerged as master and he was shaking, trembling with excitement and joy. He had shown none of the traditional reluctance in accepting the awesome burden, and there had been none of the lengthy debates regarding the choice of a pontifical style. In place of the sober "Volo" of acceptance he cried out, like a child unexpectedly gaining a long-awaited desire, "I am pope! I am pope!" Immediately he announced that sonorous papal style of "Alexander" and instructed the master of ceremonies to prepare the little slips of paper which would circulate through Rome, the first tiny break with convention. Shortly afterward Alexander displayed himself to the crowd which suddenly gathered, beaming, laughing with undisguised joy, making his graceful, sweeping benediction to the city and to the world. The crowd eventually dispersed, the cardinals went back to their palaces, the curial machinery began to pick up the rhythm of a new pontificate—and the rumors started.

The rumors grew steadily over the following years. They were based on sophisticated truths, expanded half-truths and hairbreadth legalism. They were the result of honest indignation, of devious opportunism and of outright hatred. They were summed up and expressed at last in that bitter epigram which winged its way around Rome. "Alexander sells the keys, the altar, Christ Himself. He has a right to, for he bought them." Years later when the man himself was dead and all that he had worked for had crumbled and disappeared, the Florentine historian Francesco Guicciardini set down, in his precise and luminous prose, a classic syllogism which sought to account for the curious nature of the Borgia pontificate. "As his accession to the papacy was foul and shameful—for he bought with gold so high an office—so similarly his government was in agreement with its vile foundations."[17] Guicciardini towered above all other Italian historians, for his work was the first truly national history yet devised in his fragmented nation, a history that placed in broad and majestic perspective the fantastically complex pattern of Italian events. His judgments achieved the status of historical truth, no matter how partisan their ultimate foundation, for there was no historian of equal stature to oppose them. In this matter he, Italy's historian, had spoken with finality and there was nothing left for posterity to do but reframe the charge, in more or less emotional language, that in the Conclave of 1492 Rodrigo Borgia had committed a unique crime whence all else flowed.

Reading Guicciardini's confident, unqualified statement, no one could guess that the conclave was among the most mysterious ever held, that its inherent contradictions totally confused contemporary Romans, much less a Florentine living and writing a generation later. The records of the conclave itself gave no certain clue. There was no Piccolomini to break the rules and transmit to posterity his priceless account of the negotiations as had been done in 1458. Johannes Burchard, the master of ceremonies, was stationed at the hatch through which food was passed and was therefore in a good position to pick up authentic information at the source. He probably recorded it in his immense diary, but that section is missing. The scrutiny lists of the conclave survived, but they merely tell how the members voted, not why. The elaborate ceremonial of secrecy whereby the conclavists were literally immured served merely to distort, not conceal, what really happened. Those conclavists who eventually talked were men intent upon justifying themselves or displaying their virtuous abstention from unholy actions. And the sum of their later accusations was that Borgia literally bought the votes of thirteen of the cardinals in order to secure a majority, carefully grading his bribes according to the voter's own chance of success, so that the ninety-six-year-old Cardinal of Venice received a mere five thousand ducats while, at the other extreme Ascanio Sforza, the prime favorite, received not only a vast quantity of bullion but also the pick of Borgia's own offices, including that of vice-chancellor.

The observer following the path of Borgia's life repeatedly encounters at vital points a curious web of contradictions, a web so tangled that the following of separate strands can lead to totally opposing conclusions. Most of these webs were of Borgia's own construction, the product of a subtle but limited mind intent upon defending its own and indifferent to the interpretations that might be placed upon his actions. It is out of these contradictions that the more lurid charges against him were to be manufactured, particularly the tangled legal web he wove around his family which made inherently credible the otherwise grotesque charge of incest. But the contradictions in the conclave which brought Borgia from the wings to the center of the stage were, for once, none of his making. Nevertheless, the pattern endures so that it is possible to argue with almost equal force and logic that he committed simony on an unprecedented scale, or that he was simply the victim of appearances.

It was not inherently improbable that naked bribery with actual money should play a part in a conclave. Piccolomini's candid evidence had made that quite clear even thirty years before, and matters had deteriorated considerably since then. Rather more complex—bordering, indeed, upon the metaphysical—was the charge that Borgia had committed simony by promising Sforza the office of vice-chancellor in exchange for his vote. If this were simony then the honorable Piccolomini had been just as guilty in confirming Borgia in that same office for the same reason, and guilty, too, was every newly elected pope who distributed his necessarily vacated benefices and offices among his friends rather than among his enemies.

In any case, Borgia could have continued his defense, what bribe could a conclavist offer to a rival that could possibly compensate him for the loss of so universal and so absolute a power? Ascanio Sforza had stood on the brink of success. His only two rivals had been Borgia, and della Rovere. Borgia was personally popular and known to be highly competent, but was compromised by his nationality, while della Rovere had not only incautiously displayed his true nature while in a position of power during the previous pontificate, but was also known to be strongly pro-French. It was rumored, indeed, that the king of France had contributed some two hundred thousand florins to his campaign fund. As usual, the favorite had emerged not so much because the conclave liked the idea of him as pope, as that it disliked the idea of one of his rivals emerging as supreme lord. Reluctantly, the cardinals were opening a path by which Ascanio Sforza could ascend the throne—and then he abruptly drew back. Why should he do this, accepting the lesser for the greater?

The Roman observers were content to accept the fact without delving into the reason. Each man, after all, had his price, and the Roman chronicler Infessura came forward with the dramatic story of how four mules loaded with bullion were seen to pass from Borgia's palace to Sforza's during the small hours of the morning of the conclave, the precious load constituting the cash element in the transaction. Infessura was a republican and bore so bitter a hatred for the papacy that, in his chronicle, the woman's milk that was administered to the dying Innocent was transformed by Infessura into blood taken from children at the cost of their lives. But liars can also tell the truth, and his charge that Sforza succumbed to bribery was endorsed by the Milanese chronicler, Bernadino Corio, a temperate and well-informed man who was naturally sympathetic toward a leading member of Milan's great family. He knew Ascanio Sforza well and so was able to give some insight into the reason why a man in such a position might sell his vote. In Corio's view, Ascanio was something of a simpleton, a man who lacked the courage to stake everything on a single throw of the dice and therefore accepted immediate wealth, together with an immensely powerful office, with the intention of fighting another day from a secure base. He made a fatal mistake, Corio believed, and so, with a certain justice, was responsible for his own ultimate destruction.

Apart from Corio's judgment and the cynical, though not necessarily inaccurate opinion of the Romans, the silence of those accused provided a powerful, if negative, indication that Borgia's election was indeed a criminal act, for that silence looks uncommonly like the silence of guilt in the circumstances. Eighteen months after the election a massive international movement was made to oust Alexander from the throne. The major accusation was that his simony had invalidated his election, and he made no attempt to counter that particular charge. Moreover, bribery was a two-way business, as Guicciardini pointed out honestly enough, and if Alexander was guilty so too were those who "without any regard to the precepts of the Gospel, were not ashamed of making a traffic of the sacred treasures, and that in the most high and eminent seat of the Christian religion." Those who had accepted the bribe also remained silent under the accusation. Objectively speaking, it seems probable that Borgia did indeed buy the majority of his votes, but that the prevailing situation of corruption made his act appear virtually normal, and it was not until a legal weapon was sought against him that the charge was formalized and thereby entered the canon of Borgia legend as a uniquely wicked act.

Hindsight has luridly colored the reaction to his election, but at the time it was welcomed heartily enough even though it had come as a surprise. The Roman populace, which had often enjoyed Borgia's lavish public entertainments, looked forward to a glittering pontificate of pleasure. The princes of Italy and Europe came to the reasonable conclusion that no pontificate could possibly be as bad as the last, a conclusion backed by the members of the Curia itself, who had nothing but good to say of Borgia's solid professional competence. Doubtless many of the compliments were the product of protocol rather than affection, but most seem to have been imbued with a genuine respect for the man and hope for the future. Ferrante of Naples sounded a sour note: "Upon hearing the news he dissembled his grief in public but with tears—which he was not accustomed to shed at the death of his children—told his queen that this creation would prove fatal to Italy and a scandal to Christendom."[18] But given Ferrante's character and the longdrawn struggle between the papacy and the Kingdom of Naples, Alexander Borgia might reasonably have concluded that a Neapolitan insult equaled a compliment from any other source.

He began his reign with a characteristic admixture of good sense and ostentation that appealed at once to the sober minority as well as the majority ever agog for new sensations. It was a secretary of the Chancery who noted that, as cardinal, Borgia had attended every consistory for thirty-seven years, a record impressive in itself and outstanding in an administration where the frivolous were increasingly in evidence. One of the results of the increasingly corrupt administration of the papacy was the complete collapse of law and order during the interregnum between the old and new pontificates. There were riots, the product of pure hooliganism, but unconnected with any political object. Over two hundred people were murdered in a little over ten days and ordinary life in Rome came virtually to a standstill. Alexander acted vigorously. Murderers, instead of flaunting themselves as folk heroes, found themselves pursued, apprehended and hanged—not from the traditional gallows near Sant' Angelo but over the razed ruins of their own homes. For a brief period the papal troops became the symbol of law instead of a weapon in a dynastic struggle; so that by August 26, when Alexander's coronation took place, Rome was as quiet and orderly as it was ever likely to be.

Borgia's supreme cultural gift was an ability to organize ceremonials. In another age and another milieu he would have been a superb theatrical producer. On the occasion of his coronation on August 26, two weeks after his election, he surpassed himself. The ceremony was the oldest such in Europe, older by far than the coronation even of the emperor. For more than a thousand years the crowning of a pope had gathered to itself a wealth of symbols, each having originally possessed a precise legal meaning now forgotten, thus becoming part of the mystery of the popedom but providing opportunity for brilliant display. Borgia turned his lively mind and deep purse upon the ancient ritual and produced a ceremony whose magnificence seems to have taken even Rome by surprise.

Bernadino Corio was in Rome that August and devoted page after page of his chronicle to it, groping for ever more adjectives to describe adequately this dawn-burst of the Renaissance over the ancient city. At St. Peter's, where Alexander was crowned and emerged to display himself, "there was an incredible crowd of prelates—a most wonderful thing to see for each was wearing his mitre and each was adorned according to his particular office. One after another the cardinals advanced to kiss his feet, his hand and his mouth and all the other prelates followed suit." 19

The second part of the ceremony, that in which Rome as a whole took part, was the procession across the width of the city to take formal possession of the ancient Lateran Palace. Corio seems to have followed it the entire way, beginning with the assembling of the procession in the piazza of St. Peter's. He cast a particular eye on the Milanese archbishop who might have been the center of all this splendor. "The first was he who was blind to his own fate

—that is to say, Ascanio Sforza—attended by twelve pages, each dressed in jerkins of crimson satin, purple capes and carrying batons bearing the arms of Visconti and Sforza." [19] Each of the cardinals who followed was attended by his official "family"—retainers dressed in his colors—so that the great square was a blaze of crimson and silver, purple, violet, gold, the colors clashing with the scarcely less gaudy trappings of the papal troops—twenty squadrons of mounted men under the command of the captain, Niccolo Orsini. There were "seven hundred priests and cardinals with their retinues, knights and grandees of Rome in dazzling cavalcade, troops of archers and Turkish horsemen, palace guards with long lances and glittering shields." Civic and papal Rome were briefly united in one dazzling splendor of pageantry.

In the center the pope himself—Alexander VI, "Sovereign Pontiff and Universal Pope, Servant of the Servants of God, Supreme Lord of Rome and of the Papal States,"—benign, reveling in the magnificence which he had conjured in a matter of days. He was an impressive enough figure in his own right but after the ailing Innocent, Borgia struck the Romans as a man capable of living up even to the grandiloquent name he had chosen. Another eyewitness, Michael Ferno, described Borgia's appearance in terms suitable for a national hero and only just this side of idolatry.

> Upon a snow-white horse he sat, serene of countenance and of passing dignity. Thus he showed himself to the people and blessed them: thus he was seen of all. His glance fell upon them and filled every heart with joy. And so his appearance was of good augury for everyone. How wonderful

is his tranquil bearing. And how noble his faultless face. His glance, how frank. How greatly does the honor we feel for him increase when we behold his beauty and dignity of body.[20]

Ferno's hyperbole was doubtless the automatic flattery of a hungry scholar keeping an eye open for preferment, but it reflected Roman opinion accurately enough, for the Romans were as quick to worship as they were to destroy.

The assembled procession moved off on its long route —past Sant' Angelo, where the great cannon boomed and the men-at-arms stationed thickly between the battlements added brilliant color to the cold stone; over the bridge and past the Torre Nona, the latter innocent of its usual dangling corpse; through the narrow streets of Parione with the sinister names proclaiming their proximity to Rome's official torture chamber—down through the Street of the Executioner, the Street of the Cord and so on—into the handsome Via Papalis. The day was hot, the crowds immense, the water with which the sweepers had cooled the streets having long since evaporated so that "there was so much dust that it was almost impossible to see the sky." Past the Pantheon, the home of the old gods witnessing the triumph of the servant of the new; past the Forum, now grass-grown, its name forgotten along with its glory so that men knew it now simply as the Cow Field, a useful place for pasturing cattle in the heart of the city, past the Colosseum; past the buried Golden House of Nero.

Corio was particularly impressed by the immense triumphal arches that had been erected in a matter of days, and though for an ephemeral purpose appeared permanent, towering over the surrounding roofs. And everywhere was visible the ox emblem of the Borgia—as a statue with water and wine pouring from it; as a medallion, embroidered on banners and gonfalons, painted on walls. That emblem would take on a ferocious character later, but the inscriptions that now proclaimed Alexander a god—Jove himself—hailed his emblem not as the destroying bull but as the benevolent ox, symbol of fertility and promised abundance.

Finally, late in the afternoon, the procession reached the Lateran and there Alexander fainted, for despite his health and vigor he was sixty-one years old and much tried by that day's events. "All the court were dead with fatigue from the dust, heat and the rest," a member of the procession later remembered. "You can imagine what it was like having to ride eight or ten miles at a stretch through such crowded streets." [21] Reviving, the pope completed the ceremonies, earning the admiration of onlookers. "Alexander assumed the pontificate with the meekness of the ox—he administered it like a lion."

Rodrigo Borgia as Pope Alexander VI was not only the vicar of Christ, believed to be the unique successor of the Apostle and thus charged with the burden of all human souls. He was also the head of the world's largest organization, a bureaucracy so enormous that its functioning seemed a daily miracle. Externally, the Curia resembled a species of dinosaur lumbering along its chosen path, unaffected by outside stimuli, but internally it was flexible enough. No organization could have survived the trauma of the past century unless capable of some degree of adaptation.

The most obvious change was the increased status of

the cardinals. Princes though they were in every sense of the word, they had always been, paradoxically, the guardians of the democratic element in the Church, exerting a continual braking pressure upon the theoretically absolute power of the pope. Over the past century, when councils convened by cardinals had dared to pronounce upon the validity of this or that pope, the cardinals' power had increased. Before each election now, each member of the conclave signed an agreement that should he emerge as pope, he would recognize the privileges of the cardinals, refrain from adding to their number without their approval and contribute, if necessary, to their financial upkeep. Alexander automatically had signed that agreement—and as automatically made a mental reservation, for who could tie the universal pope, to whom had been given all powers of binding and loosing, to a promise made when he had been but cardinal? Nevertheless, the wise man moved cautiously in these uncertain times. It was not his intention to exert his will in a head-on clash with these proud men but, rather, through the smoother, surer method of simply diluting the power of the college by packing it with his own supporters.

The declared annual income of the cardinals varied widely, from a minimum of two thousand ducats a year to Giuliano della Rovere's income of twenty thousand ducats. But the overt wealth of a cardinal, even his family connections, was of less direct importance than the influence he enjoyed in an organization which had to delegate power in order to operate at all. The administration of the Church was divided into three concentric rings. The outer ring was Christendom itself, with the apostolic power dividing and subdividing into ever smaller channels until at last it passed through the humble parish priests from Iceland to Africa.

There, the permanent representative of the pope was the bishop, but there was always the danger that he might identify himself too closely with local patriotism or succumb to the pressure of the local monarch. In moments of crisis, therefore, the cardinal legate was dispatched to the locality, armed with the absolute powers of the pope himself for a limited period.

The second ring of the temporal Church was composed of the Papal States themselves. It was not for the sake of prestige or even military defense alone that the papacy battled to maintain the states. In an average year the states yielded a revenue of some one hundred thousand florins, less than the annual income enjoyed by the great mercantile powers of Milan, Venice and Naples, but far more than that of the papacy's smaller neighbors in Italy. Power in the states was concentrated almost entirely in the hands of the so-called vicars in the various cities, a system which was creaking ominously as more and more of the vicars contemptuously ignored their suzerain and acted as though they were independent lords.

The third ring was in Rome itself and this was divided into two: the civic government of the city, now almost wholly under the control of the pope; and the papal Curia, a series of great departments of state, each virtually autonomous and headed by a cardinal. The most prestigious was the chancery, which now had Ascanio Sforza as its vice-chancellor. His income of eight thousand ducats—handsome but not immense—was perhaps four times what he could have earned as a professor of law at a university. The chamberlain of the treasury probably wielded more immediate power in day-to-day matters, but the vice-chancellor's general political influence was immense. He worked in close contact with the pope himself, and through his department passed the tens of thousands of legal documents which regulated the whole enormous structure of the Roman Church in its purely temporal affairs. Here were drafted the bulls which affected the lives of millions of people; here arrived the pleas or threats of monarchs together with the petitions of little men who craved the exercise of the Apostle's power in their favor. The Chancery became the goal of every hungry scholar who could turn an elegant Latin phrase. Scores found employment, for it was growing at a greater rate than any other department, so great that eventually the larger part of it migrated from the Vatican to Borgia's old palace on the left bank of the Tiber. The vice-chancellor, as the papacy's lawyer, was therefore president of the Roman Rota, a supremely vital office. The Rota was the ultimate court of appeal for the ecclesiastical affairs of all Europe. Altogether, there was small wonder that the vice-chancellorship should be looked upon as the traditional penultimate step to the papal throne itself.

Parallel with the Chancery was the Apostolic Chamber, the department of state responsible for finances. The chamberlain, like the vice-chancellor, chose all his own officials—with one exception. The papal treasurer was appointed directly by the pope, and Alexander, always preferring to achieve his ends by outwardly legal means, gratefully took advantage of the system and appointed his cousin, Francesco Borgia, to the office. Rumor had it that Francesco was the son of old Calixtus, an unlikely story that was Francesco's only claim to fame. But Alexander needed a loyal, competent and pliant man in this delicate post. Francesco occupied it throughout the pontificate, receiving a cardinal's hat as reward.

Papal revenues were in two forms, spiritual and temporal, faithfully reflecting the dual nature of the papacy itself. Spiritual income was received from all Europe. Originally, it had taken the conventional form of gifts from the faithful together with such customary payments as the annates, one year's income from each new occupant of a benefice whether he were bishop or parish priest. Gradually however, a new, far more lucrative and ultimately more damaging form of spiritual revenue began to appear, the sale of indulgences and of offices. Even before Alexander's time the sales had increased to such an extent that a recognized sub-department, the Datary, came into existence to control it. The Datary proved an ideal instrument for Alexander. He already had perfectly legal access to a secret treasury, a fund which allowed him to finance his personal expenses without the necessity of gaining the chamberlain's approval. But though the fund was generous it could not keep pace with Alexander's demands upon it as his ambitions for his children grew ever greater. The treasury machinery was too complex and too public for his purpose. It was, after all, a little embarrassing to see milliners' and jewelers' accounts solemnly set down in the Apostolic registers. But the newly evolved Datary existed in a kind of no-man's land, and Alexander brought it under his direct control. Unsophisticated people might complain that the sale of offices was simply another version of simony, but it was just possible to argue that the sale constituted a loan, the buyer recouping his outlay by receiving the revenues of the office. The technique provided the legal cloak which Alexander ever preferred to wear, and what actually happened to the money was known only to a very select few.

Temporal income—the revenues which the papacy

derived from its position as one of the major European landlords—had inevitably declined disastrously during the Schism but had recovered with the return of normality, when the papacy was again in a position to enforce its rights. These revenues, in addition, had received a curious and wholly unexpected boost when the Florentine, Giovanni di Castro, discovered alum in Italy. To the uninitiated there was no reason why this dull, unglamorous mineral should cause the stir it did in European banking circles. But alum probably made more fortunes than did more obviously precious metals, for it was a vital element in both clothing and tanning, Europe's major industries. Outside Italy, European alum mines had long since been exhausted, and for centuries manufacturers had been obliged to import it from Asia Minor, particularly from the mines near Constantinople, paying heavy tolls for the privilege. Long before the fall of that great city to the Turks, Europeans had been looking for another, less vulnerable source, and Giovanni di Castro found it through a combination of sheer luck and acute observation. Exploring the hills behind Civitavecchia he noticed a locality where vegetation was similar to that growing near the alum mines of Constantinople. Prospecting further, in 1462 he discovered what was to prove the immensely rich deposit of the Tolfa mines. Thus there was justification for the exuberant letter which he wrote to Pope Pius:

> Holy Father, today I bring you victory over the Turk. Every year the Turks extort from the Christians more than three hundred thousand ducats because Ischia produces but little and the alum mines of Lipari have been worked out since the times of the Romans. Today I have found seven moun-

tains so rich in alum that they could furnish seven worlds.
You will be able to supply alum enough to dye the cloth of
the whole of Europe and thus snatch away the profit from
the infidel.[22]

By great good fortune for the papacy, Tolfa happened
to be situated in the Papal States, and thereafter the Apostolic Camera exercised a virtual monopoly in the supply of
alum to Europe. Merchants were threatened with the heavi-
est spiritual penalties if they should again turn to the infidel
for alum supplies, but there was hardly a need to create an
artificial protection for a source which was hundreds of
miles closer to production centers. Revenues mounted to
some fifty thousand florins per year from this single source,
and it was a revenue not only rich but constant. No matter
what went on in the world, regardless of which princes rose
or fell, people needed clothes, clothes had to be dyed, and
so long as there was money enough to satisfy this basic
need, the stream of gold moved steadily from the choking
alum mines of Tolfa to the quiet rooms of the Camera.

Combined temporal and spiritual incomes provided
Alexander with some four hundred thousand florins annually. Compared with other European monarchs his income
was only moderate; in terms of sheer spending power, indeed, the papacy was very low in the European league. The
king of France enjoyed an income the equivalent of at least
a million florins. His powerful vassal, the duke of Burgundy, followed with an income of some nine hundred
thousand. Even England's king could boast of seven hundred thousand annually, while in Italy the only major power
with a smaller income than Alexander's was Florence with
two hundred thousand. The largest single charge on Alex-

ander's purse was the upkeep of the standing army necessary to defend the Papal States. It cost one hundred thousand florins, a quarter of the entire revenue. In bookkeeping terms, the states simply paid for themselves. The next major charge on his purse was the half share which each cardinal levied by right upon the revenues of the Patrimony, the area immediately surrounding Rome. This accounted for a further thirty thousand florins or more, reducing the revenue to some 250,000 florins even before the scores of lesser payments were made.

The papacy, outwardly so magnificent, was in fact in a state of chronic penury. A pilgrim in Rome saw only the fixed assets. Gaping at the accumulation of more than a millennium's existence—the priceless vessels, the gorgeous robes, the splendid palaces and churches—he might reasonably conclude that the Church was the fount of all wealth as well as all wisdom. But the clerk, adding up his figures in some airless cubicle, could see the reality: the papacy was balanced on the knife-edge of solvency, with revenues only just equaling expenditures. The speed with which the Tolfa windfall was assimilated into ordinary income showed how narrow that margin was. A pope who wanted to raise a large sum of money for an unusual purpose had only limited options. He could increase the taxes on the Jews, the only wealthy group who could be treated with impunity, he could borrow, he could appeal to Christendom generally (the usual course when he wanted to finance a crusade), or if he were fortunate in his timing, he could wait for a jubilee year. Every fifty years, at the turn of the century and of the half-century, the faithful were summoned to Rome and arrived in tens of thousands to make a great public demonstration of faith at the tomb of the Apostle and at the mother churches of Christendom. Alexander, as ever, was fortunate, for the next jubilee was scheduled for the year 1500. Nevertheless, though he could then count on a certain addition to income, it would be less than the splendid outward appearances betokened. Jubilee expenses were heavy and the Roman shopkeepers rapacious, taking a very large share of the pilgrim's purse. Money was in short supply throughout Europe. It would be at least another twenty years before Aztec gold circulated in any quantity, and the pope was in direct competition with the gold-hungry monarchs of the continent, each of whom needed ever more specie to maintain their growing armies and the increasing splendor of their courts. Alexander had every pressing reason to look elsewhere for money, and under pressure of need, progressed almost imperceptibly from unconventional to actively criminal means of obtaining it.

The papal budget was heavily in the red at the time of Alexander's election. Indeed, it could hardly have been otherwise, considering the mixture of incompetence and corruption that had characterized the previous pontificate. Alexander succeeded in balancing that budget, for he brought to the office of pope the same frugality with which he had run his household as cardinal. Even in later years when his son Cesare forced him to find ever larger sums to match the young man's ravenous ambitions, Alexander maintained a careful watch over the curial machinery itself, so that it functioned more efficiently, more economically than it had for many decades past. Under Alexander's rule, the Vatican became the center of gaudy entertainments, but the observant noticed that they cost Alexander very little indeed. The profusion of costly, but inherited, plate and the glittering company at banquets obscured the fact that the meal itself usually consisted of a single course and that wine, though abundant, was of inferior quality. Alexander loved theatrical entertainments, provided that they were not intellectually demanding. And actors were cheap, a stage could be erected for a few ducats, and the artists who created the spectaculars were glad enough to work for little or nothing in return for the immense prestige gained. Alexander had no intellectual pretensions, no particular ability or desire to seek out and reward original talent, but that admixture of affability and majesty which all men noticed about him gave him an immense personality so that he seemed to confer where, in fact, he received. His court became fashionable and, in the manner of successful fashions, created its own standard. His guests scarcely noticed that it was they, striving to outdo each other with glittering entourages and splendid gifts, who actually created the glamorous atmosphere. His household expenses rarely rose above ten thousand florins per year, an impressive figure when compared with the thirty thousand florins that the Medici deemed necessary to run their household in Florence or the one hundred thousand florins that the papal household itself would need in a generation's time when a Medici pope sat on the throne.

The
Court
of Rome

4

At sixty Alexander was still an extraordinarily
attractive man. He was by no means handsome, as his
sons Cesare and Juan were. His head was too fleshy, the
nose and mouth too heavy for formal good looks. But
all who came in contact with him, men and women alike,
testified to a magnetism which made mere regularity of
features an irrelevance. The portliness of middle age
had developed into an undeniable stoutness, but
Alexander was tall enough to carry the weight of flesh
so that it gave him genuine majesty. There was nothing
stiff or pompous about him. The small plump hands
gesticulated energetically in conversation, the black eyes
sparkled; the sensuous, generous mouth under the great
beak of a nose smiled easily. Perhaps the most
impressive thing about Alexander was his voice. He
loved taking part in the sonorous rites of the Church,
his vigorous, full-bodied chanting sounding beautiful
even among professional choristers, for his voice was

resonant and rich. In conversation his voice could hypno-
tize, now falling beguilingly, now lashing out venomously
in anger, now urgent, now pleading, but always alive.

Alexander brought to the business of being pope a
certain gusto, a certain larger-than-life quality which was
the product of immense self-confidence. He never seemed
to have any doubts either in religion or politics. A less
confident man might have displayed some diffidence when
the Portuguese and Spaniards came to him to complain
about each other's trespassing in the New World. Alexander merely called for a map and, with a splendid gesture,
divided the world between the two nations. In religion he
was orthodox and, if anything, inclined to be old-fashioned. He displayed an unusual degree of veneration for
the Madonna, and in her honor instituted that sounding of
the angelus bell which was to echo throughout Catholic
Europe down the following centuries. It was precisely the
rather showy, theatrical gesture which he liked to make,
and gave no real indication as to his true religious beliefs.
Canon lawyers contemplating the bizarre temporal prece-
dents he established, and forced to disentangle their consequences, could perhaps count themselves fortunate that he
did not similarly experiment with the spiritual side of his
office.

Tolerance was undoubtedly Alexander's most obvious
good point. One of the first acts of his pontificate was to
take official notice of the new art of printing and establish
the Index of prohibited books as a bulwark against the
spread of heresy. It would have been a natural act, one
which could have been legally justifiable, to extend the
censorship to cover the political pamphlets which attacked
him personally. He did not do so even though some of the

propaganda leaflets were remarkably vile compilations, accusing not only him but also his children of every imaginable lust of the flesh and mind. "Evil is often spoken of me but I let it pass," he remarked to the Venetian ambassador on one occasion, and it was true enough.

Alexander's curiously long-suffering patience with the turbulent Girolamo Savonarola in Florence bore ample witness to that fact. He had summoned Savonarola to Rome "to give an account of the prophecies for which he claimed Divine inspiration," prophecies which were causing dangerous political upheavals. It was a perfectly legitimate act on the part of Savonarola's spiritual superior, but the monk ignored the summons, defied the excommunication which followed and garnished the defiance with a personal attack on Alexander and the Rome over which he presided.

> They only ring their bells for coin and candles. They sell their benefices, sell the Sacraments, traffic in masses. When the evening comes one goes to a gaming table, another to his concubine. They are steeped in shameful vices. Formerly it used to be said "if not pure, at least demure." Now no one need try to keep up appearances. No one talks now of his nephew but simply of his son or daughter. All veils are cast aside.[23]

The most obvious person in Rome who might have more fittingly termed his own son his nephew was Alexander, but he ignored the personal barb as he ignored the ever more vicious ones which followed. Even the Florentines wearied of their self-appointed leader's violent language and ever wilder denunciations and claims, but when Alexander did move against Savonarola it was simply on the grounds of insubordination and of acting as priest while excommunicated. "Does this friar think that he alone was excepted when Our Lord conferred the power of binding and loosing on our predecessor St. Peter? Our duty as pastor of the flock forbids us to tolerate such conduct any longer." Alexander was still prepared to absolve Savonarola "if the monk will prove his obedience by abstaining from preaching for a reasonable time,"[24] but by then Savonarola had totally departed from reality and was shortly afterward abandoned by his followers to his thronging enemies in Florence itself. Alexander merely had to approve what was virtually a fait accompli.

The eulogies which attended Alexander's accession to the throne no more reflected truth than did the execrations and legends which followed his death. Both eulogies and execrations alike were political products, the work of men with axes to grind or grievances to work óff. But he was well liked by those who came into humdrum, daily contact with him, by the servants or court officials who had nothing to hope or fear politically from him. All other things being equal, Alexander preferred to be liked rather than disliked, preferred laughter to tears, preferred doing a favor to a disfavor. In return he was served cheerfully enough and with what seems to have been real affection—sufficient on one occasion to save his life. In the summer of 1500 he happened to be seated in the throne room, talking to the datary Ferrari and the chamberlain Gaspar, when a freak storm broke violently overhead. Ferrari and Gaspar dashed to the windows to close them and as they did so lightning struck the building, collapsing a large part of the roof and the story above the throne room. When the two men turned back into the room all they could see was an enormous mound of rubble burying the throne with Alexander still seated in it. Crying for help, the two elderly clerks threw themselves on the mound dragging away the stones and timber and plaster. They found Alexander alive, but bleeding and unconscious. The canopy of the throne, in collapsing, had protected his head but he would probably have suffocated had it not been for the prompt action of Ferrari and Gaspar.

Alexander much preferred the living arts to the static, singing and dancing being his favorites. Nevertheless, he was sufficiently sensitive to contemporary currents to try his hand at architecture, commissioning permanent work on the Vatican palace. The previous fifty years' work on the palace had progressed spasmodically, stopping or starting according to the aesthetic appreciation of the reigning pope and the state of his treasury. Sixtus had built the Sistine Chapel, a gaunt forbidding building ideally suited to its primary purpose of providing a secure place for conclaves, but which added little of architectural beauty. His successor, Innocent, had ignored the main block altogether and built himself a beautiful little summer palace, called the Belvedere, at a distant point in the garden. Now Alexander took a hand, erecting the structure called the Torre Borgia. His architectural contribution was little more attractive than Sixtus's for, externally, the Torre Borgia was simply a massive tower built as much for defense as for the enlargement of the existing accommodation. But internally the two ground-floor rooms became part of a glowing jewel of early Renaissance art. The rooms adjoined three existing chambers in the old palace which Alexander had obviously long had his eye upon as possible private quarters, should

he ever become pope. Almost immediately after his coronation he commissioned Pinturicchio to decorate the rooms
in the shortest possible time. Pinturicchio worked speedily.
The plaster on the new rooms of the Torre Borgia could
hardly have been dry when he began work on them, because he finished the whole work in a little over two years
after Alexander's accession. The speed betokened his own
skill in organizing the elaborate work and Alexander's
burning impatience for quarters that would bear his own
imprint.

Fashion rather than artistic sensitivity probably led
Alexander to choose Pinturicchio, for at thirty-eight the
wizened little man with the big head had emerged from the
ranks of the anonymous and was now much in demand
among the wealthy, more conservative Roman patrons.
There was something rather old-fashioned about his style,
as though he lacked the confidence to plunge headlong into
the exciting new world unfolding around him—a defect in
the eyes of the intelligentsia but a trait which rather appealed to someone like Alexander with his own un-
developed and provincial tastes. "Deaf and undersized,
mean in person and appearance," a contemporary dismissed Pinturicchio. He also had the bad luck to be married
to a shrew and altogether passed as a figure of fun among
the swaggering gallants of Rome. But it was this same wizened, hesitant, henpecked little man who explored the
buried past and brought back, at considerable physical danger, a lost art of the classical city. Over the past half-century
cautious and thoroughly haphazard excavations had revealed that beneath the ground-level of the present city
there lay another Rome: the halls and chambers of the
imperial Caesars, wrapped in darkness now, choked with

rubbish, dank, populated only by giant rats, but bearing upon the walls the fantastic decorations wrought by men dead fifteen hundred years. The early excavators were searching for salable treasure, either in the form of the fabled gold of the equally legendary emperors, or the more prosaic marble statuary which could now fetch a high price due to the prevailing passion for all things classical. Pinturicchio sought and brought back less tangible treasures. Later searchers were to leave dramatic accounts of the excitement and dangers of this subterranean exploration— the encounters in the dark with bats and rats; the long, wriggling, scrambling journey through choked passages; their sense of awe on gaining some vast chamber whose dimensions their feeble lights were unable to disclose. Pinturicchio had no gift for language. He spoke with his brush and his brush traced onto the new walls of Rome the designs he had seen on the walls of buried Romes, "designs which are called by the ignorant 'grotesques' because they were found in certain subterranean caverns [*grotte*] in Rome, the said caverns having been in ancient times bathhouses, studies and the like,"25 Benvenuto Cellini later explained condescendingly. Rome was ever agog for novelty and the fantastic creations with which Pinturicchio enlivened his formal studies earned the attention of the great and eventually his supreme opportunity. Unwittingly, the work he executed for Alexander was to add substantially to the Borgia legend, wrapping yet another layer of mystery around the family.

Pinturicchio's murals in the Borgia Apartments, as the five chambers became known, were predominantly religious in subject, each of the chambers being devoted to a single theme. *The Seven Joyful Mysteries of the Virgin* were depicted in the place of honor, the first chamber that a visitor entered from the Hall of the Popes. Here, too, was the great *Resurrection* in which the kneeling Alexander admires a Redeemer emerging triumphantly from the tomb. Pinturicchio placed the pope in a relatively insignificant position, tucked away in a lower corner which the eye at first passes over. The artist was, as customary, working closely by instructions and, in this instance, actually under the eye of his patron. Alexander posed on the spot for the portrait, heaving his huge body to the top of the artist's flimsy scaffolding, kneeling or sitting patiently high up in the cold, new room that smelled of wet paint and new plaster. It could therefore only have been at Alexander's express desire that, in the mural, he should have been placed in pious obscurity below his Savior. The face, however, shows no such humility, and only with difficulty can it be linked genealogically with the remote, ascetic face of his Uncle Calixtus. Plump, self-confident, self-satisfied, the mouth full-lipped and sensual beneath the enormous nose, Alexander regards his God not as an equal but, perhaps, as a junior partner might a senior—conscious of a gap in status but not overwhelmed by the knowledge. In that portrait Pinturicchio touched greatness, reflecting precisely the character of a man untouched by self-doubt and its product, conscience.

The themes for three of the four other chambers were also conventional enough. Murals here were dedicated to *The Seven Arts, The Apostles,* and *The Sibylls* and were clearly the work of a competent painter fulfilling a straightforward commission. But in the chamber which led directly from the Room of the Seven Mysteries the unassuming little artist embodied a mystery which would give a wholly unlooked-for quality to his work, turning a common enough religious painting into an enduring enigma. In this room he seems to have gathered his confidence up and, in one great swirling act of creation, transmuted into his own idiom the essence of those long-buried murals before which he had stood entranced candle in hand. The chamber was later called the Room of the Saints after the seven great murals he painted, depicting seven legends of the saints. But it might better have been called the Shrine of the Bull, for on the ceiling and in the wall spaces between the painting of the legends, the Borgia emblem was repeated hundreds of times—not the benevolent ox of the coronation procession, however, but the sacrificial bull of the god Osiris.

Pope and painter met briefly on common and curious ground. It was in precisely this fantastical representation that Pinturicchio excelled and thus reflected faithfully that trait of non-realism which lay behind Alexander's matter-of-fact façade. It was a common Renaissance conceit to give a pagan coloring even to Christian symbols and the kind of scholar who saw nothing odd in describing Christ as Apollo would see nothing strange in identifying the family symbol of Christ's current vicar with the symbol of one of the greatest of pagan gods. But to the more sober, more conventional Christians, it seemed as though the occupant of Peter's chair was already falling victim to its occupational hazard, giving more weapons to the enemy of the Borgia.

Six of the seven legends which Pinturicchio illustrated in this beautiful little chamber were unexceptional enough, but around the seventh legend—that depicting St. Catherine disputing before the pagan Emperor Maximinius—a mystery developed overshadowing even that of the Osiris bull. The overt story depicted was of Catherine of Alexandria disputing the philosophers of the emperor in theological debate, impressing him so greatly that he cut off her opponents' heads. Alexander may have approved the subject, either because of the coincidence between his pontifical name and that of the saint's city or, as the uncharitable suggested, because Catherine was also the patron saint of bastards. Whatever the reason, Pinturicchio gave undue prominence to the painting. The scene he shows is straightforward enough although he follows the usual custom of putting classical figures in contemporary dress and also includes in the background a triumphal arch similar to those erected for Alexander's coronation. The saint stands before the throned emperor, ticking off her debating points on her fingers, and behind each of the two main figures are others which represent the philosophers and courtiers of Maximinius. For nearly five centuries controversy has centered on the two central figures of emperor and saint and, on the right, the mounted horseman and the boy and girl standing in front of a bearded Oriental. These five figures are firmly claimed to be the daughter, sons, and daughter-in-law of Alexander—and the claim has been as vigorously refuted.

Lucrezia Borgia was only thirteen or fourteen years old when Pinturicchio was working in the Apartments, whereas the model he used for St. Catherine seems to be a mature woman. At about this period Lucrezia was described as being "of middle height and graceful in form. Her face is rather long, the nose well-cut, the hair golden. Her mouth is rather large, with brilliantly white teeth, her neck is slender and fair, the bust admirably well-proportioned."[26] The description could apply closely enough to the figure of St. Catherine in the fresco, in particular to the relatively uncommon golden hair and the long, slender neck. In addition, a little over a year after the mural was painted Lucrezia obtained a divorce from her first husband on the grounds of his non-consummation of the marriage. Given Alexander's legalistic mind it is highly unlikely that his canon lawyers would have cited, as grounds for the divorce, the husband's inability to consummate if the wife was obviously immature. The probability is that Lucrezia achieved maturity earlier than was common, and there is therefore no inherent improbability in seeing in St. Catherine "whose lips seem to part for sighs rather than words," the beloved daughter of Alexander Borgia.

The identification of the three sons, Cesare, Juan, and Joffre with the emperor, the mounted horseman and the boy respectively, raises additional problems whose tentative solution in turn raises more. On the grounds of age alone the identifications seem unlikely. Juan could not possibly have been more than seventeen years old when the mural was painted, whereas the horseman identified as him is clearly a man at least in his thirties. Similarly the figure identified as Joffre has the face of a mature man, and Joffre was no more than twelve years old at the time. Cesare was about eighteen years old, whereas the emperor in the mural is at least ten years older. There is an additional problem here in that the bearded face resembles very closely the reasonably authentic portraits of Cesare in his maturity. Hence, the observer regarding the supposed portraits of Alexander's son is forced to the conclusion that they can be accepted as genuine only if it is assumed that the faces were repainted years later when one of the supposed subjects, Juan, was dead.

But to reject the portraits as genuine is to raise the

insoluble problem as to why Alexander, who doted upon his children, did not instruct the artist to include their portraits with his own among the decorations of what was virtually the family home. Pinturicchio did indeed paint a series of family portraits in the Castel Sant' Angelo. But by that curious irony which seems to attend all Borgia affairs, these portraits—the only authentic ones of the Borgia children—were the only ones destined to disappear.

Time was to add an additional element of mystery, and contribute further to the legend, of the Borgia portraits. Despite the high quality of Pinturicchio's work, despite the size and importance of the rooms themselves, the Borgia Apartments fell into a centuries-long neglect after Alexander's death. That neglect supposedly arose from the evil reputation they had acquired. Giuliano della Rovere, who succeeded his hated enemy as pope, vigorously declined to live in the same quarters. But thereafter their unpopularity was caused by the fact that, as more buildings were added to the Vatican complex, the Apartments became dark, unfashionable and inconvenient. Neglect produced obscurity and obscurity inevitably produced legends. Among them was that invented by the Florentine writer Giorgio Vasari who, writing fifty years after Pinturicchio and his patron had died, stated confidently that one of the murals showed Alexander adoring his mistress, Giulia Farnese, thinly disguised as the Madonna. Yet the only mural portrait of the pope shows him unequivocally adoring the risen Christ. And over the centuries after Vasari's own death, those richly glowing murals disappeared almost entirely from public view behind clumsy partitions and cupboards. They were brought back to light in the nineteenth century, but by then the Disputation of St. Catherine was an enigma and the Borgia name encrusted with legend.

Some ten minutes' walk from the Vatican Palace rose the enormous cylindrical mass known as the Holy Angel Castle. The Emperor Hadrian had erected it as a family tomb nearly fourteen hundred years earlier, but he built too well for his purpose, since the tomb was almost custom-made as a fortress. Not content, it seems, with the existing seven hills of Rome, Hadrian determined to build an eighth as sepulchre. That vast drum, rearing up directly from the bank of the Tiber, resembled a circular hillock, for the platform on its top circus was laid out by the emperor as a garden, complete with pine trees. It commanded the major bridge over the Tiber, and from that convenient garden suspended in the sky, missiles could be hurled outward—or into the heart of the city itself. Romans made use of that fact very rapidly and the Holy Angel entered upon its long and bloody history as the major castle of Rome.

Only the most determined of cave dwellers would have wanted to live in the main sepulchral chamber, situated in the heart of the drum and reached by way of a winding, ascending passage. Air vents pierced into this passage for the convenience of funeral cortèges, but there was no other source of lighting whatsoever and the sepulchral chamber itself was in darkness. Rising from the surface of the drum, however, was a tower designed to support the enormous monument of Hadrian. Within the tower were more chambers intended for the dead but capable of being transformed for the living, as it was relatively easy to pierce windows through the walls of the tower. This was done sometime before the tenth century, and the monument entered upon its second phase as a fortress-palace. By now its origins were forgotten. Legend had it that the Archangel Michael had appeared on the tower, sheathing his sword as a sign that a current epidemic of plague was ending. Gratefully the Romans erected a statue of the archangel on the tower in place of the long-vanished monument of Hadrian, and the structure was ever after known as the Castel Sant' Angelo.

Rome was so fragmented that it was impossible to say he who held Sant' Angelo held Rome. Nevertheless, it was certainly true that whoever was installed in Sant' Angelo could defy Rome as long as he pleased, provided he was well stocked with food. Sant' Angelo was impregnable. There were bigger castles in Europe; there were also castles which were impregnable because of their inaccessible site. But no other military structure in Europe combined impregnability with close proximity to a vital area. There was only one tiny entrance, set down at the very base and leading directly into a narrow tunnel, so that any hope of battering an entrance was utterly impracticable. An assault tower could perhaps be set against the drum, but the continuous curve meant that contact could be made only along a very limited area. The advent of cannon had little impact on Sant' Angelo. A prolonged cannonade would doubtless make life unpleasant for anyone in the tower or elsewhere on the surface of the drum; but in such an emergency it was easy enough to descend to the main sepulchral chamber and there await the end of the bombardment. The only possible way to get at the vulnerable interior was to demolish the thousands of tons of stone that protected it on all sides, but there was probably not sufficient gunpowder in Europe to hurl the number of cannon balls needed to do the job.

Sant' Angelo had passed into and out of the hands of the papacy, depending on the ebb and flow of papal power in the city, until two centuries before Borgia when the then occupant of the castle, an Orsini, became pope, and thereafter Sant' Angelo remained as the main defense of the Vatican. Successive popes had tinkered with it, adding a few low buildings atop the drum and strengthening the outer defenses; but not even such great builders as Nicholas and Sixtus seemed to have grasped its full potential. Alexander, during his long years as a cardinal, must have occasionally idled away an hour planning what he would do with Sant' Angelo should he ever have the chance, for within a few weeks, possibly even days, of his election he was discussing a major project for the ancient building with the Florentine architect Antonio San Gallo. At about the same time that Pinturicchio began work on the Borgia Apartments, San Gallo brought in his army of masons and laborers who were to convert the vast, battered hulk of an emperor's tomb into a pope's elegant castle.

Alexander had two main aims in mind: He wanted to exploit the full military potential of the structure in terms of modern theories of siegecraft, and he also wanted a home. Rome had been relatively quiet the past few years; certainly no external enemy had battered at the city gates within living memory. But the time would indubitably come again when perhaps his very life would depend upon his ability to put stone between himself and the mouths of cannon, and he had no intention of roughing it in the gaunt, haunted caverns of Sant' Angelo while his enemies luxuriated in the Vatican. San Gallo was therefore working not only as a military engineer but as domestic architect in partnership with Pinturicchio.

The fact that Alexander was both portly and aging had a direct effect upon the drum itself. He declined to puff his

way up the long, winding passageway to the top but also
disliked being carried in a litter. San Gallo therefore hewed
a corridor diagonally through the drum with an access to
a raised walkway outside. The new corridor passed directly
through the central sepulchral chamber, and for the first
time in fourteen hundred years daylight penetrated, if
wanly, into the heart of the mausoleum. That apart, there
was little to be done with the enormous drum, and San
Gallo directed his attention mainly to the defensive fortifications ringing it, and the surface of the drum itself. The
castle was an easy stroll distant from the Vatican, but if its
shelter were urgently required then that quarter of a mile
or so could be a lethal journey. Years earlier there had been
a raised walkway running high over the roofs of the inter-
vening houses, leading from the first floor of the Vatican to
the top of the defensive outer walls of Sant' Angelo. San
Gallo restored and extended the walkway so that, in an
emergency, the pope could proceed in dignity and safety
from palace to castle. On the river side of the castle, the
defenses were extended and given a new, enormous round
tower: all wanting to cross the bridge automatically came
under the direct surveillance of the castle itself. Near the
top of the drum, stores for oil and grain were hewn out of
the stone; the architect designed them to hold at least 185
tons of grain and some 5,000 gallons of oil respectively—
rations enough to last the garrison at least three years.
Adjoining the stores was a row of windowless cells. Some
had already witnessed the despair of entombed prisoners
for perhaps a thousand years but others were newly
adapted cells. One of the big triangular air vents which
penetrated the surface of the drum to ventilate the winding
passage below was made use of by San Gallo. The bottom

was sealed off, creating a peculiarly horrible kind of oubliette into which a prisoner was lowered by rope. Benvenuto Cellini came to know this particular cell; at least it was dry, a marked improvement over another which that connoisseur of prison cells also experienced in Sant' Angelo. This was "a gloomy dungeon below the level of a garden which swam with water and was full of spiders and many venomous worms. They flung me a wretched mattress of coarse hemp, gave me no supper and locked four doors upon me. In three days that rotten mattress soaked up water like a sponge. I could hardly stir because of my broken leg and when I had to get out of bed to answer a call of nature I crawled on all fours with extreme distress in order not to foul the place I slept in. For one hour and a half each day I got a little glimmering of light which penetrated that unhappy cavern through a very narrow aperture. Only for so short a space of time could I read, the rest of the day and night I abode in darkness." [27] He survived largely because "my vigorous temperament became adapted to that purgatory." Others were not so vigorous or fortunate, but the Tiber ran conveniently close to dispose of the remains of those, the majority, for whom imprisonment in Sant' Angelo was simply a long-drawn-out death sentence.

But the fortifications, the walkway, the stores, the cells were only the expression of the military aspect of Sant' Angelo; almost incredibly San Gallo managed to turn part of this forbidding monument into an attractive, elegant residence. On the riverfront of the castle he created a roof garden which became one of Alexander's favorite spots. Eventually the garden disappeared, for it made a vulnerable point in the otherwise sheer front of the castle, but the low halls that San Gallo built on the surface of the drum remained to form a nucleus for what was to become a city in the sky. The great central tower remained but the chambers within it were turned over to the treasury and archives. The line of new buildings divided the surface of the drum into two semicircular courtyards, the whole forming probably the safest residence in Europe. Once a visitor had penetrated the lower defenses and made his way up the ramp, he passed a final guardroom on entering the first of the two courtyards. The main mass of new buildings rose to the left, and here Alexander held court during visits. Surrounding the top of the drum was a wall, high enough to ward off arrows of the ill-disposed, low enough to provide a superb panorama during peace. Here Alexander loved to walk, cool above the choking heat of the city, secure among a handpicked garrison, attended by his beloved family. From this vantage point the vast, forbidding drum of stone below seemed a natural feature supporting an independent community—an intimate, self-contained little city tucked under the broad iron wings of its protecting archangel. In 1497 lightning struck the angel with an effect like a bomb burst, destroying most of the buildings beneath it. Alexander ordered their immediate reconstruction, and in one of them Pinturicchio painted the authentic portraits of the Borgia children. Later, these rooms were demoted, becoming simply the guard commander's apartments, and the murals, the only certain representation of the most notorious family of Renaissance Rome, disappeared.

The court over which Alexander presided was not the largest in Europe. The king of France, for one, would have regarded life as insupportable unless his most trivial needs and wishes were the sole responsibility of some nobleman proud to bear a menial's title, so long as it gained him proximity to the royal person. But the papal Curia was undoubtedly the oldest court. For more than a millennium it had evolved an extraordinary complex of rituals and offices on a purely ad hoc basis, creating a jungle of etiquette only the adept could penetrate. Alexander's guide through the jungle—where a false step could embroil the papacy in deep embarrassment—was the German master of ceremonies, Johannes Burchard, whom he had inherited from his predecessor. Alexander was fortunate, for Burchard was as competent as he was unlikeable. Never would Burchard make the mistake of offending some powerful ambassador or encouraging an unimportant man by some error in precedence. Posterity was perhaps even more fortunate because Burchard kept a voluminous diary and it is through this diary that the Borgia can be seen as human beings going about their daily affairs, not the incredible monsters of propaganda delivering the world to Satan. Yet even as Pinturicchio's painstaking murals unwittingly created a mystery around the Borgia, so Burchard's pedantic diary added another enigmatic dimension. Unlike the painter's, however, his motives were deliberate.

The little of Burchard's own personality that emerges from his pages is remarkably unattractive. He was a courtier in the fullest, pejorative sense, permanently on the lookout for his own advantage, as avid for four ducats as for four hundred, capable of launching a complicated scheme to blacken a rival's character. A man who could not merely retain, but increase, his power under three such different popes as Innocent, Alexander and Julius must certainly have been an operator of rare skill. Nevertheless, in Burchard's work and the diary that made it possible, he displays impressive professional integrity.

His reason for keeping the diary is succinct. "Seeing that it behoves a master of ceremonies to pay heed to individuals I, Johannes Burchard, Master of Ceremonies to His Holiness our lord the pope, will note below the things which happened in my time which appeared to be connected with ceremonies together with at least some external affairs, so that I may the more readily give account of the office entrusted to me." [28] He was obsessed by detail, for not only were the complex rituals of the Roman rite his responsibility, but also the ceremonies of a most ancient court which was, above all, bound by precedent and custom. He records more than once how visiting ambassadors would come to the verge of blows even in the chapel on a question of precedence. At even minor ceremonials Burchard would record exactly what the pope wore for future reference in order that continuity might be maintained.

Despite the impression Burchard gives of being simply a recorder, he in fact seems to have enjoyed considerable influence in the Curia. At a meeting of Congregation during the reign of Innocent VIII a discussion arose as to the correct ceremony for the reception of the holy lance, the priceless relic which Sultan Bajacet had sent the pope. It was decided that a public fast would be an appropriate gesture, until Burchard pointed out that if the Romans were given a fast instead of the feast they were expecting there would be trouble. He behaved imperiously with equals, and even superiors, in the performance of his duties. "The bishop of Glasgow had a tunic of faded crimson under his cape, which was most unsuitable. I therefore advised him not to appear in public with it again." During an argument with a cardinal over a question of ritual, Burchard proved himself right by citing precedent. "So saying, I dismissed the cardinal." It is difficult to imagine any other court official dismissing a prince of the Church.

Burchard's decision to keep a journal was personal; no one in his position had ever troubled to do so before, and it was long before it became a formal part of the office of clerk of the ceremonies. Nevertheless, he appears to have expected it to be read by eyes other than his own and went to considerable lengths either to substantiate his statements or give their provenance when he was writing from hearsay or long after the described event. After noting the appointment of Robert Sanseverino as gonfalonier he added, "I should say that the above account of the creation of the gonfaloniere was noted down or rewritten by me long after it occurred, from a memorandum made by me for it long before." Elsewhere he notes on another matter, "I do not report the proceedings in greater detail because I was not present, but I have understood from others that it was as I have described." The painstaking search for accuracy and precision was undoubtedly merely the self-protective device of a bureaucrat, but the result was the creation of a record virtually unique in Renaissance Rome. Compared with the lush fantasies of his contemporary, Infessura, or the more sober but still imaginative despatches of ambassadors seeking to glean information to justify their expensive presence in Rome, the diary of Johannes Burchard achieves almost actuarial status.

The first section of the journal, that dealing with the eight-year pontificate of Innocent VIII, is devoted almost entirely to ceremonial—tens of thousands of words exclusively concerned with the problems of who should sit where, precede whom, wear what. It is therefore under-standable why references to the Borgia family should be sparse in this section, despite the fact that Rome was becoming very much aware of them. But with Alexander's pontificate, the nature of the diary changes totally. Natu-rally, ceremonial still occupied a very large part but, follow-ing his plan to give information concerning external affairs as they affected the Vatican, Burchard produced an aston-ishing number of vivid sketches of both persons and events. He still acted as recorder, giving little or no indication of his personal opinion of any particular affair, but the reader is able to follow the twists and turns of policy in terms of human personality, gaining an unusually clear idea of the motives of those concerned. Except those of the Borgia family.

Burchard's reticence arose from no sense of delicacy, for he gives not the slightest indication of surprise or disap-proval that the Holy Father of Christendom should also be the earthly father of a flourishing family of bastards. Bur-chard had, after all, been hardened in the previous pontifi-cate. His main problem with the Borgia was how to inte-grate the mistress, daughter and daughter-in-law of the pope into ancient ceremonials intended exclusively for males. Breach of tradition alone could shock him and pro-duce a disapproving note. He remarked the occasion when Giulia Farnese, Lucrezia, and her sister-in-law Sancia, bored by a lengthy sermon, scrambled out of their seats and parodied the speaker, much to Alexander's delight and Burchard's shocked dismay. Efficiently and without protest he organized Lucrezia's wedding in the Vatican, for a precedent had been established in the previous reign when he had planned the wedding of Innocent's granddaughter in the same place. Burchard did note, however, that the girls in Lucrezia's train, overcome by excitement, did not genuflect to the pope. That solecism was grimly noted to ensure that such a breach of the proprieties should never occur again, nor did they when Lucrezia was married for the second time in the same place.

It was not the existence of the Borgia children which restrained his pen, nor does he appear to have feared repercussions from using blunt words. Quite casually he could refer to Giulia Farnese as "the pope's concubine" although, in general, he employed colorless terms. But later in the reign, when Cesare's influence grew paramount, Burchard became correspondingly tight-lipped. When Cardinal Orsini died in prison in 1503, almost certainly at the behest of Cesare, Burchard noted, "Our Holy Father commanded Bernard Gutteri, my colleague, to arrange the funeral. I myself will not attend the ceremony nor have anything to do with it, as I do not wish to learn aught that does not concern me."[29] Nevertheless, his very act in recording his decision to keep his hands clean argues forcefully that he had good reason to do so, giving substance to the specific accusations of other, overtly hostile, writers. None knew better than he that the Vatican and, hence, Italy, revolved around the Borgia family. In accordance with his own intention he should have left a record of them fuller than the bare accounts of their presence in certain places at certain times. He did not do so. What he did was to outline a series of portraits and then leave it to other hands to paint in the details with increasingly lurid colors. Johannes Burchard, master of ceremonies to three popes, had brought the art of survival to a very high level indeed.

The
Dynast

5

In the spring of 1493 Ferrante, king of Naples, unburdened himself to his kinsman Ferdinand, king of Spain.

> This pope leads a life that is the abomination of all, without respect for the seat he occupies. He cares for nothing save to aggrandize his children by fair means or foul, and this is his sole desire. From the beginning of his pontificate he has done nothing but disturb the peace. Rome is more full of soldiers than of priests and when he goes abroad it is with troops of men-at-arms about him, all his thoughts being given to war and to our hurt. . . . In all things he proceeds with the fraud and dissimulation natural to him, and to make money he sells even the smallest office and preferment.[30]

No one reading that letter could have guessed that just six weeks earlier, Ferrante had been eagerly trying to arrange a marriage between his own children and those of the abominable pope, nor that in a year's time he would succeed in doing exactly that. The letter was pure propaganda, produced by his uneasy awareness of the close relationship between Alexander and Their Catholic Majesties of Spain, who still looked upon Ferrante as a usurper in Naples. In Italy the hard-won balance of forces was on the point of destruction, and a sensible man like Ferrante had long since learned to get in the first blow. But like all good propaganda, the letter had its basis in fact and Ferrante at least had the honor of being the first to voice that accusation which was to be the leitmotif of Alexander's enemies: "He cares for nothing save to aggrandize his children."

That was true enough as the world saw it. Certainly the most conspicuous feature of his pontificate, and one which gave the impression of a fixed and constant purpose, was that aggrandizement of his children. But Alexander VI was essentially a man of moods and emotions, ever swinging from one extreme to the other. At the beginning of his reign he gave the impression of one who desired to put the past behind him, to discharge as well as he could the awesome responsibilities of the role which he had grasped so eagerly. No matter that society, and Roman society in particular, accepted the existence of his children as something unworthy of note. The fact remained that their existence was a standing reproach to a man in his situation. With rather remarkable self-discipline, this man who loved his children above all other human beings deliberately excluded them from his coronation festivities. The most outstanding testimony to that desire for a new start was the fact that his eldest son, Cesare, was not even officially summoned to Rome.

Cesare was not quite eighteen years old when his father became pope. Apart from a few brief visits home, he had been absent from Rome for the past four years on that wandering course of studies prescribed for a young man of good family. At the age of fourteen he went to Perugia to study canon law at the famous Sapienza. He had no particular interest in the subject. His father intended him for the Church, and canon law was therefore an inescapable study. Nevertheless, even in this unattractive field he acquitted himself brilliantly, displaying at this very early age his ability to grasp the essentials of a situation and present it with logic and eloquence. His tutor and all the fellow students in his call were Spaniards, and among them he made the first of those friends and allies who were to remain with him, in a curiously strong attachment, throughout his brief, fantastic career. From Perugia he went to the university at Pisa and it was there, at about midnight on August 11, 1492, that a courier arrived from Rome with the news that his father had been elected pope. Cesare left Pisa a few days afterward and took the road south. Doubtless he went on to Rome, but quietly, discreetly—a private citizen whose presence in the city went unnoticed. Immediately after the coronation he moved on to Spoleto, the beautiful little hill city which was papal territory, and there he remained until March of the following year when, officially, he entered Rome and took up residence at his father's side.

By this time, Alexander's brief-lived desire for respectability had waned and died, and as rapidly the Romans began to revise their original optimistic forecast for his reign. The usual swarm of kinsmen and compatriots had flocked into Rome on news of the election; and though Alexander refused to let his love of kin affect his judgments as statesman, and appointed only competent men to high office, there was evidence enough to justify the old hatred and fear of the Catalan. "Ten papacies would not be sufficient to satisfy this swarm of relatives," the Ferrarese ambassador wrote to his master as the outlandish Spanish names reappeared in the Apostolic registers. And if the Spanish pope was generous to men whose only claim on him was their common birthplace, how much more generous should he be to those who were of his own flesh? The children of Alexander's first family were already provided for: Pedro was dead and the two girls decently married off. It was the turn now of the children of the second family, and Cesare was the first to receive the full fruits, although they were fruits that tasted bitter in his mouth for they were not of his choosing or desire. On the first anniversary of his coronation, Alexander made his son a cardinal of Holy Church.

Cesare had always been intended for the Church and therefore, from a very early age, Church benefices had been showered upon him. Before he was twelve he was a protonotary of the Church, treasurer of the cathedral of Cartagena, bishop of Pampeluna and, when his father became pope, he inherited almost automatically the family seat of the archbishopric of Valencia. His illegitimacy technically disqualified him from holding any Church office, but Pope Sixtus had obligingly granted Cesare a dispensation when he was only six years old. Nevertheless, the dispensation did not apply to the immensely powerful office of cardinal, an office which was vital to Cesare's career. His father found a way out of the impasse, and in so doing threw a curious light on Borgia family affairs. A commission headed by no less a person than the vice-chancellor Ascanio Sforza deliberated on the problem and solemnly reported that the young man generally known as Cesare Borgia was, in fact, the lawful child of Domenico d'Arignano and his wife Vannozza Catanei. Cesare was therefore not a bastard, and therefore not a son of Alexander. The pope, out of consideration for the love he bore Cesare's half-brother Juan, had taken Cesare into his family and permitted him to bear the name of Borgia. The report was published as a bull in 1493, thereby permitting Cesare's entry into the Sacred College in the same year. Simultaneously a secret bull was drawn up which disclaimed Alexander's responsibility for the published statement and specifically claimed Cesare as his natural son.

The duplicity was necessary to satisfy the letter of the law, but it must have contributed considerably to the bitter hatred which Cesare felt for his brother Juan, a hatred born of the contrasting roles which their father planned for them. Cesare was to make the family fortune through the Church, whereas Juan was to have the glamorous role of founding the family dynasty. Cesare's prospects would have dazzled most young men. Even at the age of eighteen he was probably one of the richest young men of his generation, although he possessed no land. Splendid though his Church preferments were, they implied nothing further than the passive receipt of income, and the one certain fact known about Cesare Borgia in his youth was that he was not a passive person. Looking ahead, all he could see was the career of an ecclesiastical courtier; by contrast, the range and speed of his achievements when he was given a free hand shows clearly that his talents lay elsewhere. He excelled in the bold, dramatic stroke rather than in patient, devious intrigue, preferring the glamor of force to the drudgery of bureaucracy.

A year after his father's coronation, Cesare Borgia seemed just another young Roman dandy, immensely wealthy, bedecked with titles, with his own establishment but doing nothing in particular apart from the usual round of boisterous pleasures. It must have been an intensely galling experience for a vigorous, highly intelligent young man but it was the role cast for him by his father. He could, and did, disguise his true feelings. Later, at the consistory in which he pleaded to be released from the cardinalate, he displayed a sudden flash of hatred for the brother he believed had robbed him. But meanwhile, during the long period of waiting, Cesare gave the impression of being totally satisfied with his life, accepting the boredom of a future ecclesiastical career for the sake of the present income. Andrea Boccaccio, the ambassador from Ferrara, sketched a lively picture of the young man pursuing his pleasures about town. "I met Cesare yesterday in the house in Trastevere. He was just on his way to the chase dressed in a costume altogether worldly—that is to say, in silk, and armed. He had only a little tonsure like a simple priest. I conversed with him for a while as we rode along—I am on intimate terms with him. He possesses marked genius and a charming personality, bearing himself like a great prince. He is especially lively and merry and fond of society. The archbishop never had any inclination for the priesthood— but his benefices bring him in more than 16,000 ducats annually."[31] Boccaccio incidentally conveyed a picture of himself as a toady of some magnitude, but though he was mostly concerned to let his master know that he was on such cordial terms with the great, his portrait of Cesare at the beginning of his career was borne out by others—the portrait of a highly intelligent young man with more than sufficient vigor and charm to exploit his opportunities, but seemingly content to fritter them away.

The house in Trastevere where Cesare and Boccaccio met in that spring of 1493 was the palace of San Maria in Portico, a building not far from the Vatican where lived the three most important people in Alexander's life; his cousin Adriana, his mistress Giulia Farnese, and his daughter Lucrezia, then in her thirteenth year. It was Lucrezia, more than any of the four children, who felt the full force of her father's curious domestic arrangement. Her young brother, Joffre, was still only a child; her two elder brothers Cesare and Juan would, in any case, have left the family home for the studies custom dictated. Thus it was around Lucrezia that their mother's lamentations centered. Vannozza made the best of the situation, but she did so with a deep and lasting sense of grievance. Even after Lucrezia had finally severed her links with Rome and was a duchess in her own right in Ferrara, Vannozza's sighs followed her —"your fortunate and unfortunate mother" was the manner in which she usually signed her letters to Lucrezia. It is expecting too much of Vannozza's passive nature to suppose that she would have defied Borgia's plans for their daughter in any significant manner. But it was another woman who supervised the upbringing of her child during a vital period of the girl's life—and that woman was notorious for having acted as bawd to her cousin. There was excellent reason for Vannozza Catanei to have grave doubts about her daughter's future and to pity herself as she drifted out of the Borgia story.

But the household in San Maria was a remarkably

happy one. Lucrezia and Giulia Farnese were close enough in years to pass as sisters and, given their enforced and curious propinquity, they were fortunate in that they enjoyed each other's company and became close friends. They were markedly similar in character—light-hearted, quick-witted, rather shallow but essentially generous. Their home, so discreetly presided over by Madonna Adriana, was only a step or so away from the Vatican. It became Alexander's personal sanctuary, the place where he could escape those tedious rituals of church and state which could make him explode with boredom, a place beyond the penetrating eye and disapproving sniff of his master of ceremonies. A kinsman of Giulia's, a certain Lorenzo Pucci, paid a visit to the palace on Christmas Eve 1493 and left a charming picture of the domestic life which so strongly attracted Alexander. "Today I called at the house of San Maria in Portico to see Madonna Giulia. She had just finished washing her hair when I entered. She was sitting by the fire, with Madonna Lucrezia, the daughter of our master, and Madonna Adriana and they all received me with great cordiality." Pucci had called, significantly enough, to thank Giulia for certain favors she had obtained for his family, and after an exchange of compliments, the conversation turned to domestic matters. They admired Giulia's new baby, the little girl called Laura:

> She is now well grown and, it seems to me resembles the pope for truly it is always possible to tell the fruit from the seed. Madonna Giulia has grown somewhat stouter and is a most beautiful creature. She let her hair down before me and had it dressed. Never have I seen anything like it before —she has the most beautiful hair. She wore a headdress of

fine linen and over it a sort of net, light as air, with gold thread interwoven in it. In truth, it shone like the sun! I would have given a great deal for you to be present to see her for yourself. She wore a lined robe in the Neapolitan fashion as also did Madonna Lucrezia who, after a little while, went out to remove it. She returned shortly after in a gown almost entirely of violet velvet.[32]

Pucci had eyes only for Giulia—La Bella Giulia, Christ's Bride, as the wits called her—the celebrated beauty who had captured the most powerful man in Rome. Lucrezia, homely by contrast to that dazzling feminine glory, was worth only an afterthought in his letter. But she was by no means unattractive in person or in nature. A year or so after Pucci's visit, another correspondent describes her in highly complimentary terms: "She is of middle height and graceful in form. Her face is rather long, the nose well cut, the hair golden, eyes of no especial colour. Her mouth is rather large . . . by nature she is always happy and gay." She lacked her brother Cesare's magnetism, but otherwise she shared fully the easy charm of their father.

Lucrezia was approaching her fourteenth birthday when, in June 1493, she was married off to Giovanni Sforza, lord of Pesaro. Sforza was more than twice her age, a man possessed of few talents and less charm, but who happened to be related to the most powerful family in northern Italy and so presented immense attraction to Alexander, who was much preoccupied in establishing himself securely during this first year of his reign. This was Lucrezia's first marriage but third betrothal: piecing together the ambiguous documents which marked her progress to full marital status, it would appear that at one stage she was in fact legally betrothed to two men simultaneously. Like her brother Cesare, she experienced to the full the devious interweavings that characterized Alexander's policy for his family, a policy that arose from his desire to protect his illegitimate children at every conceivable legal angle, but produced also a tangled obscurity in which legends would flourish abundantly.

Lucrezia was eleven years old when she was first betrothed in that solemn ceremony which for most people was an act almost as final and unbreakable as marriage itself. The prospective groom was a young nobleman of Valencia, and contracts between the pair were exchanged in February 1491, eighteen months before her father became pope. Then, in April of that year, further contracts were exchanged binding Lucrezia to marry another Valencian noble, Don Gaspare d'Alversa, whose father held estates in the Kingdom of Naples. It was perhaps these estates which enhanced young Gaspare's value as a potential husband, for despite Alexander's abiding affection for his native Spain, he saw clearly that his own family's future lay in Italy. No one ever seems to have troubled formally to dissolve the first contract. But the young man proved accommodating, his family accepted a modest cash sweetener for their offended honor, and Lucrezia seemed destined to become a Spanish matron whose children would some day possess a modest fief in southern Italy.

Then, sixteen months later, her father became pope and her entire future altered. Simultaneously, she was a highly valuable pawn for her father to use in his role of papal monarch seeking to defend the Papal States and, as his daughter, she was the means whereby he could place the Borgia dynasty on a sound footing in its adopted country. In the light of Alexander's later actions and his ever-soaring plans for his children, it seems unlikely that he ever viewed Lucrezia's marriage with Giovanni Sforza as other than an expedient in the fluid and potentially dangerous political conditions of the first eighteen months of his reign. But the Borgia were always able to keep their own counsel and in the eyes of the world Giovanni Sforza, the insignificant count of Pesaro, was suddenly a very important person. His splendid kinsman, Ludovico Sforza of Milan, who hitherto had barely noticed Giovanni, now gave him a high-ranking, well-paid sinecure in the Milanese army. Giovanni's neighbor, the marquis of Mantua, lent him some of the magnificent Gonzaga jewels to bedeck himself at his wedding. And Roman society was prepared to accept a provincial with thirty thousand ducats of dowry money, even if the more knowledgeable were inclined to doubt the extent of the influence Giovanni Sforza, count of Pesaro, hoped to yield.

There was but one sour note to mar the wedding preparations. Don Gaspare, Lucrezia's second betrothed, less a gentleman than the first, came to Rome swearing vengeance. "There is much gossip about Pesaro's marriage," an ambassador noted. "The first bridegroom is here, raising a great noise as Catalans do, saying he will object to all the princes and powers of Christendom. But willy-nilly, he will have to submit." The Alexander Borgia who was capable of outwitting the great monarchs of Europe was more than equal to dealing with a minor Spanish family, and the bewildered Don Gaspare found himself not merely consenting to Lucrezia's marriage, but even agreeing not to marry for at least a year afterward—a characteristically devious action of Alexander's, presumably with the object of keeping Don Gaspare available should he yet be required for Lucrezia.

But Don Gaspare was not needed, and whether or not he remained in Rome to witness his betrothed's splendid wedding to another man, no one was sufficiently interested to record. Johannes Burchard had the responsibility of arranging the wedding, carefully recording the details in that diary of his in case it should ever prove necessary to repeat the performance, for precedence was all. The ceremony took place not in the private Borgia Apartments but in the great public halls of the Vatican, Burchard correctly interpreting his master's wishes that the marriage of the daughter of a pope should be a state occasion, intimately affecting the apostolic Church. To reinforce that point the great consistorial throne was set up in the Sala Reale, the hall normally used for solemn consistories of the Church, with smaller thrones for the bride and groom before it. A hundred cushions for the principal guests were scattered on the floor, and the room, like all the other chambers, was specially decorated for the occasion with rich tapestries and hangings of velvet in a color scheme of gold and blue and green.

Lucrezia had already transferred her household to the palace of Cardinal Zeno, a friend of the family, because the somewhat ambiguous nature of the menage in Adriana's house was now thought unsuitable. Her brother Juan escorted her from the cardinal's palace to the Vatican. A Negro slave bore her train and she was followed by about one hundred and fifty maidens and matrons of Rome, including Giulia Farnese and Battistina, the granddaughter of His late Holiness, Innocent VIII. The bride's mother, Vannozza Catanei, was not present. Battistina's wedding in

these solemn halls had established a useful precedent for
Burchard to follow, and she had therefore earned her position in the most glittering wedding procession Rome had
seen in years. Vannozza, by contrast, had no status, for the
post of pope's concubine was now adequately filled by the
delightful Giulia. Despite his care, there was that indecor-
ous moment which shocked Burchard. As the procession
entered the wedding chamber, where Alexander was already seated in state, the excited women forgot their manners and rushed to their places instead of first genuflecting
before the enthroned vicar of Christ. Only Lucrezia and
those immediately around her made the correct obeisance,
Burchard noted disapprovingly. But nothing else occurred
to mar the ceremony. Camillo Beneimbene, the notary who
had put the formal questions to Lucrezia's own mother on
her wedding day nineteen years before, now performed the
same office for Lucrezia herself. Lucrezia agreed that she
was willing to become Don Giovanni Sforza's lawful wife,
rings were exchanged and a naked sword, held by the Captain-General of the Holy Roman Church, was slowly lowered over their heads. "There followed a well-constructed
sermon by the bishop of Concordia dealing with the sacra-
ment of marriage."

So Burchard recorded precisely, impassively, for his
own pedantic purposes. But among the guests was a far
livelier chronicler and that was Andrea Boccaccio, ambassador to the duke of Ferrara. Eight years hence Boccaccio
would be inspecting Lucrezia with considerably closer interest as the potential bride for his master's son, but today
he was more concerned with depicting for his master a
ceremony which very few persons have ever witnessed—the
wedding of a pope's daughter in the apostolic palace. The

little ambassador bubbled with delight at the splendors around him, avidly noting the names and office of those great people with whom he was rubbing shoulders:

> The union was publicly celebrated in the palace, with the greatest pomp and extravagance. All the Roman matrons were there, also the most influential citizens and many cardinals—twelve in number—stood near her, the pope occupying the throne in their midst. The palace and all the apartments were filled with people who were overcome with amazement. The only ambassadors present, however, were the Venetians, the Milanese and myself, and one from the king of France.

There was a tricky question of etiquette as to the correct moment to present the duke of Ferrara's gift. The pope himself solved it by decreeing that it should be presented at a private dinner party he was giving that night. Boccaccio, again present, supplied his master with a guest list, mostly family and friends of the family. The ambassador skated delicately over their peculiar relationships.

> There was Madonna Giulia Farnese—of whom there is so much talk . . . then the wife of Angelo Farnese, Madonna Giulia's brother. Then came Madonna Adriana Orsini. The last is mother-in-law of the above-mentioned Madonna Giulia. She had the bride educated in her own home, where she was treated as a niece of the pope. Adriana is the daughter of the pope's cousin, Pedro de Mila, now deceased, with whom Your Excellency is acquainted.

The supper table was cleared at four o'clock in the morning and the presents brought in: brocade and jewels from the duke of Milan; a drinking service of silver and gold from Ascanio Sforza; more gems from the Spanish Cardinal Monreale; a wine cooler from the bride's brother Juan; vases and cups of jasper and gold from two papal officials.

> These were all the gifts presented at the time. The other cardinals, ambassadors, etc., will bring their presents with them later. In conclusion, the women danced and, as an interlude, a good comedy was given with songs and music. What shall I add? There would be no end to my letter. Thus we passed the night, and whether it were good or bad Your Highness may decide.[33]

There was one outstanding omission in the long catalogue of ceremonies and entertainments: no one seems to have formally witnessed the bedding of the bride and groom. An occasion for much crude humor, it was also a vital component in a dynastic wedding on the reasonable assumption that a naked young couple who shared a bed would proceed without waste of time to the proper end of matrimony. The omission of the coarse, essential bedding ceremony was to have profound consequences for Lucrezia's unfortunate bridegroom Giovanni Sforza.

A point which Boccaccio overlooked, but which was picked up by the coldly observant eye of Burchard was that the pope's eldest son Cesare was merely "among those present." It was the favorite second son, Juan, who had the honor of leading the bride in the procession even though he should have been in Spain, at his own wedding, and had specifically postponed his departure for the purpose of giving his sister away.

The honor granted to him, at Cesare's expense, on that wedding day was all of a piece with the treatment he had received throughout his life from his father. Carlo Canale, the third husband of Vannozza, who discreetly described himself as Juan's stepfather, once told a friend that the surest way to the pope's favor was by flattering this younger son. Alexander's preference was curious. Compared with Cesare, Juan was a nonentity—boastful, arrogant, empty—reviving with his contemporaries the old hatred and fear of the Spaniard. He shared Cesare's auburn hair, good looks and fraternal hatred but little else. There was a mean, petty streak in him, well demonstrated by an incident which took place in Ascanio Sforza's palace. During a reception Juan, lolling about, was loudly criticizing the appearance and manners of the other guests. One young man took exception to being called a pig and made some remark about a "priest's bastard." Juan leaped to his feet, but instead of striking the man down as Cesare would have done, he rushed to the Vatican and complained to his father. Alexander promptly ordered a detachment of the palace guard to arrest the guest and hang him. The order was executed despite the fact that the victim, as a guest, was under the powerful protection of the vice-chancellor of the Church.

It was perhaps typical of Juan that he should make a friend of Djem Sultan, the brother of the Sultan Bajacet. Djem was now part guest, part hostage of Alexander because Bajacet paid a very useful forty thousand ducats annually into the papal coffers as long as Djem, a potential rival, was kept in Rome safely out of the way. He both fascinated and horrified the Romans.

> The appearance of this barbarian prince is fierce and cruel, his body is well knit and strongly built. He is above medium height, has one defective eye and a head which is never still as he gazes threateningly around. If this venomous serpent breaks his bonds and escapes from the cage in which Christians have secured him alas—what destruction and wounds he will inflict upon us if only he have power.[34]

At thirty, Djem was nearly twice Juan's age and exerted an extraordinary influence over him. Romans had a double cause for scandal, witnessing the seventeen-year-old son of the pope, dressed in oriental turban, robes and slippers, with a large curved dagger at his belt, walking arm-in-arm with the brother of the Grand Turk, the implacable enemy of Christendom. No one, however, was unwise enough to complain to the pontiff. The execution of Sforza's wretched guest had shown clearly the limits of Alexander's tolerance.

At the age of fourteen Juan had inherited the estate and title duke of Gandia from his dead half-brother Pedro. No empty title, it carried with it a great palace in Spain and large territories to uphold that dignity. He inherited more, for Pedro had been betrothed to Maria Enriquez, cousin of King Ferdinand, and Ferdinand now agreed that she should be transferred to Juan. It was the first major dynastic coup of Alexander's pontificate, for it linked him intimately with the royal house of a united Spain. Queen Isabella deeply disliked the idea, partly as a result of her long-standing suspicion of Alexander, but mostly, it seems, from a contempt for Juan himself. "He was a very bad man," the Spanish chronicler Bernaldez recorded flatly. "Proud, puffed up with arrogance and evil thoughts, cruel and entirely unreasonable." Nevertheless, Isabella gave way to her husband as she did in most things concerned with the Borgia, and Juan was duly accepted as the bridegroom. In 1492, during the crowded months following Alexander's coronation and in the midst of a most delicate political situation, the pope found time and energy to prepare his son's debut in Spain. Juan was not only his beloved son, but also the means of consolidating the Borgia base in its native country and Juan's circumstances were to be correspondingly magnificent. Andrea Boccaccio, that ubiquitous Ferrarese ambassador in Rome, was keeping a close watch on the emergence of this new family, informing his master of trivial and major events alike so that a composite picture could be formed in Ferrara. Juan would depart like a potentate, he wrote. "In a shop under my house there is a famous goldsmith who for months has done nothing but set jewels in rings and necklaces and buy every kind of precious stone. He showed me everything. There are great pearls in infinite numbers, rubies, diamonds, emeralds, sapphires, all in perfect condition."[35]

Juan was ready to leave by the late spring of 1493, but Alexander insisted that he should stay for Lucrezia's wedding and it was not until September that he finally left Rome. His cortège was enormous. Extravagant gifts for the bride and her royal relatives, clothes and equipment for Juan and his huge personal household, ornaments in precious metals and woods, many of them wrought by the splendid new race of artists—together they represented not merely a prince's suite but one of the vital channels whereby the new culture that had risen in Italy flowed out and began to irrigate Spain. But in addition to priceless artifacts, Juan took with him his father's concern. If a plenitude of advice could make a man, then Spain should have received the ideal prince in the shape of Juan Borgia. Alexander's letter to him was a curiously touching admixture of hard-headed political instructions and a fatherly care that his son should be at home in a foreign land, with much earnest advice as to the right method of dressing the hair in the Spanish mode, the correct form of dress and the like. The pope prided himself on his knowledge of Spanish customs and affairs, and though that knowledge was outdated, for over twenty years had passed since his last visit to Spain, it could have still been of value to a young man whose entire life had been passed in the sophisticated world of Rome.

Juan gave no evidence of profiting from that advice. It was not altogether his fault for, apart from the inherent weakness of his character, he was condemned to be eternally an alien—a Spaniard in Italy and an Italian in Spain, lacking either the intuition to identify himself with the society in which he found himself or the strength to force respect from it. Within a few weeks of his arrival in Spain, Alexander was obliged to write to him again, this time in fierce anger, for Juan's loutish behavior imperiled the delicate balance of Borgia influence in Spain. He had treated his highborn bride with the ultimate insult, not bothering to consummate the marriage, instead preferring to roam the streets of Barcelona with a gang of highborn rowdies. Italians, and particularly Romans, would have laughed; the Spaniards were incensed, and thereafter Alexander kept the closest watch on Juan, empowering his envoys to discipline him if necessary. Juan was never to learn political sense, but he was a good-looking young man, possessing sufficient of the Borgia charm first to mollify his indignant young wife and then to turn her into his willing slave.

In September 1493, at about the time when Juan's immense caravan was leisurely traveling south and at about the time when Lucrezia was unenthusiastically inspecting her new home in Pesaro, Alexander married off his fourth child by Vannozza, the eleven-year-old Joffre. The bride was Sancia, the illegitimate daughter of the heir to the throne of Naples and this time Juan did not bother to defer his departure to Spain: there were no priceless gifts; there was not even a bride, for the marriage in the Vatican was by proxy. The Neapolitan nobleman who took the part of the bride put on a splendid act of buffoonery, exhibiting an excruciating coyness as the vows were changed. But that was all which enlivened a purely paper transaction. The cold little ceremony, however, marked a moment of far more importance than Lucrezia's splendid wedding to a nonentity; of greater importance even than Juan's match with a Spanish heiress. Joffre's marriage shows Alexander, as pope, finally tackling the nagging papal problem of Naples which every pope, sooner or later, had to face. The marriage has Alexander, as a Spaniard, entering into an alliance with the major Spanish power on the Italian mainland. And the marriage is the moment when Alexander, as a Borgia, united his family with King Ferrante of Naples and his son Alfonso, perhaps the most evil and certainly the most hated men in Italy.

Over half a century had passed since the Spanish House of Aragon had thrown out the French Angevins from Naples and settled down to rule in their stead but, as far as the ordinary Neapolitan was concerned, the Aragons

THE ARAGONESE
HOUSE OF NAPLES

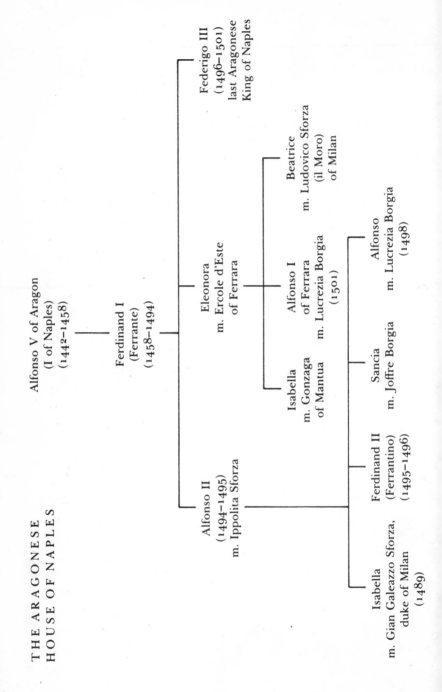

Alfonso V of Aragon
(I of Naples)
(1442–1458)

Ferdinand I
(Ferrante)
(1458–1494)

Alfonso II
(1494–1495)
m. Ippolita Sforza

Eleonora
m. Ercole d'Este
of Ferrara

Federigo III
(1496–1501)
last Aragonese
King of Naples

Beatrice
m. Ludovico Sforza
(il Moro)
of Milan

Isabella
m. Gonzaga
of Mantua

Alfonso I
of Ferrara
m. Lucrezia Borgia
(1501)

Isabella
m. Gian Galeazzo Sforza,
duke of Milan
(1489)

Ferdinand II
(Ferrantino)
(1495–1496)

Sancia
m. Joffre Borgia

Alfonso
m. Lucrezia Borgia
(1498)

were, and remained, as alien as the dynasty they had supplanted. The Neapolitans had rather liked the first Aragonese king, old Alfonso I—flatterers called him The Magnanimous and it was accurate enough as such sobriquets went. He abandoned all claims to his native Aragon and devoted all his energy to Naples, incidentally giving a Renaissance veneer to its polymorphous culture. A strong man, ruthless when necessary but on the whole a good man —such was the general verdict on Alfonso I when he died in 1458.

The nature of his son and successor, Ferrante, therefore came as a considerable shock. Italians, even Neapolitans, rarely took active pleasure in cruelty but there was about Ferrante a quality of refined evil that pointed up his alien ancestry. It was a cruelty which surpassed even that expected from a Spaniard and gave substance to the whispered charge that his unknown, unacknowledged mother had been a Moor. He gloated over torture and preferred mental to physical pain. His aged secretary, who had served both him and his father for decades, desperately tried to buy his master's continuing favor with gifts of land and money when he suspected that his days were numbered. Ferrante smilingly accepted everything until all had been given and then struck the old man down. Those enemies who fell into his hands were chained in cages among which he liked to stroll as at a zoo. Legend had it that when death at last released their souls, Ferrante still kept their bodies, embalming them so that he could continue to gloat over them.

But Ferrante, unfortunately for his subjects, was not only skilled in cruelty: He was also a statesman of supreme ability, surviving in the approved manner by playing his enemies off one against the other. For forty years, the enormous kingdom of Naples lay quiet in his grasp, its turbulent barons seemingly hypnotized by the nature of their monarch. Innocent VIII, Alexander's immediate predecessor, had tried to exert the papacy's theoretical right of control over Naples by stirring up trouble among the barons. Ferrante crushed the incipient rebellion with sickening cruelty, fought the papacy to a standstill and declined to pay any other tribute except the traditional annual gift of a white horse.

Much of Ferrante's power derived from the fact that he was skilled and fortunate in those marriage negotiations which bound the states of Italy into an intricate web. His daughter, Eleonora, was the wife of Ercole d'Este, the tough old duke of Ferrara. Her two daughters, the beautiful Beatrice and Isabella, had married Ludovico Sforza of Milan and Francesco Gonzaga of Mantua respectively. The daughter of Ferrante's son Alfonso was, by title at least, the duchess of Milan although both she and her husband remained in the shadow of Ludovico, the regent of Milan. At the age of seventy, Ferrante could congratulate himself on a stable kingdom at home supported by a network of dynastic alliances.

Then, abruptly, this new family had risen above the horizon, these part-Spanish Borgia with their ravening ambitions, backed by the enormous power of the Keys, creating their own wide-ranging alliances that might, in time, throttle even the House of Aragon. Ferrante's first instinct had been to try and outflank them; that was why he had written to his kinsman the king of Spain in the spring of 1493 protesting against Alexander's mode of life. That move failed, for Ferdinand of Spain was not yet ready to interfere in Italian affairs. Almost immediately afterwards the long-standing alliance between Milan and Naples collapsed when Ludovico Sforza usurped the throne of Milan and, as if that were not enough, Alexander then married his daughter Lucrezia into the Sforza clan.

Ferrante found himself floundering wildly for balance after years of manipulating the balance of others. He could not outflank the Borgia; he could not attack them; could he perhaps join them by the recognized means of a matrimonial alliance? His first move was to try and obtain Cesare as husband for Sancia, the illegitimate daughter of his son Alfonso. Alexander toyed with the idea but then stuck to his decision to retain Cesare in his holy calling and obligingly offered the boy Joffre instead. The youngest, instead of the eldest son, represented by no means so good a match but Ferrante, by now thoroughly off balance, had no choice but to accept. He had to accept, too, the knowledge that should a better political alliance occur to Alexander before the eleven-year-old Joffre was eventually bedded with Sancia, then that marriage would go the way of other proxy Borgia marriages.

In January 1494, just five months after that proxy marriage, Ferrante died—"sine luce, sine cruce, sine Deo" as Burchard tersely put it. The fate of Ferrante's heir, Alfonso, and of the entire Spanish dynasty in Naples now lay in the plump bejeweled hands of Alexander for he alone, as pope and suzerain of Naples, had power to crown the next king of Naples. But if Alfonso lay, quite literally, at the mercy of Alexander, Alexander himself had most urgent need of Alfonso. The uneasy—the unnatural—calm that had prevailed throughout Italy since Alexander's election was on the verge of breaking up, the traditional enemies of the papacy having joined hands with the Spaniard-haters to threaten his very survival. Worse, far worse, was the news that yet another French campaign to conquer Naples was

being planned. Such plans were commonplace enough, but
this one differed from the rest in that the leader was the
idealistic young king of France himself, Charles VIII, whose
ultimate aim was nothing less than a Crusade to recover
Jerusalem. Charles had already announced his intention of
claiming the crown of Naples as a descendant of the legitimate Angevin dynasty. A standard move that. But he had
also announced his intention of reforming the papacy as a
by-product, and the only way the papacy could be reformed
was by removing its current head. A large army was being
formed in France, and the French ambassador in Rome had
already appeared before Alexander mingling threats with
promises in an attempt to persuade him to abandon Alfonso and restore the legitimate Angevin dynasty in the
person King Charles of France.

Alfonso, closely watching events from Naples, was well
aware of the changed position and in February 1494 despatched a splendid embassy to Rome. The ambassadors
presented the traditional white horse to the pope, humbly
recommended their master, and heavily hinted that it
would be as well to settle matters while both parties had
freedom of movement. Alexander agreed that the proxy
marriage between Joffre and Sancia should now be consummated as swiftly as possible but, aware of Alfonso's
vulnerable position, he drove a very hard bargain indeed,
a bargain which would not only enrich Joffre but his two
brothers also. The proxy marriage had already made Joffre
prince of Squillace and lord of Cariato with a guaranteed
annual income of ten thousand ducats. Now the boy was
invested with one of the seven great offices of Naples, that
of Grand Protonotary, and received in addition a further
income of ten thousand ducats annually in recognition of
his services as a military commander. His brother Juan,

then strutting in Spain as the duke of Gandia, became a Neapolitan nobleman—prince of Tricarico—with appropriate estates and income plus a salary of thirty-three thousand ducats for military services which were as purely notional as were Joffre's. In the bargaining Cesare received less glamorous and marginally less lucrative appointments. Four days after the contract was signed, his head had been shaved in its first tonsure, the physical manifestation of his father's determination to make him a priest. Nevertheless, there were many rich benefices in Alfonso's hands and Cesare was able to pick up a comfortable four thousand ducats a year to add to his income. The most loyal of Alfonso's advisers might have pondered the curious potency of matrimonial alliances in state affairs. In exchange for the honor of uniting the bastard daughter of King Alfonso with the bastard son of Pope Alexander, the Neapolitan treasury was not only committed to paying out nearly seventy thousand ducats a year for the next generation, but in the kingdom itself two more foreign territorial lords had been established.

The crowning of King Alfonso of Naples, and the wedding of Don Joffre Borgia with Donna Sancia d'Aragona were affairs of great enough state to warrant the presence in Naples of the papal master of ceremonies himself. Accordingly, Burchard left his familiar quarters in the Vatican palace on April 20, 1494, accompanied by four servants newly dressed at his own expense and, despite vile weather, journeyed to Naples in four days. Both the coronation, on May 7, and Joffre's wedding, which took place four days later, went smoothly. Burchard had a lively argument with his Neapolitan opposite number regarding the exact nature of Alfonso's oath of fealty to the papacy, but Johannes got his way so that the king was obliged to acknowledge specifically that he ruled only by grace of the pope. At the wedding Burchard noted, shocked, how the queen's attendants openly helped themselves to the golden ducats which Joffre ceremonially offered his bride. Joffre aroused considerable amusement with the hastiness of his reply to the formal question "Do you accept this woman," a quickness which was totally out of keeping with his childish face and form and which was certainly not shared by his bride.

Sancia was sixteen years of age, a beauty even in this court of voluptuous women, rather less innocent than her unmarried status implied and wholly contemptuous of the child with whom she was about to be bedded for the greater glory of the papacy and the kingdom of Naples. Her discontent was temporarily reduced by the sight of the rich presents her bridegroom brought her: the necklaces of pearls, the ornaments of rubies and diamonds and emeralds, the golden rings set with immense gems, the lengths of brocades and silks and velvets, all warming the feminine eye and heart. But one needed no worldly knowledge to predict that this particular marriage was unlikely to run smoothly. That, however, was no concern of His Holiness's master of ceremonies. Johannes Burchard, his duty done, turned tourist, gaping at the natural steam baths, the sulphur springs and other abundant marvels of the landscape around Naples before returning to Rome, well content with himself and his world, leaving Don Joffre Borgia to make himself at home as well he might in the kingdom of Naples. But elsewhere in Italy the uncertain calm was about to break into a full storm, menacing not only the much-threatened kingdom itself but also Don Joffre's father and the whole future of the Borgia clan.

The
French
Invasion

6

Milan, the state destined to fall and drag the others to ruin with it, was to all appearances the most solidly based of those five powers which dominated Italy. Unlike Venice, it was unaffected by the rising power of Islam. Unlike Florence, it drew its wealth from an immensely fertile region, and its subject cities had long been rendered truly subordinate. And unlike Naples and Rome, Milan possessed a ruler who could reasonably be argued to be of native and of popular stock.

Technically, Ludovico Sforza was merely the regent of Milan, ruling on behalf of his young nephew, Gian Galeazzo Sforza, the true duke of Milan. But the ailing, spiritless boy and his vivid but helpless wife, Isabella, were being pushed ever further into the background by the splendid Ludovico, epitome of the Renaissance prince. "Born for the ruin of Italy," was the pronouncement of his contemporary and biographer, Palo Giovio, an opinion echoed and elaborated until the entire responsibility for the Italian tragedy was placed upon Ludovico's plump shoulders. He was just twenty-nine years old when he settled himself in his illegal throne. His nickname, "Il Moro," was simply a version of his baptismal name, Maurus, but flatterers gave it a special significance. One meaning of the word "Moro" was "mulberry," supposedly the wisest of plants because it is the last to put out leaves after the winter and the first to bear fruit. Delighted, Ludovico adopted the mulberry as part of his insignia; mulberry became the fashionable coloring among the ladies and gentlemen of the Milanese court, and the fruit itself appeared repeatedly in frescoes and carvings. But "Moro" could also be interpreted as "Moor"—the skilled, cunning and resourceful native of Africa—and this interpretation, too, Ludovico adopted. Sometimes both interpretations were used, together, as in that hypocritical painting in which Ludovico—half Moor, half mulberry tree—shelters his helpless young nephew, the duke of Milan. But usually it was as a Moor that Ludovico appeared in iconography, such as in his favorite propaganda painting, in which he is shown in the guise of a Moorish servant brushing the hem of Italy's dress.

For it was as arbiter of Italy's fate that he saw himself —and as others saw him in the first years of his rule, dazzled as they were by the splendor of his court. Milan's great wealth in the blooming years of the Renaissance enabled it to attract fashionable talent to the court; so that in the eyes of contemporaries, it was Milan rather than Florence that was the home of the new culture. Ludovico possessed a genuine sensitivity and love of the new world of the mind, to which he gave expression not only through the obvious means of commissioning frescoes and sculptures, but also in the less glamorous maintenance of scholars and writers whose works by no means automatically flattered their patron. Leonardo da Vinci came to Milan, bringing with him his lyre shaped like a horse's head, his notebooks, his schemes for fortifications, waterworks and strange new weapons; and found good employment as musician, court painter and deviser of entertainments. The historians, lawyers and philosophers at the University of Pavia had their salaries doubled. The great castle of Porta Giovia in Milan, the home of the prince, was renovated and decorated in the glowing colors of the new art. The streets of the city, too, were cleaned, the casually built obstructions of many years removed, the houses painted.

Despite his nickname of the Moor, Ludovico had the fair good looks of the Lombard Italian. Naturally inclined to plumpness, his face had been fleshed out by good living to an almost feminine softness, a gentleness of contour oddly at variance with the massive nose and chin of the Sforza. The contrast reflected something of his dual nature: When fortune favored him he was strong, resolute, confident; but in adversity he crumbled—rapidly. Philip de Comines, whose master King Louis XII of France was to destroy this glowing court of Milan, summed up their victim's character in a single sentence. "This Ludovico was a wise man but very timorous and humble when he was in awe— and false when it was to his advantage. And this I do not speak by hearsay but as one that knew him well, having had many transactions with him."

Those who later sought a single, dramatic explanation for the root cause of the destruction of Italian freedom claimed to find it in the jealous rivalry which Ludovico's beautiful, ambitious and much-loved wife, Beatrice d'Este held for Isabella d'Aragona, the wife of her husband's nephew. Certainly the explanation simplified a fantastically complex situation, substituting for an incoherent tangle of political and personal motives the classic simplicity of feminine jealousy triggering off the French invasion which, in turn, was to lay Italy open to more foreign adventurers. There was an added poignancy in the fact that Ludovico's wife and his nephew's wife were cousins, for both were granddaughters of old Ferrante of Naples—an excellent example of the dynastic web which was throttling Italy. But there parity ended between the young women. Beatrice was a daughter of the brilliant—and nearby—court of Ferrara and married to a powerful man who doted upon her: Isabella's closest relatives lived at the other end of Italy and her husband was an invalid youth. Beatrice d'Este was not only a great beauty with an infectious charm of manner, she was also an intellectual in her own right and so an ideal partner for Ludovico. Her early death—a few months after the French invasion—shattered him and may well have led to the undermining of his will to resist at a critical moment. There was nothing he would not do for her; but there was only one gift that she, the most favored of women, really wanted. For all practical purposes she and Ludovico ruled Milan, but the ducal crown still remained legally on the head of Ludovico's ailing nephew Gian Galeazzo and, while he lived, Beatrice could never call herself duchess of Milan.

It is probable that in the private chambers of their imposing castle, Beatrice prodded her husband toward the brink, to some solution of the galling situation. But had she never existed, even had she been as humble and submissive in practice as in the theory of her marriage vow, Ludovico would have inevitably trodden that path by himself. In order to enjoy his illegal power, he had to place his nephew under increasing restraint, amounting at last to virtual imprisonment, as the boy grew to manhood. Later, after the invasion and all the tragedy that came from it, he opened his heart to the Venetian ambassador, Marco Foscari. "I confess that I have done great wrong to Italy, but I had to act because of the position I was in. I did it most reluctantly." The ambiguous situation in Milan could not have continued indefinitely. The Milanese might have accepted the situation equably enough, but Isabella's Neapolitan kinsmen, her father Alfonso and her grandfather Ferrante, would sooner or later abandon diplomatic protest for armed threat. Isabella herself, as spirited as her husband was supine, objected strongly. She was being robbed of a crown and she let the world know. In 1493 she wrote a bitter letter to her father, spelling out the humiliations imposed upon a princess of Aragon, describing how she and her husband, the true duke and duchess of Milan, depended for the very necessities of life upon Ludovico's charity.

> Everything is in his power, while we are left without friends or money and are reduced to live as private persons. Not Gian Galeazzo but Ludovico is recognized as lord of the kingdom, the true duke. His wife has lately born him a son, whom everyone prophesies will succeed to the dukedom, and royal honors were paid to him at his birth while we and our children are treated with contempt. We live here at risk to our lives. . . . If you have fatherly compassion, if love of me and the sight of my tears can move your soul, I implore you to come to our help and deliver your daughter and son-in-law from the fear of slavery, restoring them once more to their rightful kingdom.[36]

Isabella's father Alfonso wanted to wage outright immediate war upon the Milanese upstart but her grandfather Ferrante, seasoned by thirty-five years of Italian intrigue, declined to do anything so foolish. He worked in the approved manner, steadily undermining Ludovico's position while putting on an appearance of perfect friendship. It had been an alarming time for Ferrante when Alexander had married off Lucrezia to Giovanni Sforza, even though Giovanni, lord of the dreary little city of Pesaro, was small fry. But Ferrante had neatly countered that by bringing about the proxy marriage between his illegitimate granddaughter Sancia and Alexander's son Joffre, if at a rather higher price than he had wanted to pay. That was the correct way of doing things, countering threat with threat and plot with plot. Only fools went to war when the same results could be obtained by judicious bribery. Then in January 1494—"the first year of the miserable years"—he died. Alfonso succeeded him. And Ludovico found himself faced with a man who combined political enmity and personal hatred with an unpredictable impetuousness. Given Ludovico's position and his supreme self-confidence, there was little surprise that he, a political dwarf, should have attempted to wield a giant's club. He invoked the enormous power of France and precipitated a French invasion with all its incalculable consequences, to distract his enemy Alfonso. As inevitably he overbalanced, the delicate equilibrium of Italy collapsed and nearly brought down Alexander Borgia with it.

The current owner of the giant's club was another political dwarf, King Charles VIII of France. Italian writers vied with each other to execrate his memory, their judgments ranging from the coldly corrosive portraits created by professional diplomats to the spontaneous, astonished reaction of a bystander who saw him on his entry into Rome. "The king of France was the ugliest man I have ever seen in all my days—tiny, deformed with the most appalling face that ever man had." Philip de Comines, who served King Charles as well as his successor King Louis, was considerably kinder to his memory for he knew the empty-headed young man well. Comines could not but admit what everyone knew, that "neither his treasury, his understanding nor his preparations were sufficient for such an important enterprise." But Comines thought Charles meant well, desiring not only the glory of another crown but also the honor of cleansing the papacy. "He was the most affable and best-natured man in the world. I verily believe that he never said a word to any man that could in reason cause displeasure. I do really think I was the only person in the whole world he was unkind to—but being sensible it was in his youth I could not resent it."[37]

To the Italians who experienced the invasion, the eruption of an immense French army across the barrier of the Alps appeared as some natural force, inevitable as an avalanche, inescapable as a swarm of locusts. But Comines had a considerably different viewpoint. He was closely involved in the affair from its cloudy beginnings to its tragic end; from the moment when Charles announced his decision to conquer Jerusalem, occupy his ancestor's throne in Naples, and reform the papacy, to the time when the remnants of the once-proud army straggled back across the Alps. And it was Comines's impression that the invasion was a deplorable accident that probably would never have happened had Charles been taken seriously at the outset.

"To all persons of experience it was looked upon as a very dangerous undertaking nor indeed was anyone for it but himself and one Stephen de Vers, a man of very mean extraction and one who had never seen or had the least knowledge of military affairs. There was also one Briçonnet, who was of the council—but his nerve failed him and he shrunk his neck out of the collar."[38] Even when Charles's counselors became aware that he really intended an invasion, they seem to have assumed that he intended sending a token force; and it is possible that at this stage he did not plan to go in person. Then in rapid succession two Italians arrived at his court. The first was a Milanese bearing a letter in which his master, Ludovico Sforza, promised fullest support to the French. The second visitor was a Genoese, the cardinal of San Pietro in Vincoli, Giuliano della Rovere, "fatal instrument then, before and after, of all the calamities of Italy." Sforza's letter promised a smooth passage through the easily defended Alpine gateway into Italy, della Rovere's presence offered the means of an attack upon the Neapolitan king's major ally in Italy, the pope himself.

The relationship between Guiliano della Rovere and Alexander adds, for posterity, another twist to the Borgia story, creates one more mystery that cannot be resolved even by conjecture, for the elements are self-contradictory. The College of Cardinals was by now almost wholly a political arena in which representatives of the embattled city-states of Italy and their transalpine allies sought to overcome each other. Apart from one or two men who had, almost miraculously, maintained the Christian impulse that had originally brought them into the Church, the cardinals themselves had entirely abandoned the last pretense of exercising a spiritual office, the means having obscured the ends of office at last. The cardinals might have claimed, in their defense, that their roles were thrust upon them, the inescapable result of the papacy's position as a major Italian power which they, either as good sons of the Church or loyal citizens of their own states, had to defend or attack as with any other power.

Guiliano della Rovere was an excellent example of the new breed of prelate which, during the next two centuries, was to embroil the papacy ever deeper in the battles of Europe; a breed in which it is impossible to determine where personal ambition ended and loyalty to the state began—and where it is equally impossible to detect any activities with a purely spiritual motivation. Della Rovere was, primarily, a realist for whom "treachery" and "loyalty" were synonymous with "expediency," and who added to that convenient definition the Italian ability to equate honor with survival. After losing the battle of the conclave to his enemy, Borgia, della Rovere should have followed the established pattern and attempted either to weaken his enemy from within or—and the alternative was the more popular and sensible—gone over to him, and in exchange for the promise of powerful support, built up his position in readiness for the next conclave. He did neither. Almost immediately he turned to open, direct hostility, and except for a few occasions when his own definition of expediency obliged him to support Alexander, della Rovere maintained contemptuous hatred throughout the pontificate. It obliged him to move counter to his own personal preferences. He allied himself with the devious Ludovico Sforza, the natural enemy of his own state of Genoa, and summoned into Italy those foreigners whom he was to spend the greater part of his own pontificate in chasing out. Della Rovere's uncharacteristic reaction intrigued his contemporaries. It could hardly arise from any Christian abhorrence of the character of Christianity's high priest, for no sensible cardinal would allow such an objection to influence his political actions. The reaction did not seem to rise from the common dynastic rivalry that colored most people's reaction to the Borgia. Della Rovere held nothing but contempt for his cousin, Girolamo Riario. No children were credited to della Rovere; and when he at last ascended the papal throne, Italians were astonished by the fact that he seemed almost free from nepotism. Seeking an explanation for della Rovere's actions, the gossips claimed that Borgia had supplanted him in the affections of Vannozza Catanei, and that the young man who went by the name of Cesare Borgia should, by rights, have borne the name of della Rovere. The viciousness with which Giuliano attacked Cesare when eventually he had the power could as forcefully affirm as negate the rumor; but otherwise his dour, harsh, character gave no indications of such a motivation. All that Rome knew for certain was that Giuliano della Rovere held such a personal hatred for Alexander Borgia that he would defy the normal canons of political behavior to satisfy it.

Immediately after Alexander's coronation, della Rovere had left Rome for his own city, the port of Ostia at the mouth of the Tiber whose control enabled him to cut Rome's communication with the sea. Ostia became the center of the opposition to Alexander, and both cardinal and pope took extraordinary precautions against the possibility of either assassination or armed attack. Once when Alexander, returning to Rome from a tour of the states, was greeted by the customary salute from the guns of Sant'

Pope Alexander adoring the risen Christ
Painting by Pinturicchio in the Vatican (Mansell Collection)

Details from The Disputation of Saint Catherine
Painting by Pinturicchio in the Vatican (Mansell Collection)
The figure 1 is thought to be Cesare Borgia

From The Disputation of Saint Catherine
The figure 2 is thought to be Lucrezia Borgia

From The Disputation of Saint Catherine
The figures below 3 are thought to be Joffre and Sancia

From The Disputation of Saint Catherine
The figure 4 is thought to be Juan

Giulio della Rovere
Painting by Melozzo da Forli (Mansell Collection)

Caterina Sforza
Painting by Marco Palmezzani (Photo Alinari)

Ludovico Sforza
Painting attributed to Leonardo da Vinci (Mansell Collection)

Angelo, persons with him thought he was going to faint, so convinced was he that the cannonade signaled an attack. The two men were briefly reconciled, for each still maintained allies in the same camp—notably Naples—but the fragile relationship was shattered by the most bitter quarrel of all between them when, in the Consistory of September 1493, Alexander bestowed cardinal's hats upon his son, Cesare, and upon Alessandro Farnese, the young brother of his mistress Giulia. When in the following March, Alexander made his compact with Alfonso, the new king of Naples, Giuliano della Rovere took himself to France.

He arrived in Avignon at a critical moment. The difficulties and dangers of the French expedition were daily becoming more apparent. Few informed Frenchmen had any faith in Ludovico Sforza; and it was common knowledge that Stephen de Vers, the most consistent advocate of the expedition, if not actually in Ludovico's pay, had certainly been promised much; so that de Vers's advice to his king had been rendered other than disinterested. The more cautious, or less bribed, members of Charles's council seemed on the point of succeeding in pounding good sense into his head; and the vanguard of the army had actually been recalled, when della Rovere arrived in Avignon and immediately hastened to the king's camp. There, according to Guicciardini, the cardinal upbraided the king in a speech "which according to his nature was delivered more with efficacious reasoning and expressive gesture than with ornamental words." Della Rovere told Charles what a fool he would look in the eyes of Europe were he to draw back now after all his boasting. What had the king to fear? With the contempt of the Italian for the Italian, della Rovere pointed out that his fellow countrymen "being accustomed rather to a show of war than its reality will not have vigor enough to sustain the French fury. What fears, then, what confusions, what dreams have possessed your royal breast? Where is the fierceness with which you boasted, only four days ago, that you would overcome all Italy united?"[39]

Throughout the long speech attributed to him, della Rovere made no direct reference to the real reason for his presence in France: the promise that through him, a leading member of the Sacred College, a blow could be delivered against Alexander Borgia that would either topple him from the throne or force him to place the crown of Naples on Charles's head. But it was this knowledge, rather than the scathing sarcasm, that restored the young king's courage; so that at last he gave the order for the march into Italy.

It was this knowledge that emboldened his ambassador in Rome to demand audience of the pope and address an openly threatening speech to him. Alexander smiled grimly at the routine reproaches regarding his libidinous nature and the scandal of his ways; wrapped in his impermeable self-satisfaction, he allowed a remarkable freedom of speech to those around him. But he paid rather closer attention to the ambassador's threat that if he did not place the crown of Naples on the head of Charles, then a council would be called to investigate the charge that, simonaically, he had bought his high office. It was open, unabashed blackmail but nonetheless effective. No matter that this simony had been common knowledge within a few hours of the conclave, only now had della Rovere used the power of his position to threaten his enemy with the council that all popes feared. No matter that few of the cardinals who would form that council had clean hands; the issue was legal, not moral. Ascanio Sforza, who had benefited from that simony more than any other man apart from Alexander himself, piously joined his voice with those of his brethren who sought to expunge the stain. Sforza's opposition to his one-time friend and benefactor Borgia was, in a way, involuntary, for he had no choice but to follow his brother Ludovico into the opposition camp. But, incredibly, Sforza —the seller—had high hopes of following Borgia the purchaser in the chair of St. Peter.

Few took much notice of King Charles's evident sincerity. "It's no business of his to reform the Church," Ludovico Sforza told the silent, outwardly admiring Venetian ambassador. "Speaking between ourselves, the king has more need to reform himself than setting about reforming other people." But if Alexander's simony could be used to lever him out of the throne, then a gap would be created which a large number of people would gain great profit by filling.

The progress of the French army through Italy was not so much unopposed as virtually a triumphal procession. Alexander for once shared an opinion of della Rovere's — contempt for the Italians. "The French conquered Italy with wooden spurs and a bit of chalk," he remarked later, and certainly in city after city the only military activity was the billet master moving from lodging to lodging, placing his chalk mark upon the doors to indicate a billet. There had been some embarrassment in Milan when Isabella threw herself before the king's feet, begging him to right the injustice and restore her husband to the ducal throne. Charles, with all his faults, had a kind heart and might even have indulged in some impetuous action had not his counselors edged him aside. There was another queasy moment when he remarked curtly to Ludovico that the French had as strong a genealogical claim to Milan as they had to Naples. But that also passed, for Charles's counselors had no intention of fighting this war as preliminary to another. Florence proved a little difficult, for Charles had been stupid enough to enter the city with couched lance, the universal sign of conquest; and there had been a moment when it seemed that the great bell, *La Vacca*, would toll its summons to the citizens to throw out yet another enemy. But a concord was reached and the army continued its march upon Rome.

Throughout the menacing advance of the French, Alexander had been tormented to distraction by a purely domestic problem. The beautiful Giulia Farnese had decided to remember her marriage vows and took herself off to her husband, leaving Alexander raging in Rome. Apparently he valued his mistress far higher than his tiara. The avowed purpose of the French invasion was to take that tiara from him, but he barely spared a glance to the advancing army, so furious was he with Giulia and her confidantes, so intent was he upon her return. Giulia's brother, Cardinal Farnese, threw up his hands in horror. He had been happy enough to accept his red hat through his fortunate relationship, but the matter was now an open scandal and even a Farnese could blush. Alexander ignored the cardinal's protests, thundered against Giulia, against her husband, even against the favored Adriana da Mila, who was torn between obedience to her cousin and a belated sense of guilt toward her son. Orsino Orsini himself resolved the matter. He lost his nerve and agreed that Giulia should return. At about the time that the French army was leaving Florence, she and Adriana took the road to Rome.

They chose a bad day for traveling. Little more than three hours after setting out, they encountered a forward patrol of the French army under Yves d'Allegre. Giulia's beauty, the stateliness of Madonna Adriana and the sumptuousness of their equipment intrigued him; it was obvious they were no ordinary women. They were escorted with great politeness to d'Allegre's temporary base at Montefiascone, and there Giulia disclosed that she was, indeed, the legendary Giulia Farnese and that her duenna was none other than the pope's cousin and confidante, Adriana da Mila. A messenger was hastened to Charles with the news that ideal hostages had fallen into French hands. Charles was shocked; the French did not fight against women, he declared. But d'Allegre, though an accomplished gallant, did not share his master's high ideals of chivalry. Another messenger was dispatched this time for Rome, with the information that the freedom of the ladies could be bought for three thousand ducats.

Alexander had been awaiting their arrival with impatience and then increasing apprehension. He wasted no time in bargaining when he learned what had happened. A papal courier was sent with a strong escort to d'Allegre, carrying the demanded ransom. Simultaneously another messenger was sent to Charles himself, bitterly upbraiding him for the action of his servants. D'Allegre kept his side of the bargain, providing Giulia and Adriana with an escort of four hundred knights to take them safely the rest of the way to Rome. So impatient was Alexander to be united with his mistress that he was actually waiting at the city gate as the party rode in at nightfall on December 1. He dressed carefully for the occasion, wearing cloak, boots, sword and dagger in the Spanish fashion. Giulia was young and impressionable, and her escort of dashing young Frenchmen might very easily eclipse an elderly ecclesiastic in her esteem.

Rome laughed at the opera buffa, but in Milan Ludovico Sforza was indigant. "These ladies were the heart and eye of the pope: they would have been the best whip for compelling him to do everything which was wanted of him for he could not live without them. The French received only three thousand ducats as ransom although the pope would gladly have paid fifty thousand or more simply to have them back again."[40]

Alexander had little time to enjoy Giulia's company. He went to bed each night with the knowledge that the French army was another fifteen miles closer to Rome. He awoke each morning with the knowledge that more of his allies would abandon him during the coming day. The city was in a ferment of fear and excitement; never within living memory had Rome been the object of an attack. Those who could leave did; all day long the slow processsion of laden oxcarts made its way through the city gates. At first Alexander also decided in favor of flight, and Burchard hurriedly organized the packing of the more portable valuables. But then his master changed his mind. If the bishop of Rome could not find safety in Rome, where could he find it? The citizen militia was called out; they responded tardily, sullenly. It was obvious that, if it came to a fight, they would not lift a hand in defense of the Borgia pope. Burchard was summoned. If the native militia would not fight could he, perhaps, persuade his fellow nationals, the local German colony, to form an emergency bodyguard? The situation was hopeless and Burchard bluntly said so. Still Alexander did not despair, for outside Rome was his first line of defense, the expensively maintained papal army under its commander, Virginio Orsini. But Virginio not only refused to fight, he actually went over to the enemy, taking all the troops with him. He and Giulia's husband were cousins, but it was not through any family feeling that Virginio acted as he did. In common with most of the Orsini, he rather despised the spiritless Orsino and personally he held nothing against Alexander. But he, too, was convinced that the pope's situation was hopeless and, in the practical Italian fashion, Virginio had joined what seemed to be the stronger side. For his miscalculation he and the Orsini clan were to pay dearly.

The French army, its monarch at its head, marched into Rome as darkness was falling on the last day of 1494. Burchard rode out to meet the king, exchanging stiff greetings with della Rovere who, with two fellow cardinals, was about to enter the city. Charles chatted eagerly with the papal master of ceremonies, the one man in Rome who could give him accurate information about the state of affairs in the Vatican. What ceremonies would he, Charles, have to go through? What precisely was the role and influence of Cardinal Cesare Borgia. Burchard answered the tumbling questions the best he could as they rode through tumultuously cheering crowds to the palace that had been set apart for the king. There, the royal bodyguard took over, drawing a ring of steel around the palace, sealing it off from the rest of Rome.

A few hundred yards away at the Castel Sant' Angelo similar preparations were underway. At the last moment Alexander had followed the example of so many of his predecessors and set up his court in Rome's unconquered and unconquerable castle. His family were with him; even Vannozza had abandoned her comfortable house for the safety of Sant' Angelo. There might have been an embarrassing confrontation between the past and present mistresses, but Cardinal Farnese took advantage of the situation to whisk his sister out of Rome and Alexander, for once, did not object.

Yet, after all the frantic preparations and bloodthirsty threats came merely anticlimax. "Twice our great guns were ready to fire on Sant' Angelo but both times the king opposed it. I will not pretend to say whether he acted well or ill, but I think his best way was to compose matters amicably as he did," Comines recorded. He was in Venice at the time, struggling to keep his master afloat in the treacherous crosscurrents of peninsula politics and he, for one, was unsurprised by that anticlimax beneath the massive walls of Sant' Angelo. "He was a young man and incapable of performing so important a work as the reformation of the Church."[41] In Rome the taciturn Burchard for a change displayed almost a sense of humor as he recorded the contest between pope and king; between the veteran politician toughened after forty years of running battles with his equals and the inexperienced, romantic young man bred in the mystique of monarchy, that belief that the king had only to wish and it was ordained. Alexander adopted any device that would help throw his adversary off balance: feigning faintness at a difficult moment, entangling Charles in the trivia of protocol, pretending to be unaware of his approach so that the unfortunate young king was forced to go down on his knees twice while the court looked on. The impression of Charles conveyed by Burchard is that of a lost puppy, scampering with increasing bewilderment from one chamber to another of the Vatican Palace. "They will make another pope with the intention of reforming the Church," Briçonnet had written confidently to the queen of France on the day that Charles had triumphantly entered Rome. Three weeks later that was all forgotten. Ascanio Sforza's name was raised briefly as the only possible successor to Alexander, but even Charles could not quite see how Alexander could be deposed for simony in favor of Ascanio, "the principal merchant for it was he that drove the bargain, and received most of the money." The question of a council dropped quietly into the background in favor of Charles's real ambition, the possession of the Neapolitan crown. Alexander twisted out of that problem with some skill. It did affect another party, he argued—the current wearer of the crown—but he would consult with his cardinals as early and as fully as possible. Even Charles must have been aware that Alexander intended doing nothing about the matter once pressure had been removed, but neither was it possible for the French to remain indefinitely while the futile negotiations dragged on. The temper of the ever-fickle Romans changed, less from any affection for their bishop than from hatred of a contemptuous foreign army that looked upon itself as a conquering force. In Spain, the Catholic Majesties talked loudly of their blood relationship with Alfonso of Naples and their sudden filial reverence for Pope Alexander VI. Caught between the immediate threat of a city on the edge of open warfare, and of the distant but far more terrifying threat of a Spanish move at his rear, Charles could no nothing but complete the attack on Naples before his army's strength was expended in street battles, or before the delicately balanced alliances collapsed beneath him. He and Alexander signed a virtually meaningless pact: all past mutual offenses were to be forgotten; Charles was to be invested with Naples, when that should prove possible; a handful of castles were to change hands and Briçonnet, Charles's adviser, was to receive a cardinal's hat. Altogether it was a derisory end to a megalomanic project, and Alexander could well permit himself a feeling of deep satisfaction. The forces opposing him had been tested to their utmost and had collapsed.

Charles left Rome on January 28, taking with him Cesare Borgia, ostensibly as papal legate, in reality as a hostage while the army was crossing papal territory. For Cesare it was undoubtedly a humiliating debut on the international stage, but he seems to have assumed his role with an impassivity which totally deceived Charles. A few days' march out of Rome Cesare disappeared. His carefully sealed and guarded wagons in the baggage train were promptly impounded—and found to be empty of any valuables. A courier was sent galloping back to Rome, bearing the king's bitter accusations to Alexander. The pope declared he knew nothing of the matter, deplored his son's breach of faith, agreed that he ought to be returned—but no one seemed to know where he was. Cesare remained discreetly out of public sight until the end of March, but when he did eventually appear openly in Rome the entire situation had altered radically. Charles, after ascending to the pinnacle of triumph—so effortlessly and undeservedly that Comines his loyal servant was convinced it was by the direct hand of God—was hurled down as swiftly.

Alfonso of Naples seems to have been as convinced as Comines that the Neapolitan adventure was in supernatural hands. Rumors sped around the capital that the ghost of old Ferrante had appeared to his son, lamenting that the days of Aragon were over for they were paying the price of their sins. A Sibylline prophecy was discovered, foretelling the doom of the house. "Alfonso was seized with such a panic fear that in the night he would cry out he heard the French, the very stones and trees cried 'France, France.' "[42] His fear was rather less likely to have been produced by messengers from the other world than from the prosaic knowledge that it was a Neapolitan tradition to contemplate, passively, the destruction of Neapolitan kings by ambitious foreigners. The Italian chroniclers sought to prove that the crimes of Alfonso and his father Ferrante had cost them the loyalty of their subjects. When Alfonso hurriedly abdicated in favor of his son, Ferrantino, the situation remained unchanged, although everybody agreed that Ferrantino was a virtuous young man, much loved by all who knew him. The Neapolitans could not find a reason, as ever, for defending one foreigner against another merely because both claimed to be kings of Naples. Ferrantino fled, Charles's army entered Naples, and the Neapolitans courteously cheered the advent of their newest monarch. Charles enjoyed himself as king in the beautiful, treacherous, wholly enigmatic city for some three months and then, rather like a sleeper awakening, turned his thoughts to the problem of getting home—only to find the path closed.

At the other end of Italy in Venice, Comines had been watching the incredible adventure first with surprise, and then with mounting dismay as reports came to him of Charles's lotus-eating approach to Italian politics. Comines filled his journal with a reproachful catalogue of the king's stupidities. "From his first arrival at Naples to his departure, he minded nothing but his pleasure and his ministers

nothing but their own advantage." He partly excused the
king on the grounds of youth, laying the blame on the
avaricious, incompetent ministers—they should have fortified the castles; they should have kept better discipline;
they should have known that Italian alliances were built on
sand. But Comines himself, despite his competence and
loyalty, despite the fact that he was actually resident in the
city that hatched the plot against the king, knew nothing
whatsoever about it until it was a fact, as he had the honesty
to record. When he became aware of the constant coming
and going of ambassadors—papal, Milanese, Spanish and
even imperial—all of whom avoided him, he taxed the Senate with plotting against his master. "I was told that I ought
not to believe all the flying reports of the town, and that in
Venice people had the liberty of saying what they pleased."
Experienced as he was in Italian ways, the smooth reply
convinced him that a league was undoubtedly being formed
against Charles and, with increasing desperation, he sent
messengers hastening south to urge the king to begin his
return before the Italians closed ranks. Charles delayed, an
anti-French alliance came into being, and the French, after
their triumphal tour of Italy, were now faced with the prospect of fighting their way back home against a briefly
unified nation.

Despite his humiliating experience in Rome in the past
winter, Charles seems to have believed that a man-to-man
talk with Alexander would solve all his difficulties. He returned to Rome still hopeful on June 1, to find that the
pope had discreetly removed himself and his family to
Siena, leaving a courteous message to the effect that he was
vacating the Vatican only to provide Charles with suitable
lodgings. Charles, at the head of his large army, took the

road to Siena. Alexander nimbly moved the papal court to Perugia and then, circling behind the French, re-entered Rome on June 27 to the admiration and enthusiasm of the Romans. He was home in the Vatican, comfortably established with his family and court again in their familiar surroundings, when news arrived of the great battle of Fornovo.

Fornovo was hailed by the Italians as an important victory, a stirring demonstration of the effect of national unity against the barbarians from beyond the Alps. The Italians were, in fact, badly mauled, and Ludovico Sforza personally demonstrated the efficacy of Italian unity by making his own treaty with Charles: the French were to forget that embarrassing claim to Milan, and Ludovico would help Charles in the next round against Naples. It so happened that on the very day of Fornovo, Ferrantino returned to Naples amid the practiced cheers of the Neapolitans, an event which seemed to hammer home the fact that the first French invasion had ended in total failure and humiliation. Nevertheless, the French carried home with them not only the memory of Italian mockery but the knowledge, too, that Italians were their own worst enemies; that Italy would fall prize to whoever could exploit the Italian genius for dissension.

The
Rise of
Cesare Borgia

7

Cardinal Cesare Borgia was just twenty-one years old
when Fornovo seemed to signal the end of foreign
intervention in Italy. Ever since his brother Juan had left
for Spain he had had good reason to believe that his
father was at last contemplating a change in their roles.
Alexander could hardly help turning to the vigorous,
intelligent elder son, physically present in Rome, when
problems of state arose that affected the Borgia dynasty
as well as the papacy. More and more Cesare came to
believe that responsibility for the Italian affairs of the
family would, eventually, be placed in his hands while
Juan, perhaps, continued to handle the Spanish aspects.
The public knew little about Cesare apart from the fact
that, as a cardinal, he took part in a number of religious
ceremonies. Nevertheless, those at the center of things
who were sensitive to the meaning of the minutiae of
protocol were aware of his increasing importance in
Vatican affairs. He was very rarely far from his father; he

had been created a legate; he had abandoned the palace
that had been bought for him to take up residence in the
Vatican. The rooms allocated to him were above the great
chambers painted by Pinturicchio, and they formed a ceremonial suite which allowed him to receive important guests
as though he were a prince. The number and stature of
those guests reflected his own increasing influence, ambassadors as well as fellow cardinals thinking it politic to bend
the knee to the young man whose priest's tonsure was
utterly at variance with his splendid layman's costume. It
seemed to the hypersensitive courtiers that Cesare had at
last got his way, that the tonsure was as irrelevant in theory
as in fact, and that Cesare Borgia was moving slowly but
steadily toward a purely secular career.

Then in August 1496 he was again eclipsed by his
brother Juan. Alexander had at last felt himself free to
begin the extermination of the Roman barons—those fet-
ters of the pope, as he called them—and summoned his
beloved second son from Spain to undertake the task.

The Orsini were slated as the first victims, for it had
been they who had opened the road to the French and
openly allied themselves with Charles. The expedition
against them was launched with a ceremonial and solemnity
that better befitted the opening of a major crusade than the
continuation of a dynastic struggle for a few square miles
of territory. It ended in fiasco for, despite Juan Borgia's
resounding titles of gonfaloniere of Holy Church and commander of the papal host, he was still a feckless, inexperienced young man and the Orsini were veterans in this
kind of warfare. A prolonged siege of Bracciano, their great
fortress on its beautiful lake to the north of Rome, was
abandoned in disarray; and in a counterattack upon the

papal forces in the field, Juan was slightly wounded and promptly fled back to Rome.

Juan's humiliation was equaled by his father's fear for, suddenly, the military situation seemed as threatening as it had a year earlier. The Orsini believed, with justice, that they were fighting for their continued existence. Too, there remained strong pockets of French resistance, survivors of Charles's expedition who had dug themselves into fortified cities, and the two in combination could yet break the Borgia grip on Rome. Ostia, Rome's port, was still in the hands of a French garrison; and now with a land blockade added to the sea blockade Rome took on the character of a beleaguered city. Alexander despatched a call for help to the Spanish monarchs, and they authorized their commander in Italy, Gonzalo de Cordoba, to march to his aid. Gonzalo hastened north from his base near Naples and in a short but bloody engagement he threw the French out of Ostia. Italy's helplessness was never better demonstrated than in this assault upon Ostia when foreigners hurled themselves on foreigners in Rome's defense. Gonzalo's tiny force was wholly Spanish. Even the reinforcements he was able to pick up in Rome were Spanish, for Garcilaso de la Vega, the Spanish ambassador in the Vatican, threw aside his protected status and with a handful of volunteers marched with his compatriots. Gonzalo, on his return to Rome, was hailed hysterically as savior of the city by Romans who could see nothing unusual, nothing sinister in the fact that only a Spaniard had the ability to defend them. Alexander welcomed Gonzalo in the Borgia Apartments, gave him the Golden Rose—and at the same time created his discredited, incompetent son Juan duke of Benevento, investing him with territories that Gonzalo's skill and courage had gained for the Holy See.

It is probable that this event marked the beginning of the deterioration of Alexander's vital relationship with Spain, for Gonzalo bitterly resented the beggarly reward for saving Rome. The event also denoted the fact that Alexander considered nothing to be unjust or ludicrous if it led to the aggrandizement of his children. His attempt to eradicate the Roman baronies was, in Roman eyes, both praiseworthy and expected. Successive popes had struggled with the task of suppressing this greedy, unscrupulous class which regarded Rome as its personal property, and whose virtuous condemnation of the papal monarch was largely the product of envy. Alexander's decision to create a Borgia barony was, in the Roman view, again to be expected, for those cynical eyes had long ceased to observe the fine distinction between the pope as papal monarch and as head of a dynasty. But Gonzalo de Cordoba was a Spaniard newly arrived from a country that still bore the scars of its long battle with the archenemy of Christianity, a provincial who lacked the practiced Roman ability to reconcile the irreconcilable, a Christian who could still be shocked by the antics of Christianity's priest. He also happened to be perhaps the greatest living general in Europe, a man who combined the chivalry and courtesy of the fast-vanishing breed of Christian knights with a flexibility of intellect amounting to genius, that enabled him to exploit the new forms of weapons and warfare and thus dominate in a tradition-bound field. Finally, de Cordoba was not only the general of Their Catholic Majesties but also the friend and confidant of Queen Isabella, the dominant member of that Spanish partnership, who already nursed a suspicion and dislike of Alexander Borgia that was only imperfectly concealed. Burchard assumed that de Cordoba's resentment was aroused by the contrast between his reward for saving

Rome and Juan Borgia's reward merely for being Juan Borgia—a pretty, perfumed metal flower worth a few hundred ducats compared to the reward of a dukedom. Burchard was probably right, but de Cordoba's personal resentment resulting from the shabby incident was, in the long run, far less important than the effect it had made on him as a loyal and experienced Spanish statesman. The arms of Spain, it seemed, were being employed not in the defense of an independent papacy which could hold the balance of power in Italy, but simply to bolster up yet another Italian princeling. It was a piece of information, from an unimpeachable source, which Queen Isabella received with great interest.

Gonzalo's resentment and disquiet were shared by Cesare, although for a totally different reason. There was now no doubt whatever that the incompetent Juan was indeed intended by their father to play that role which Cesare passionately desired and could fulfill far more adequately. Juan was already established as a duke in Spain, possessed of a loving wife who had already given him two children—and one of them the vital son—to perpetuate the Borgia dynasty. And now he was to be established in Italy. The rivalry between the brothers, hidden while Alexander had control of Cesare, dormant while Juan was in Spain, now became so obvious and so ferocious it figured in the despatches of resident ambassadors as news of sufficient political importance to pass on to their masters. Then, in June, a bitter edge was added to the rivalry when Cesare was made the instrument to secure for Juan the newly awarded dukedom of Benevento to be carved out of the kingdom of Naples. Natural death had contributed to the already dizzy twists and turns of Neapolitan politics. Ferrantino, the last king, had died after a reign of little more than a year and his uncle and successor, Federigo, eagerly agreed to Juan's dukedom in exchange for his own recognition as king. Defying the College of Cardinals and the Spanish ambassador, Alexander nominated Cesare as his legate to perform Federigo's coronation in Naples. It was an honorable distinction for a young man who had made no particular mark as a papal statesman. But Cesare was perfectly well aware that as a result of his legateship, Juan would be established as a powerful territorial lord not, as hitherto, in a distant land, but in Italy itself, while Cesare himself remained a purely ceremonial figure. Nevertheless, he seems to have hidden his thoughts with his customary skill, preparing for the splendid ceremony as though outward form were all that mattered.

Cesare maintained his equanimity at the small family party which his mother Vannozza gave on the evening of June 14, 1497, at her villa near the baths of Diocletian. It was an intimate and sober affair, attended only by Juan, Cesare, their cousin, Cardinal Juan Borgia-Lanzo, and one or two family friends. The party broke up before midnight, the guests parted amicably, and Juan was never again seen alive. On the morning of June 16, his body, frenziedly hacked and with the hands tied, was fished out of the Tiber.

The murder of Juan, duke of Gandia, duke of Benevento, lord of Terracina and Pontecorvo, gonfalonier of Holy Church, might have been designed as a key scene by a master dramatist, for it contained within it all the contradictory elements that were to make the Borgia story one of the great legends of Europe. The murder occurred at the precise moment needed to free Cesare and place him on his desired path, yet it is impossible to prove his responsibility. Details of the murder were subjected to an immediate and lasting blaze of publicity, yet its origins remain rooted in impenetrable obscurity. Its motives can be ascribed equally to political, sexual, dynastic, or frankly personal hatred. Persons closest remained silent, those more distant evolved their own explanations to account for the contradictions, and out of those contortions arose legend that fatally besmirched the moral character of the entire family even while it gave Cesare almost superhuman stature.

Juan's movements on the last night of his life and, probably, up to a few hours before his death are known. He, Cesare, their cousin Cardinal Juan and their attendants rode back from Vannozza's villa in the suburbs and remained in company until they reached Alexander's old house, now the residence of the vice-chancellor, Ascanio Sforza. There Juan parted, but not alone. Accompanying him were his servant and a man wearing one of the common festive masks. This man's name and identity are unknown; but he must have been known by face at least to the Borgia family, for Burchard reported that he had been Juan's constant companion over the past month or so. Why no search was ever made for this mysterious masked man is only one of the enigmatic aspects of the murder.

Leaving his companions, Juan had declared he was headed for an assignation with a certain Madonna Damiata, according to subsequent accounts. His household, therefore, was not troubled by his absence and even Alexander, when the fact was reported to him later in the day, was unworried, for he assumed that Juan was discreetly remaining in hiding until darkness. Late that afternoon, however, Juan's horse was discovered wandering riderless, one stirrup cut off as though by a sword-blow. At the same time, it was reported that the servant accompanying Juan had died from terrible wounds received during the night. Supposedly, the man had been discovered shortly after daybreak and died without speaking after his removal to a house. Again, it is inexplicable why news of a mortally wounded servant wearing Juan's livery was not conveyed to the Vatican until several hours after the man's discovery. He was found not in a back alley but in the busy Piazza della Giudecca, and he must therefore either have lain dying in front of dozens of passersby, or those who found him at dawn kept the news to themselves for some unknown reason.

The discovery of the horse and the dying servant placed a sinister interpretation on Juan's absence and, thoroughly alarmed now, Alexander ordered the most rigorous search made. The search did not, apparently, disclose the whereabouts of the masked man nor of a group of men supposed to have been seen loitering near Juan about half an hour after he left his companions; but it did bring to light a man who gave a curiously detailed account of an event he had witnessed the night before. Burchard gave the witness's name simply as Giorgio, describing him as a timber merchant who had a woodyard on the riverside. According to Giorgio, at about two o'clock on the morning of the murder he had seen a man on a white horse, accompanied by four men on foot who appeared to be his servants, approach the river with a dead man slung across the horse. Giorgio seems to have been remarkably well hidden and have had extremely good hearing and eyesight, for he described in some detail the conversation which passed between the men and the precise method by which they threw the body into the Tiber. The witness's account was vindicated when a massive dredging operation produced the corpse of Juan Borgia, still dressed in its finery, including valuable jewels, and with a purse of gold pieces intact on his belt.

Such were the meager details which allowed only the sketchiest reconstruction of the murder. Presumably, Juan had been attacked sometime between midnight and 1:00 A.M. near the Piazza della Giudecca, where his servant had been left for dead. Juan's attackers must have been on foot, for a mounted troop would have attracted considerable attention at midnight, and he must therefore either have been led into an ambush—and the only person who could have so led him was the masked man—or the attackers were known to Juan and did not arouse his suspicions. He was seized, bound, conveyed to a private house, tortured there with a sword or dagger, and then slaughtered. His body was conveyed to the Tiber a little over an hour later.

The contradictory elements in the story remain irreconcilable for posterity. Giorgio's lushly detailed account, contrasted with the paucity of all other information, sounds like a carefully rehearsed tale, even down to the reason why he had not bothered to report the matter. He had seen hundreds of corpses thrown into the river at that point, he claimed, and no one had ever troubled about them. Burchard, the prime witness, is silent, for his diary breaks off at this point. Meticulously he recorded Giorgio's dramatic evidence, the dredging of the Tiber, Alexander's passionate grief when the corpse was brought to the Vatican, the obsequies for the dead man. Then the diary breaks off and is not continued again until August, nearly four months later. The only certain deduction that can be made is that Juan's murder was not the result of a nocturnal brawl but a carefully planned and skillfully executed operation. But who profited?

Alexander himself carefully named those he believed to be innocent but whom gossip had associated with the crime. For three days after the murder he was, quite literally, demented with grief. On the evening that Juan's body was borne across the Tiber for interment, his shrieks in the Vatican could be heard by members of the cortège as they crossed the bridge of Sant' Angelo. On June 19 he was sufficiently recovered to formally notify the College of Juan's death at a special consistory and to declare his intention of reforming the Church. His speech of penitence and remorse carried a ring of terrible sincerity that echoes even through the medium of the formal report of the Venetian ambassador who recorded it.

> The duke of Gandia is dead. A greater calamity could not have befallen us for we bore him unbounded affection. Life has lost all interest for us. It must be that God punishes us for our sins, for the duke has done nothing to deserve so terrible a fate. We are resolved without delay to think of the Church first and foremost, and not of ourselves nor of our privileges. We must begin by reforming ourselves.[43]

The manner in which Alexander unbared his soul to the apprehensive college of cardinals, lacerating himself, gave the clearest possible evidence of the reason why he had so favored Juan: he loved his son with a fierce, all-consuming love. His speech also provided posterity with a brief and almost uniquely undistorted insight into the true character of the man himself. All other actions of Alexander can be shown as simply the product of a ravenous worldly ambition; his desire to reform both the Church and himself could spring from no other source but spiritual remorse. The immense psychic shock of Juan's death opened his eyes, if briefly, to what he had become, and his reaction was on a typically extravagant scale. It could not last. It was impossible for a man of sixty-seven not merely to abandon the habits of thought of a lifetime but to extricate himself from a situation that he had inherited with the tiara. But it showed that the spirit behind the splendid presence was not entirely atrophied, that under different circumstances he could have been a different man, and that it would not have been wholly blasphemous or ludicrous to predict that the Borgia family would, a generation later, give a saint to the Roman Church.

As to the murder, Alexander specifically exculpated those upon whom suspicion had immediately fallen. First there was Guidobaldo Montefeltro, duke of Urbino, the gentle condottiere who had fought with Juan against the Orsini and who, through Juan's cowardice, had fallen into their hands and been abandoned by Alexander. Juan had received lavish honors but there was not, it seemed, sufficient money to pay Montefeltro's ransom and he had languished in prison until his fortunately loyal subjects raised the money themselves. But he was no murderer, declared Alexander, and neither was Ascanio Sforza nor his nephew Giovanni though both had motives. The whole Sforza clan had been caught up in the disgrace of the French fiasco. Ascanio himself, although the vice-chancellor, had briefly seen the inside of Sant' Angelo. In addition, he had recently quarreled furiously with Juan and altogether had thought it advisable not to attend this particular consistory.

Giovanni, the unfortunate first husband of Lucrezia, not only had been caught up in the same political catastrophe produced by the French invasion but had also recently been divorced on the grounds of his alleged impotence.

The last person to be cleared by Alexander was his own son Joffre. The inclusion of Joffre's name was curious, for he was only fifteen years old at the time and his only possible motive arose from a separate family scandal of a type which Alexander never made public. In naming Joffre he was tacitly admitting that the scandal was so notorious as to give the boy a motive for fratricide, and a public denial was therefore necessary. Rome believed, and with excellent reason, that both Juan and Cesare had made a cuckold of their young brother.

Joffre Borgia, the youngest son of Vannozza, plays a pathetic figure beside his glamorous brothers and sister, his activities appearing as a mere postscript to theirs. A drab, spiritless young man whose apathy so goaded Alexander that he had been heard to declare in anger that he could not claim him as son, it was peculiarly unfortunate that Sancia of Aragon, of all women, should have been chosen as wife for him. Four years older than her boy-husband, she was a beauty, had considerable spirit and no morals. The marriage to Joffre was forced upon her and she had no choice but to accept. But from the beginning she declared she had no intention of playing the passive role expected, of being only the means of transferring titles and land and, in due course, providing an heir for them. It is possible that had Joffre been of stronger character or older when he married her, he might have been able to restrain her. Possible—but unlikely. Brought up as she had been in the corrupt ambience of the Neapolitan court, herself the product of an illicit affair and her chastity therefore of little dynastic importance, Sancia was notorious in Naples even before she married. Joffre, colorless even in favorable circumstances, became a nonentity among the swaggering, arrogant nobles who formed Sancia's social world; and her attitude toward him was one of open contempt tinged with malice. That the boy collapsed and wept on his wedding night was common knowledge, which regaled the courts of both Rome and Naples. That choice information could have come only from one source. Alexander, always wanting to have his children around him, insisted that Joffre and Sancia should come to Rome- -with results that might have been expected. Sancia—black-haired, with a glowing olive-tinted skin and startling blue-green eyes—was reckoned extraordinary even in a city sated with beautiful women. Brought into intimate and prolonged contact with a twosome such as Juan and Cesare Borgia and sharing their amorality, Sancia, through her activities in the weeks before Juan's death, gave grounds enough for Alexander's anxious disclaimer. No one believed that the puny Joffre himself could have wielded the sword that slashed open Juan's throat, but there were any number of men who might have played upon his impotent hatred and used him as a cover for the slaying. The Orsini, who had been feuding with the Borgia for a generation now, some other enraged cuckold, a disappointed social climber—it could have been anyone.

Neither Alexander nor anybody else in Rome the summer of 1497 mentioned as suspect the man whom posterity was to condemn almost unanimously as the murderer. Nothing is known of Cesare's activities on that June night, nor during the days immediately following. After he left Juan he presumably continued on to his suite in the Vatican. He remained in Rome until July, when he went to Naples to carry out the postponed coronation; but he played no part in the investigations. The fact that gossip touched the characterless Joffre and ignored Cesare is extraordinary. The only possible interpretation is that those who were best in the position to know accepted as axiomatic that Cesare had nothing to gain from the murder. Certainly, their father did not think it necessary to exonerate Cesare publicly, although in the tangled affair any one of the brothers had motive for murdering either of the others. Rome knew, as did Cesare, that Juan's titles and estates would pass to Juan's son born three years earlier. But Rome did not then know that Cesare intended to relinquish the hated cardinal's hat and, succeeding, would draw exclusively to himself the secular honors that would otherwise have fallen to Juan. It was only when this became apparent that rumor sought to link Cesare with the murder and which, in the manner of gossip, became fact after it had been repeated and elaborated upon through a chain of correspondents and chroniclers.

Examining the sparse, contradictory evidence regarding the murder itself, dubiously assessing the testimony of contemporaries, of whom none were disinterested and few even moderately well informed—the only verdict at which posterity can arrive is a cautious "not proven," leaving in permanent abeyance the question of Cesare Borgia's guilt or innocence. There is no doubt that he had the ability, and little doubt that he had the desire, to plan; and surely he gained considerably, if indirectly. Apart from the opinion of people in Rome at the time, there are two later pieces of evidence—one negative, and one positive—which can be adduced in Cesare's favor. Federigo of Naples, who dis-

liked him intensely, nevertheless did not protest receiving
his crown from Cesare's hands a few weeks afterwards—
had urged, indeed, that the coronation be postponed so
that Cesare could attend as planned. Federigo was a truly
religious man, and although politics forced him to accept
his crown from an illegitimate cardinal—it seems unlikely
that he would have taken part in a religious ceremony conducted by a fratricide. And it was Cesare whom Alexander
appointed as trustee to administer Juan's estate on behalf
of the dead man's infant son. Alexander would have been
indeed the monster of his legend had he charged the murderer of his beloved son with such a pious task.

But there was one person who, from the beginning,
believed implicitly in Cesare's guilt—his sister-in-law Maria
Enriquez, Juan's widow. Grief undoubtedly poisoned her
mind. Her marriage had lasted less than four years, but she,
it seems, had found qualities in Juan that others did not
suspect, for they were unusually happy together. Then,
brutally, that loved husband had been taken from her, the
two little children left fatherless. The court of Spain was,
on the whole, neutral with a mild bias in favor of Cesare's
innocence. It was to be his misfortune that the only Spaniard to convict him should have been in a position to do him
immense harm, for Maria was high in favor with her royal
relatives. Better than anyone else in Spain she knew the
bitterness of the dynastic rivalry between the brothers.
How much she was aware or believed of that other rivalry
for Sancia's favors cannot be conjectured. It is unlikely that
what was openly spoken of in Rome was unknown in Aragon, but the knowledge seems not to have affected her
feelings for her worthless husband. He appears almost
saintlike in the group portrait she commissioned ten years

later to commemorate his murder. Paradoxically, the painting also provided Cesare with a species of immortality for
it shows one of the few reasonably authentic portraits of
him, although even here exists the enigma attached to all
Borgia portraits. Juan is unequivocal, a beautiful flower-
crowned figure kneeling in adoration before the Virgin,
unaware of the brutal figure behind him about to plunge a
dagger in his back. Facing him are his brothers Cesare and
Joffre, Cesare apparently surrendering his sword while
Joffre turns to him. The somewhat pedestrian painter may
have intended Cesare's act of surrendering to be interpreted as an admission of his inferiority to the noble figure of
Juan. Alternatively, it could be a near-literal depiction of
Cesare's catastrophic end. But either interpretation shows
clearly where Maria Enriquez placed the blame for Juan's
murder, and how she kept its memory green years after
persons in Rome had discreetly tucked it aside.

Investigations were still being pursued in Rome nearly
a year after the murder, but they became increasingly desultory, almost certainly because Alexander was truly convinced that he knew the murderer and was biding his time.
Naturally buoyant, he had in any case rapidly persuaded
himself, or been persuaded, that in Cesare he had a far
more fitting heir than Juan. What arguments Cesare used
or what pressure he exerted were unknown outside the
Borgia Apartments, but they were sufficient to overturn
within two months the plans for him which Alexander had
cherished more than five years. In August the remarkable
news sped around Rome that Cardinal Cesare Borgia,
whose head was still regularly shaved in the tonsure of the
priest, was looking for a wife and had apparently found her
—none other than Sancia, his sister-in-law. The plan was

admirably economical, involving a simple exchange. Joffre was to obtain Cesare's hat and Cesare was to have Joffre's wife. Doubtlessly, Joffre would have made a somewhat better cardinal than Cesare, and Sancia would have been considerably improved as the wife of Cesare; but Cesare had set his sights higher than the illegitimate princess of Squillace.

The bride-to-be now canvassed was the widow of Ferrantino, the late king of Naples. But no sooner had the tongues of Rome got to work on this new aspect of Cesare's ambitions when they again changed. The widow of an ex-king and the bastard of another had not the status commensurate with that in the heady future envisaged for the eldest son of Pope Alexander. Cesare sought now a legitimate princess with prospects: Carlotta, daughter of King Federigo of Naples, through whom he could hope to clutch at the crown of Naples itself. And at the same time negotiations were started to bring about a marriage between Lucrezia and Alfonso, the brother of Sancia.

King Federigo appeared unimpressed by the double honor offered his house. From his viewpoint it more nearly resembled a pincer movement than the opportunity to ally himself with the dominant family in Italy. In the previous three years he had had opportunity to learn how precarious was his family's hold on Naples: two reigning monarchs had been bundled off the throne by the mere threat of invasion. Too, he was aware that no other state in Italy offered the unscrupulous quite such an attractive package of vast wealth and extreme vulnerability. The gift of the crown lay in the hands of Alexander, and Federigo's peculiar problem was to placate the pope and yet prevent his getting a toehold in the state as a result of that placation. The negotiations for Lucrezia's betrothal went slowly but smoothly enough, for her intended Alfonso, though bearing the splendid style of duke of Bisceglie, was also illegitimate. But Cesare's offer for the hand of the Princess Carlotta, Federigo's own daughter, encountered steady if hidden opposition from the outset.

Throughout the lengthy, tedious negotiations, Federigo impresses as a weak but honorable man; loath to antagonize his all-powerful suzerain, seeking to escape the impasse by somewhat feebly leaving to his daughter the responsibility of accepting or rejecting her suitor, but who ultimately made his own courageous decision on largely moral grounds. That Carlotta was absent from Naples throughout the negotiations considerably strengthened Federigo's hand, for though the daughter of a great house was self-evidently a piece of merchandise to be bartered for dynastic gain, nevertheless, the Christian ceremony which sealed that bargain required her personal and explicit assent. Carlotta was a lady-in-waiting in the court of France, following that custom whereby the children of one house were brought up in another to widen their horizon and their marriage market; and each embassy sent to her in France comfortably ate up weeks of time. Negotiations dragged through the autumn and winter of 1497, and the spring of 1498. Then, in June the Venetian ambassador reported to his senate that the all-important marriage had "gone up in smoke," giving as reason an explanation that must have caused raised eyebrows even in Venice. "Nothing more is spoken of about this marriage because Federigo has said, 'It seems to me that the son of a pope, who is also a cardinal, is not the ideal person to give my daughter to wife. If the pope can make it possible for a cardinal to marry and keep his hat, I'll think about giving him my daughter.' "44

It was the first open rebuff the Borgia ever received, and Federigo was to suffer for it. Initially, his objection was founded on the reasonable grounds that two Borgia relatives in the house of Aragon were enough, even though both were bastards. He had good reason to know that, once the Borgia were fastened on to the vitals of Naples there was no getting rid of them; for he had been obliged to agree to the transference of the Neapolitan estates of the dead Juan to Cesare, whose claims were not so much sketchy as non-existent. In addition he had learned from France that Carlotta objected strongly to the idea of becoming "la cardinala," as she put it, refusing even to consider marrying "a priest and the son of a priest"—an unfair and sweeping criticism, for Cesare was not yet quite a priest. Carlotta could not have then known him personally but, apart from her religious scruples, enough of the Borgia reputation had percolated into France to make Cesare appear somewhat less than an ideal husband. She was, moreover, in love with a young Breton nobleman. Dynastically considered, all her objections were frivolous and under normal circumstances she should have met the brief but effective family coercion which usually resolved such difficulties. But Federigo seems genuinely to have loved Carlotta and her refusal, in any case, echoed his own moral and political objections. He passed the rejection on to Rome with the equivalent of a shrug. Alexander and Cesare received the humiliating snub without public comment, but almost immediately a papal envoy left for France with instructions to employ upon the recalcitrant princess the most powerful instrument of all, the king of France himself.

Alexander had made other attempts to use this obvious leverage, but the king had then been Charles VIII of the Italian invasion, an unhappy young man, uncertain of himself and of the incomprehensible world which mocked his knightly endeavors. In addition Charles nursed the wounds of his previous encounter with Italy. He had promised vaguely to do what he could in the matter of Carlotta, but nothing had come of it. Then he died in March 1497, still a young man, the victim neither of disease nor of war but, appropriately enough, of his own clumsiness. He struck his head on the lintel of a door although, as Comines remarked caustically, Charles was short enough to pass through with ease. His cousin Louis succeeded him, and almost immediately appealed to Rome for help of the kind that only Alexander could give.

Louis was entangled in one of those common matrimonial problems that made of European politics a complex dynastic web. He wanted a divorce from his present wife so he could marry Charles's widow, Anne of Brittany, and thus secure his hold over the province. Repeatedly, pure chance was to give Alexander the kind of opportunity for which more skilled men worked in vain. It was in the grasping of these opportunities and turning them to his own advantage that Alexander supremely displayed his expertise. Louis's matrimonial problems not only helped him solve Cesare's but also provided the means to release Cesare from the burden of a cardinal's hat.

At the
Court of France

8

Juan's death totally altered Alexander's plans for his
family. There was now no other person but Cesare upon
whom the dynasty could be built. Lucrezia was a woman,
destined eventually to be absorbed into another family;
Joffre was far too weak and young. Only through Cesare
could Alexander's ambitions be fulfilled; even if the
young man had enthusiastically embraced his religious
career it would have been necessary to separate him
from it now. And fortunately Cesare, for the past five
years, had displayed nothing but irritation at his
gorgeous but meaningless Church role; only the desire
to create himself a prince in the outside world.

There had been one obstacle to such a
renunciation: the bulk of Cesare's revenues came from
the Church. In renouncing the hat he would make
himself a poor man, as the Borgia counted poverty.
Alexander could perhaps have openly robbed the
Church to maintain his son in a secular status, but

consistent throughout his career was his passion for legality; every ducat that passed into the Borgia coffers was paid
out, in theory, on behalf of the papacy for services rendered. He could, perhaps, have tried to secure for Cesare the
Dukedom of Benevento that had been intended for Juan.
Cesare was already receiving most of its revenue, and it
would have been little more than turning a *de facto* into a
de jure situation. But that would consume time as would the
search for another barony in the states of the Church itself,
for the current occupant would have to be dispossessed.
Then suddenly, Alexander found himself talking to the
French ambassador, hearing of Louis's urgent needs and
assessing the price that he could be made to pay for them.
Louis could only promise to use his influence on Carlotta,
but he could contract outright to grant Cesare an appropriate honor as repayment for the much-needed dispensation
to remarry. The bargaining was swiftly concluded. In August 1498, just four months after Louis had become king,
he agreed to invest Cesare with the duchy of Valentinois
complete with revenues befitting a royal duke of France.
The Italians, with their love of nicknames, already had
dubbed Cesare "Valentino," from his bishopric of Valencia
in Spain; the outlandish "Valentinois" received an identical
change in the Italian tongue and it was as Duke Valentino
that Cesare at last emerged upon the secular stage.

On August 17 Cesare attended a full consistory,
dressed for the last time in the crimson of a prince of the
Church, to make his formal plea to be allowed to renounce
his priestly role. The argument he put forward—presumably that was placed in his mouth by the canon lawyers with
Alexander's approval—explicitly branded his father a liar
and himself a bastard. The opening of his speech was unex-

ceptional enough. It was well known, he said, that he had never been blessed with a sense of vocation and that his preferred path of life was at variance with that considered appropriate for an ecclesiastic. Then Cesare turned to the circumstances under which he had originally entered the Sacred College. It had been stated then, he said, that he had been the legitimate son of Domenico d'Arignano. This was not the case; he was, in fact, the son of Pope Alexander and therefore, because he was illegitimate and his election the result of a "misstatement," he was automatically disqualified from office. It was a curious plea. The statement that the cardinal of Valencia was the son of the reigning pope could hardly be classed as one of the great discoveries of the age, and the fact that the bull which legitimized him was a tissue of obvious lies must have been known before the ink on the parchment dried. Alexander's passion for the outward forms of legality now led him yet again into an unsavory situation. Possibly, he had expected a greater degree of opposition from the Spanish cardinals than, in fact, Cesare encountered. Garcilaso de la Vega, the Spanish ambassador, did indeed register a strong protest, for not only was Spain losing a cardinal but France was gaining a duke. Cesare's sacred colleagues accepted his loss without sign of grief, and Alexander smoothly blocked the Spanish protest by employing his spiritual authority. It was necessary for the good of Cesare's soul that he should cease to bear the burden of an office unsuited to him. Ferdinand and Isabella perforce also accepted the situation, but with a very bad grace.

A few hours after the consistory had come to its expected conclusion, the French envoy, Monsieur de Villeneuve, arrived in Rome and sought immediate audience with Alexander. It was immediately granted, for he brought with him an impressive document in which Louis, king of France, invested his well-beloved cousin, Caesar Borge, "his heirs and successors in perpetuity with our comtes and seigneuries of Valentinois and Dyois, their appurtenances and dependencies, together with all powers regarding the administration of justice therein. . . ." The document had been drawn up before Villeneuve left the royal court at Amboise and, reading it, Cesare might have come to the reasonable conclusion that, over the past few days, he had been simultaneously cardinal of Valencia and duke of Valentinois. Louis, however, had exceeded the generous powers of even a king of France, so anxious had he been to obtain the much-desired dispensation for his own marriage.

When the Paris parlement met in October it was forcefully pointed out to Louis that he had not simply created a duke on paper, but had established in a large and wealthy area of France a foreign prince whose powers, by feudal law, were absolute under the king. An Italian enclave had, in effect, been created in France—and, far worse, given to a member of a family notoriously Spanish in its sympathies. Cesare's imminent arrival helped Louis smooth the matter over, for parlement had no desire to create the kind of situation that would have resulted if the pope's son had been turned away under humiliating conditions. But the crisis showed clearly enough what France's leaders thought of the bargain between king and pope.

Cesare left Rome for France on October 1, and in noting his departure, Burchard appears to have made one of his rare factual errors. Cesare left Rome "in secret and without pomp" according to the master of ceremonies; but the French, in fact, were astonished by the almost barbaric magnificence of Cesare's entourage. It was a curious, uncharacteristic error for a man not only in the habit of being precise, but to whom would naturally have fallen the task of organizing the ceremony of departure. If Burchard did not make such an extraordinary blunder in his diary, the implication is that Alexander feared a popular demonstration against Cesare and arranged for his entourage to join him discreetly some distance from Rome. Certainly the papal treasury had been plundered to equip the fortunate young man; by a happy coincidence the bishop of Calahorra had recently been found guilty of heresy, and his confiscated wealth paid for part of Cesare's French mission. Altogether, nearly a quarter of a million ducats were spent to provide Cesare with pocket money and dress him in suitable style. Rumor sped around Italy that the very shoes of his horses were made of silver and deliberately loosened so they should fall off as largess. Such a story belonged to fables, but it owed its origin to a genuine and widespread belief that Alexander had ignored cost in launching Cesare upon his new career.

The dead Juan might now never have existed. The letter despatched to France ahead of Cesare to prepare his way spoke of him in the terms of extravagant love that once had been aroused by Juan alone. Writing to Louis, Alexander said, "We destine to your Majesty our heart—that is, our favorite son, Duke Valentino, who is prized by us beyond all else as a signal and most estimable token of our affection toward Your Highness—to whom no further recommendation of him is required." [45] Abraham might have spoken of Isaac in rather similar terms, and the king of France was left in no doubt whatsoever that if he wanted the father's friendship, the son's desires would have to be satisfied.

Cesare arrived by sea at Marseilles on October 11, where he was received by a royal salute of artillery, and entertained extravagantly for ten days. He then took the road north for Avignon. The city was papal territory and, over the past fortnight, its parlement had been in anxious conference with the papal legate especially appointed for the purpose of Cesare's mission. There was a certain piquancy in the fact that the legate was Cardinal Giuliano della Rovere, the bitter enemy of Cesare's father, now apparently dedicating himself to the comfort and honor of Cesare himself. After three years of exile, della Rovere had discovered that the old, well-tried Italian method of expediency was to be preferred to the striking of expensive attitudes. He had failed, totally and humiliatingly, to unseat his enemy and had retired to France with the unfortunate Charles. Della Rovere, in his favored position at the French court, was well-placed to harass Alexander if he chose, but at the cost of permanently undermining his long-term prospects. Only in Rome was a man such as della Rovere fully at home. Only in the cramped and cluttered lobbies and passages of the Vatican, in the palaces and villas of the great could an ambitious man keep track of the subtle, ever-changing patterns of intrigue and policy; noting the inflection of voice, the fleeting expression of face that indicated a shift of direction which might make one man's fortune even while it destroyed another. Della Rovere had made the first move toward a reconciliation. At Juan's death he wrote a condoling letter to the shattered father. Alexander accepted the gesture; he may, perhaps, have been unusually vulnerable during the terrible days following the murder, but he was also well aware of della Rovere's high standing at the court of France. Fulsome letters passed between the two and out of them arose della Rovere's appointment as papal legate to the court.

The new legate's first duty was to arrange a fitting reception for the new duke of Valentinois, and the council of Avignon was persuaded to raise a loan for the purpose. An embassy was despatched to Marseilles to meet the duke, and the council itself debated what form the festivities should take. Avignon's city fathers were somewhat hampered by the fact that there was no precedent to guide them in the matter of entertaining the son of a pope, but they concluded, correctly, that they could not do better than by treating him as any other young, handsome prince. Rich men liked rich presents and the council therefore voted their guest a remarkable collection of valuable hardware, some eighteen pieces of silver plate valued at three thousand florins. The city's own prestige demanded that it should be splendidly decorated with hangings and triumphal arches, the processional route strewn with clean sand and dotted with selected fountains gushing carefully calculated quantities of cheap red wine. "And finally, that no expression of joy may be wanting, he shall be feted in the Maison de la Ville with ladies and beautiful girls, for the said Don Cesare takes much pleasure therein, knowing well how to dance with, and entertain them. The dances are to be morrises, mummeries and other frivolities." [46]

From Avignon Cesare moved on to Valence, the ducal town of his duchy, where he was installed with all the honors due his dual rank of royal duke and papal favorite. More days of banquets and masques, moralities and mummeries followed before he moved on to Lyons, where the sequence was repeated. It was not until the beginning of December, nearly two months after he had landed in France that, still leisurely, he took the road for Chinon and his meeting with King Louis. The scornfully slow progress irritated Louis, who was impatiently awaiting the dispensation Cesare supposedly was bringing with him, and a spirited protest was made to Rome. Alexander hastened to conciliate the king. It was not due to any lack of goodwill on his part, he assured Louis, but he was bound by his own canon lawyers. The divorce commissioners had not yet examined all the evidence, and until they had done so and come to a conclusion, he had no power to pronounce a divorce.

Alexander's well-known love for legality now gave him useful room to maneuver. There was little doubt that the commissioners were moving at a normal bureaucratic pace, and also that Alexander could have prodded them into greater celerity. He did not choose to, for the delay kept Louis in a healthy state of uncertainty. The situation was to add yet another lurid tale to the growing Borgia legend. As Machiavelli told the story some time later: "The dispensation was given to Valentino when he went to France, without anyone being aware of its existence, with orders to sell it dearly to the king. But the king learned from the bishop of Ceuta that the dispensation already existed, and so, without having received or even seen it, the marriage was celebrated, and for revealing what he did the bishop of Ceuta was put to death by orders of Valentino." [47] The bishop of Ceuta, a trusted papal envoy, was well known; and Machiavelli must have been aware that he did not, in fact, die until over a year after the French mission—in Italy, of wounds received in battle. And Machiavelli, an experienced diplomat, must also have known that Louis was not the kind of man to risk his crown for the reasons given. In fact in early December Cesare and Louis were simultaneously informed of the divorce commission's findings, the bull of nullification was published throughout France on December 17, and Cesare was then free to meet Louis and begin his own negotiations. But Machiavelli's story would have lost its point without the twist at the end, and it was accordingly woven in its totality into the web of legend. Thus Cesare was credited with two murders in a little over a year.

That autumn in France was bitterly cold, with almost ceaseless gales of wind and rain lashing to tatters the expensive decorations of the municipalities on Cesare's route. Nevertheless, his progress attracted astonishing attention. Crowds followed wherever he moved, staring silently for the most part as though at some rare and dangerous animal. A member of Cesare's party wrote home saying they had seen nothing of trees and houses in France, nothing but people pressing around and an occasional glimpse of watery sunlight overhead. The experience seems to have gone to his head, for he lacked the maturity to recognize it for what it was: a fascinated but unsympathetic interest in him as a member of a notorious family. Humility was never Cesare Borgia's outstanding characteristic, and under the heady influence of apparent fame he became peremptory, insufferably haughty; alienating those Frenchmen who might have been disposed to assess him apart from his family's reputation, even while confirming in the rest the belief that nothing but trouble ever came out of Italy. He completely misjudged the society in which he found himself. In Italy his gaudy magnificence went almost unnoticed among men who assessed power and wealth by its outward display of velvets and jewels. France, provincial by contrast, still tended to measure a man by older, more sober standards; and Cesare's display, intended to impress, aroused only derision particularly in the royal court which took its standards from the parsimonious Louis.

Louis's restlessly moving court had established itself temporarily at Chinon in the same fabled castle from where, seventy years earlier, his cowering ancestor had been dragged by Joan of Arc to receive a crown. That shameful episode was forgotten now, for the English had long since been thrown out of France; and Louis was the most powerful monarch in Europe, undisputed lord of the largest united state between the Arctic and the Mediterranean. Toward Cesare there was, therefore, a delicate point of etiquette to be resolved. His enigmatic status again posed a problem in a society where precedent and precedence counted for everything. How did a monarch such as Louis receive a pope's bastard? It was known that Cesare was, deplorably, planning some sort of triumph for his entry into Chinon; and while it would be embarrassing for the king of France to be overshadowed by the magnificence of a private person without official status, it could also prove a grave mistake to welcome him in like regal style. The problem was solved ingeniously. It was decided that Louis and Cesare would meet "spontaneously" at the head of the castle's great staircase as though one man were simply welcoming another into his home.

One of the towers of the castle directly commanded the main street of the little town; and it was there on the morning of December 19 that Louis stationed himself to watch, with open scorn, Cesare's gaudy advent. But though the king himself mocked the display, an anonymous member of the crowd was sufficiently impressed to record, in painstaking detail and lamentable verse, the appearance both of Cesare and his retinue. The unknown poetaster lacked both the ability and interest to attempt any description of the man himself and of the crowd's reaction to him, but the laborious catalogue provides clear enough evidence of what Cesare considered appropriate for a state occasion. The impression conveyed is of bottomless vulgarity, the desire of a parvenu to obscure his origins behind a blaze of displayed wealth. Cesare was never to make that mistake again; it stemmed mostly from lack of experience and Cesare was, above all, capable of learning from experience. But it did him considerable harm during the first vital days of his contact with the French court.

The lengthy file of heavily laden sumpter mules that led Cesare's cavalcade were expensively decked out in his colors of scarlet and yellow, each animal conspicuously bearing the Borgia crest of the ox and his own insignia of the flame. The crowd's attention was particularly attracted to two immense chests, each covered with a length of cloth of gold, which were borne in ritual isolation as though they were the shrines of a religious procession. Some claimed they contained the priceless jewels which had been collected for Cesare's fortunate bride; others maintained that one chest, at least, contained the equally priceless dispensation for the king. Sixteen gentlemen of Cesare's court followed on horses caparisoned, in the Spanish manner, with towering cockades of gold and furnished with silver bridles and stirrups. Behind them came twenty mounted pages dressed in crimson velvet or cloth of gold. And finally came Cesare himself surrounded by sixty gentlemen, some of whom were his personal staff, grim-faced Spanish mercenaries whose finery did not conceal the fact that they were highly efficient killers; and the rest were Roman noblemen who had considered it politic to make the long, expensive journey with the new star so suddenly risen on the Roman horizon.

Cesare appeared in a blaze of jewels. His basic costume was the curiously somber black velvet which he was afterwards to adopt habitually, but on this occasion it was slashed to show the gold brocade of the undergarment. Gold buttons, each with a ruby in the center, fastened his doublet. Pearls and more rubies were in his hat and on his boots. Diamonds flashed upon his chest. Gold caparisoned his superb warhorse—gold beaten out into leaves to overlay the harness or worked into a net, embroidered with pearls, to confine the sweeping tail.

"Altogether too much for the petty duke of Valentinois," Louis sneered, but descended to greet his guest effusively and almost snatch from him the long-awaited dispensation. The preparations for Louis's marriage had long since been made, and the ceremony accordingly took place almost immediately.

For Cesare there was no equal satisfaction. Almost the first thing he learned on his arrival at Chinon was that Carlotta of Aragon was even firmer in her intention of having nothing to do with him. Carlotta enjoyed an unusually strong position for an unmarried girl who had refused a dynastic marriage. She was a lady-in-waiting not in Louis's court but that of his new bride, Anne of Brittany. The nobleman Carlotta wanted to marry was a Breton and Anne had taken her side. The queen was a strong-minded woman with a lively awareness of her own rights and importance. Her championship of Carlotta was probably due less to a liking for feminine intrigue than from a desire to make clear to her husband that she was the loyal protectress of all things Breton. Louis, in any case, was less than ardent in Cesare's cause; and as the days passed into weeks, with Carlotta remaining stubborn and Louis displaying help-lessness, it became obvious that Pope Alexander had, for once, been thoroughly outwitted. It was natural that Louis would lose interest once the vital dispensation was safe in the royal archives; Alexander had calculated that closely enough when he employed his own delaying tactics. But what he had not known was that Louis's plans were diamet-rically opposed to his own. Louis's plans envisaged nothing less than another French attack on Naples; and it seems highly unlikely that Louis ever seriously considered bring-ing about a marriage between the Borgia, whom he needed as allies, and the house of Aragon, which he intended to destroy. Altogether, the forces brought to bear on Carlotta of Aragon neatly canceled each other, and she was eventu-ally able to indulge in the rare luxury of marrying the man she loved.

Louis had no desire openly to antagonize the Borgia clan, and a pretense was kept going that Carlotta was still open to persuasion. But Cesare knew better. In Paris the students at the Sorbonne put on an entertaining little masque in which the "son of God" pursued an unwilling bride. Though the students were traditionally, almost professionally, irreverent; and though authority acted promptly if clumsily, simultaneously closing the show and provoking a riot—it gave a sharp edge to Cesare's personal humiliation. He reacted badly, giving further grounds for offense and for mockery as an unsuccessful gallant. He sulked, accused Louis of bad faith and even withdrew from the court with the declared intention of returning home and complaining in person to his father. Giuliano della Rovere found himself in an unpleasant position as the go-between who had failed in his self-appointed task. He tried to conciliate Alexander by excusing Cesare and lavishing praises upon him. "By his modesty, his readiness, his prudence and his other virtues he has gained everybody's affection. The young lady, however, either through sheer perversity—or because she has been influenced by others, which is easier to believe—absolutely declines to hear of the wedding." Alexander refused to be conciliated, and in a furious letter to his legate he declared that he had been made a laughingstock. "All Europe was very well aware that, but for the French king's plain promise to find a wife for him, Cesare would have remained in Italy."

Almost from the moment Cesare left Rome, Alexander had been swinging between extremes of emotion. When the news from France was good, he was beside himself with delight at the brilliant future apparently opening for his son; when the news was bad or nonexistent, he was plunged into regret, amounting at times to despair, at the situation in which he had placed himself in order to bring that future into being. It was beginning in this autumn of 1498 that the ubiquitous observers detected a change both in Alexander's personality and in his relationship with Cesare, for it was in this autumn that he abandoned—or was forced to abandon—the friendship with Spain which he had so carefully cherished throughout his life. Again, the secrecy of the Borgia family councils give no hint of the pressures Cesare brought to bear upon him to effectuate this most drastic and bitterly regretted change. But those pressures must have been extreme, for even in the perilous days of 1494, when the French were at the gates of Rome and from the battlements of Sant' Angelo he had looked down into the mouths of their cannon, Alexander had remained steadfast to the alliance with his native country. Now when neutrality, at least, would have given him an advantage, he had been forced openly to support a power known to be inimical to Spain and Italy alike.

Cesare's motives are clear enough. Throughout his brief career he was to show that he was haunted by a sense of urgency, of time fleeting, of the necessity of establishing himself during the few years left of his father's life. Unlike his father, who could be influenced by other than purely practical motives, Cesare assessed every situation in terms of its immediate benefit to himself. He would have transformed himself into a Spanish duke with perfect equanimity had the opportunity existed. It did not. Isabella's long-standing dislike of the Borgia had been charged anew by the murder of the duke of Gandia, for Gandia's widow had persuaded her that Cesare was responsible. The Spanish ambassador in Rome, Garcilaso de la Vega, had also filed increasingly worrying reports about the nature and range of Cesare's ambition. Spain was therefore out— but France provided an ideal shortcut and Cesare took it, regardless of its ultimate destination.

But where Cesare—young, fresh and optimistic— could turn to France with little sense of loss, the severing of a lifetime's ties proved traumatic for Alexander. Torn between his ambitions for his son and the knowledge that he was breaking bonds which every instinct urged him to preserve, he lapsed into apathetic exhibition of uncertainty, displaying his age for the first time. Long after negotiations for Carlotta had broken down, he sent As-

canio Sforza into Naples to see if it were possible to retrieve
something from the wreck. Ascanio returned with the expected bad news and, in his turn, put some sharp questions
to His Holiness regarding the rumors that Louis was planning another invasion of Italy, with Milan as first victim.
Alexander feebly denied it—then half-admitted it—then
claimed he would be glad to join an anti-French league if
only Cesare were not virtually a hostage in France.
Throughout the winter Alexander was tormented by the
lack of news from France, pestering the ambassadors of
every power which had a representative in Louis's court,
demanding to know if they could throw any light on what
was happening there. All other affairs of state were brushed
aside.

The Venetian ambassador reported how he had tried
to obtain a ruling on a vital question which touched on
Papal-Venetian interests "But the pope said he cared little
about this for he was awaiting other news—that is to say,
from France. He is very anxious to hear and is kept in
suspense." In their turn the ambassadors daily thronged
the antechambers of the Vatican, for bizarre though it
seemed, the destiny of southern Europe apparently hung
on a young man's attempt at marriage. In addition to the
rumors that Louis intended an invasion of Italy, there was
gossip that he was shopping around for a French bride for
Cesare, a move which would intimately tie the papacy to
France—for the fortunes of the Borgia and the papacy were
now virtually indistinguishable. As tension grew, diplomatic courtesies collapsed amid threats of violence and
obscene insults. The Venetians stood on the sidelines,
ready to profit from whatever situation developed; but the
ambassadors of those other powers who saw themselves

menaced by a French alliance—the Milanese, the Neapolitans, the Spaniards, the Portuguese—dropped all pretense that Cesare was absent on a kind of courtesy call.

On December 10 Alexander and Ascanio Sforza nearly came to blows. "Yesterday in consistory Cardinal Ascanio told the pope that sending his son into France would be the ruin of Italy," the Venetian ambassador told his government. "The pope shouted in reply that it had been Ascanio's brother who first brought the French into Italy." [48] The argument grew heated with Ascanio demanding to know just what it was that Alexander hoped—or feared—from France, and ended with Alexander threatening to throw him into the river. Far worse was the unprecedented interview between Alexander and Garcilaso de la Vega. The Spaniard had joined forces with his Portuguese colleague and together the two men launched a blistering attack on the pope's whole way of life, ending it with the usual references to his illegal election and threats to call a council. Alexander heard them out and then replied, coldly, that he was not surprised that this was the view the court of Spain held of him, for de la Vega had done nothing but bear tales and gossip back to his masters. Stung, the Spaniard blurted out the unforgivable: heaven had already punished His Holiness's crimes through his children and might do so yet again. Outwardly unmoved by the brutal reference to the murder of his son, Alexander icily retorted that, in the matter of children, Their Catholic Majesties had suffered a greater blow from heaven than had he. The only child of Ferdinand and Isabella was the girl whom history was to know as Juana the Mad. On that unedifying note the audience broke up: de la Vega to prepare his report and add more fuel to Spanish rage, Alexander to contemplate the result of his contemptuous speech. Behind the bold front was a quaking heart. He, the experienced statesman, had kicked one foothold away before ensuring that another existed.

So matters dragged on through December and January. At last, in February, there came definite news from France. King Louis was to take the road south to claim his ancestors' crowns in both Milan and Naples. Accompanying him would be his dear cousin and faithful liege Cesare Borgia, Duke of Valentinois; and as soon as the small matter of chasing the usurper from the throne of Milan was accomplished, the mighty arms of France were to be placed at Cesare's disposal so he could carve a principality for himself in Italy. Cesare had also, incidentally, acquired a bride.

She was Charlotte d'Albret, daughter of the duke of Guyenne, sister to the king of Navarre and altogether an excellent match for Cesare Borgia, related as she was to the royal house of France. Charlotte was—and remained—a pawn, moving briefly from obscurity to fame, then back again. Few troubled to record their impressions of her; but dimly through the sparse, conventional flatteries can be perceived a rather attractive girl—deeply religious but not fanatically so, sweet-tempered, gentle and accounted beautiful. Charlotte, at seventeen years of age, was not an obvious match for Cesare Borgia but the negotiations were, surprisingly, crowned with rapid success once started. Cesare pursued Carlotta of Aragon for more than a year before he gave up the chase. Charlotte d'Albret was wooed, won and wed in a little over two months.

It was the cupidity of her father which brought about the marriage. Alain d'Albret was at once penurious and avaricious. He knew, as did everyone in court circles, of the humiliation the Borgia had suffered and promptly placed a fantastically high price on his daughter. The pope was to endow her with one hundred thousand ducats, while her own dowry of ninety thousand ducats cost d'Albret nothing, for it was Charlotte's inheritance from her mother and could be used only for purchasing a suitable estate in France and not in Italy. D'Albret's preliminary proposals were accepted so swiftly that he promptly squeezed harder, demanding in addition a cardinal's hat for his son. The proposal was carried to Cesare who as promptly promised the hat on his father's behalf. Even Alain was satisfied and the bargain was struck. The marriage contract was signed on May 10, 1499 and two days later Cesare and Charlotte were married with a minimum of ceremony.

The morning after the wedding Cesare's personal envoy, Garcia, left Amboise for Rome. He covered the distance in the incredible time of four days, in obedience to his master's urgent instructions, and on arriving in Rome did not even have time to change his travel-stained clothes before he was urgently summoned to the Vatican. So weary was he that Alexander gave him permission to be seated and personally ordered food and wine brought. Garcia remained by Alexander's side more than seven hours, for the pope was hungry for the minutest detail of all that had happened in France. What was the girl like? What did the French now think of Cesare? How had he conducted himself during the wedding? He roared with delight when Garcia described how the duke had "broken the lance" eight times on the wedding night, a performance which had elicited the congratulations of the king, who said Cesare had beaten him in that particular tournament.

On and on Garcia talked while the sun rose and fell over Rome and more food and wine was brought, pontiff and servant sharing the same table. Garcia told of how Cesare had been formally enrolled as an officer in Louis's army with a stipend of twenty thousand francs a year, in command of a crack company of one hundred *lances françaises;* of his induction into the order of St. Michael; of his magnificent new coat of arms in which the bull was now quartered with the lilies; of his title, splendid in its simplicity: Cesare Borgia of France. He described the estate with which Cesare had been endowed in the fairest province of France, and delighted Alexander again with his remark that it was a piece of Spain in France, since the new duke's officers there were all Spanish. And even after Garcia was at last permitted to depart, the tale of Cesare's splendor was repeated to all who had the good sense to attend the Vatican and offer His Holiness heartiest congratulations. Fireworks hissed and roared their way into the Roman night in celebration of the great honor that had been bestowed on the Roman papacy. In the palace itself the thousands of candles in the great candelabrum were repeatedly restored throughout the night so there would be brilliance here at the heart of things. The euphoria did not pass with the coming of the dawn or in the days that followed. On the heels of Garcia there came another Spanish envoy, bearing not news but a request—for a great deal of money. Somehow Louis had not got around to paying his beloved cousin Cesare any cash on account of either stipend or ducal dues. Cesare's standard of living in France was soaring, and Italy still had to subsidize his splendor. Alexander gladly found the money immediately required: thirty-two thousand ducats of it "to send to France where the duke of Valentinois is living at great expense; and this money was over and above what he took with him," so the treasury scribe dutifully recorded and the treasurer himself, the Lord Cardinal Francesco Borgia, also dutifully endorsed—for that was why he had been appointed.

Alexander's delight was in direct proportion to the misery he had experienced during the black days of waiting. Privately he had admitted to an ambassador "that he had entertained strong doubts as to the marriage taking place, but now that it was concluded he was pleased, and whereas he used to speak evil of France, he was now all French for the love the king of France had shown toward his duke." There was talk of finding more money to bring Charlotte to Rome. She had written saying how she longed to come and pay her respects to her father-in-law, adding with an engaging touch of gentle humor that she was "very well satisfied with the duke." But that particular project never came into being. Neither Alexander nor Cesare ever saw Cesare's only legitimate child, because three months after the wedding husband and wife parted forever, the pregnant Charlotte remaining in France while Cesare accompanied the king on the Italian enterprise.

Even before Louis left France with the main body of his army, the Sforza dynasty of Milan had fallen; and Ludovico Sforza, great-grandson of the condottiere who had founded his dynasty by force of arms, was fleeing without having struck a single blow in his own defense.

King Louis's claims to the Kingdom of Naples and to the duchy of Milan were at least as good as those of their present rulers. His claim to Naples was that Angevin descent which had wearied and bloodied southern Italy for over two centuries. His claims on Milan were more complex, and perfectly illustrated the intertwinings of those matrimonial alliances which throttled Europe. The first dynasty of Milan had been the Lombard house of the Visconti. A daughter of the house had married an ancestor of Louis's and had gone to live in France but, for purely political reasons, her father had bequeathed his state to her should the legitimate male Visconti die out. Nobody expected the line to fail, but it did. Nevertheless, for nearly a century the will was ignored. Ironically, it was Ludovico Sforza himself who had activated the bequest when he summoned the French into Italy. Though beaten out, they had tasted blood and were back for more.

Louis's claims were legally unobjectionable. But the plan to plunge Italy again in bloody turmoil in order to implement dusty title deeds could have succeeded only because of the fratricidal jealousy of the Italian city-states. A unified front would have stopped this second and catastrophic invasion before it had passed the Alps. But unity was again impossible, each petty prince, each tiny power believing that he or it personally would survive the holocaust with powers augmented.

In Rome, Alexander dropped the last pretense of statesmanship, the last pretense that the good of Italy was greater than the good of a dynasty. The wretched Ludovico Sforza and his brother Ascanio were hurled to the wolves of France, and the gate into Italy opened as the byproduct of family politics. Cesare needed French help to gain his kingdom; the French wanted Milan; and so the Sforza were dropped.

In despondent predawn hours Alexander might sometimes have uneasily contemplated the dizzy and ever-accelerating speed of events. Barely two years before, he had been firmly in control of his family's affairs. He, a Spanish pope, had ensured that his eldest son was a Spanish cardinal, his second a Spanish duke, his third betrothed to the daughter of the Spanish-Neapolitan king. Now the Spanish duke was dead—murdered. And the Spanish cardinal, transformed into a French duke, was marching into Italy like an invader, arm in arm with the same French monarchy which had sworn to thrust Alexander off the throne. The marriage between Joffre and Sancia of Aragon still survived but there was no sign yet of an heir. And Lucrezia's marriage to a Neapolitan was now a liability; he would have to find some excuse to annul it. Cesare was forcing the entire family to run headlong where there was scarcely space to walk cautiously. But there was nothing now that Alexander could do about it, and he turned his attention to knocking down the victims whose states would form the nucleus of Cesare's dominion in Italy.

As usual, Alexander was maneuvering with every outward show of legality when he chose the Romagna as Cesare's field of operation. The Romagna formed a major section of the Papal States, and the present vicars of most of the Romagnol cities were little better than usurpers. The vicariates had been granted to their forebears and they had no right to them without the pope's express permission. He was establishing no unusual precedent nor was he being particularly unjust when he decided to install Cesare in their place—once Cesare had expelled them with the aid of French arms. Unusual, however, was the scale of the projected expulsions. Ten cities in the northern provinces of the states, most of them in the Romagna, were marked down as Cesare's prey and a papal bull published declaring that, the vicars having fallen behind in their feudal dues, their fiefs were now reverting to the Roman Church. One of the vicars, the formidable Caterina Sforza of Forli, promptly sent her envoys to prove that, far from being in debt to the Holy See, she was some sixty thousand ducats in advance of payment. It made not the slightest difference.

In September 1499 King Louis of France entered Milan as its true duke. A month later a large detachment of his army rode out behind Duke Cesare Borgia, lent to him until such time as he had established himself as a prince in Italy, or until such time as King Louis needed it again.

Conquest
of the Romagna

9

From Piacenza the great road ran almost directly into the eye of the rising sun, so straight and flat that its perspective dwindled to the classic vanishing point. It still bore its antique name, the Via Emilia, and it ran for 150 miles from the heart of Lombardy to the coast of the Adriatic. It traveled through Parma and Modena, through Bologna, Imola, Faenza, Forli, Cesena— stringing together the beautiful cities like jewels upon a necklace. At Rimini it turned south and lost its ancient name, but continued still to run arrow-straight in the narrow strip between the last melancholy outposts of the Apennines and the Adriatic Sea. The first rains of autumn had dampened the surface, laying the thick dust but otherwise leaving the surface unaffected, for it was well paved. Lombardy's lifeblood ran along it. The merchants ensured that it was always in good repair and what was good enough for lumbering trade caravans proved ideal for military purposes.

Along the Via Emilia now, in November 1499, there moved the most recent of the countless armies that had passed down it through its two millennia of life. The army was compact and efficient looking, stretching not more than two miles from the gorgeously caparisoned mounts of the noblemen in front to the clumsy pack wagons in the rear. Apart from the armorers, blacksmiths, cooks and general tradesmen there were perhaps seven thousand men: French men-at-arms like glittering towers in their mail; Swiss pikemen moving easily, deceptively unarmored; a handful of Spanish swordsmen in soft red leggings which gave them a similarly deceptive air of carnival; and Gascon footmen, small, agile, ferocious. Safely in the center was the artillery, drawn not by the clumsy oxen of Italian artillery trains but by horses especially bred for the purpose in France. These were the guns that had at last driven the English from France, and they moved at a fast pace so that they were always with the main body. Approaching this body of seven thousand men was another army of three thousand, but they were still toiling northward through the tortuous passes of the Apennines, sent into Lombardy by His Holiness to join Duke Cesare's men.

At the far end of the road in the city of Forli, Caterina Sforza, lady of the twin cities of Imola and Forli, received news of the advancing armies and began to make certain preparations. Following the approved method of Italian politics, when it was seen that Caterina's danger was overwhelming, her friends had abandoned her and her enemies arose openly. When the two advancing armies met she would have only her skill and courage and, perhaps, the very dubious loyalty of her subjects to combat them and save her from exile or, more likely, death.

She was thirty-six years old. On reaching that age most other woman of her day would have been resigned to declining, gracefully or otherwise, into old age. Caterina Sforza merely added another dimension to that astonishing beauty which throughout her life had charmed friends and discountenanced enemies. But Caterina Sforza was altogether a remarkable woman. For eleven years, ever since the murder of her first husband, she had not merely survived but flourished in a wholly masculine society, adopting a masculine approach to life to do so and yet remaining totally and desirably feminine, as witnessed the procession of lovers through her bed. She could use her beauty coldly, as a weapon, or as a means of delighting her lovers. On one occasion, when she wanted to rid herself of an infatuated but wary official, she seduced him, appearing before him in the filmiest of gowns and lured him to where her guard could pounce upon him; afterward she charged the official with having committed an indecent offense toward her. It was she for whom the term *virago* was coined—a term used not pejoratively but admiringly, testimony to her powerful, flexible mind and steely, utterly unscrupulous will.

Caterina was the illegitimate daughter of Duke Galeazzo Sforza of Milan and the niece of Ludovico Sforza. Ludovico's fall, therefore, immediately and intimately affected her. She had been little more than a teen-ager when she was married off to Girolamo Riario, the coarse, unsavory, but favorite "nephew" of old Pope Sixtus, who had installed him as vicar of the papal cities of Imola and Forli. Girolamo survived the debacle of the Riario fortunes on Sixtus's death, but fell victim not long afterward to the daggers of aristocratic assassins. Caterina avenged his murder bloodily—she had no particular affection for her boorish husband but assassins were not a breed to be encouraged—and efficiently took over the running of the state herself. She became legendary—but a legend based firmly on fact. That fantastic ride of hers when, pregnant, she defied the howling mobs of Rome and galloped to seize Castel Sant' Angelo marked the debut of her career. Everything she did was larger than life. After her husband's murder she escaped to the castle in Forli, leaving her children as hostages to his assassins. They threatened to kill them if she did not surrender. For answer she appeared on the battlements, raised her skirts high and cried out "Fools! Can you not see that I can make more?" When her lover was murdered she slaughtered the entire families of the conspirators—forty people, including children and women. Even her eldest son feared for his life; he had been jealous of that lover.

Caterina's subjects viewed her with a mixture of admiration and unease. The periodical rebellions against her despotic authority found little popular support. As in most of these cities of the Papal States, the rebellions were directed by those who merely wanted to take her place. It was firmly believed that she had magical powers; people talked of a marvelous book in which she kept her spells. Such a book existed and did indeed exert a kind of magic, for it consisted of exhaustive prescriptions by which she maintained her incredible beauty: the special salves for her flawless white skin; the bleaches for her ash-blond hair; the unguents for her beautiful breasts, which habitually she displayed almost uncovered; the rosewater to maintain the sparkle of her blue eyes; the powdered marble and charcoal to maintain the glitter of her even, very white teeth. She spent enormously on cosmetics, costumes and personal jewelry. But the expense was also a political investment, the means whereby she turned the traditional disadvantage of her sex to very real advantage—most directly when she allied her city-state with Florence. Giovanni de' Medici succumbed to those brilliant charms and became first her lover and then her second husband. He died after giving her a child—the boy Giovanni, who was to become perhaps the greatest and certainly the last of the condottiere—but her marriage link with the Medici and the blood link with the Sforza enabled her to accomplish what few deemed possible. She was simultaneously the ally of the two traditional enemies, Florence and Milan.

But now it seemed she had exploited every possible advantage and was at last merely a woman hopelessly at a disadvantage in a man's world. Of all men, Cesare Borgia, was not likely to be deflected from his ambition by a woman's beauty. And Caterina, better than anyone else, knew the lukewarm loyalty of her subjects. On news of the advancing armies, the Forlivese gave unequivocal signs that they would stand off and watch while the lady of Forli and the upstart called Valentino fought for the possession of the state. Wisely, she retired to her squat, rose-pink castle, gave instructions to her castellan in Imola to hold the castle there at all costs—and waited.

Cesare Borgia, riding at the head of his troops, was considerably less troubled by the military than by the political problems that lay ahead. Barring a miracle, the force at his command was more than sufficient either to winkle Caterina out of her castle or, at worst, starve her into surrender. But Cesare was a politically inexperienced young man, and was about to enter an arena which had tested and

broken far more mature men. Romagna was ringed by independent states, each of them jealously watching his advance even though each of them, for different reasons, was
prepared to acquiesce in the subjection of the Papal States.
In the North lay the most menacing independent of them
all, the *Serenissima:* the Most Serene Republic of Venice.
The Venetians had very few territorial interests in Italy. All
they desired was to create a buffer between themselves and
their turbulent fellow-Italians and would act against whoever sought to remove that buffer. To the south lay the
Republic of Florence, far more vulnerable than Venice but
presenting an even trickier problem to Cesare. The Florentines, too, were allies of King Louis of France, and had had
the good sense to stiffen that alliance with Florentine gold.
Forty thousand ducats went annually into Louis's pockets,
a sufficient guarantee of his loyalty.

In between these two major states were a handful of
semi-independent princes, of whom the Este in Ferrara and
the Gonzaga in Mantua were the most powerful. Each with
their dynastic allies could have presented a threat to
Cesare. He was in the position of a man advancing down
an uncertainly marked path through a minefield. If he
strayed too far on one side, then Venice would infallibly
explode in his face. If he strayed too far on the other, then
there would be a far bigger explosion from France, turning
an utterly essential ally into an enemy. For the moment he
was safe, particularly in regard to Caterina. Her natural
ally, Milan, had fallen at a touch. The Florentines, following their ancient policy of "wait and see," had limited their
aid to comforting words. Venice was against Caterina, for
she had proved an arrogant neighbor—and whomever
Venice opposed was doomed.

Secure in the knowledge that for the moment he had a clear field, Cesare advanced down the road. Bologna welcomed him. The Bolognese had little choice, for King Louis had written personally to them, spelling out that Cesare was not merely under his protection but was acting as his arm in Italy. "At the request of our Holy Father the Pope, and wishing to help him to recover the lands, signories and domaines [of the Papal States] and especially the castles, places, lands and signories of Imola and Forli . . . we have made our very dear and much-loved cousin, the duke of Valentinois, our lieutenant." Beyond Bologna, the papal troops coming up from the south joined his own and now, ten thousand strong, the army advanced upon the first target in its path, Imola.

Like most of the cities on this lower section of the road, Imola was little more than an armed camp that had grown around a road junction. Its defensive walls of reddish brick were low, its houses jammed together in the limited space. At the northeast corner was the fort, built to the standard design of most of the forts on the lower Via Emilia—a simple square with a round tower at each corner, a massive keep in the center and a water-filled moat encircling the whole. Compared with the giant castles of the cities of the plain it was a toy fort, just as the low city walls were a laughable defense compared with the towering walls of Rome, Florence or Milan. But the fort adequately served its purpose of providing a refuge for the ruling family during frequent, brief periods of unrest; and the town wall itself deflected the casual marauder. On this occasion they were not put even to their limited test, for the citizens did not so much surrender as rush out to greet Cesare. The governor, Caterina's castellan, withdrew to the castle and there held out for two weeks, alternately parlaying and experiencing a desultory bombardment. Then, running short of supplies, he informed Caterina at Forli that he must surrender if no reinforcements came. None did and he surrendered. He was fortunate. Caterina did not execute his children, whom she held as hostages; and Cesare, anxious to make a good impression and so influence other castellans to surrender, did not execute him.

In a little over three weeks after leaving Milan, Cesare had achieved his first military victory. Two weeks later he thought he had accomplished his second when, on December 19, he entered Forli to the cheers of the people. Then came the first opposition. The city of Forli had fallen—but Caterina was safe inside its immensely strong fortress, and no city could be deemed taken until its fortress had been captured. Forli's fortress was reputedly the most advanced defensive work in Italy, employing artillery in its defense as well as conventional arms. Cesare's advance from Imola had been so rapid that his artillery had not arrived, and there was little that could be done until it did except to negotiate; and Caterina was far too wily to be caught by even the most honeyed Borgia promises.

Meanwhile, the brief honeymoon between the invaders and the citizens of Forli was over. Cesare's troops were, for the most part, foreign. To them, Forli was merely another captured city. Rape, murder, destruction, extortion —this was the usual coin with which the French paid their defeated enemies and which the Forlivese now received. They appealed to Cesare, but there was little he could do; his troops were answerable only to the absent king of France. And as supplies dwindled during that miserably cold winter, the Forlivese were forced to dig ever deeper into their scanty stocks to feed the invader. Meanwhile, the besieging troops heard sounds of laughter and music from the well-stocked fortress.

On Christmas Day, Cesare received an unpleasant surprise. A new banner was seen flying from the castle ramparts, a banner apparently bearing the crouched winged lion of the Republic of Venice. To watchers it could mean only one thing: the Republic of Venice had changed its enigmatic mind, Caterina Sforza was now under its protection—and the future of Cesare Borgia was extremely doubtful. Cesare hastened to the Venetian envoy present with his army and there received the welcome assurance that Venice had not changed sides, that the banner was not, in fact, the Lion of St. Mark. A careful inspection showed that it was the rather similar standard of Bologna, and it was later learned that a Bolognese in the garrison had hauled it up on his own initiative.

By December 28 Cesare's artillery was finally in position—some forty different pieces, including the big gun known as "La Tiverina," nine feet long and capable of hurling a stone ball some six inches in diameter—and for the next two weeks the artillery maintained a continual bombardment. Gradually the top of the keep fell into ruins, depriving the castle's gunners of a vital observation point. Caterina was occasionally glimpsed, sometimes clad in armor and wearing the great sword she affected, sometimes defiantly dressed in gorgeous raiment, spurring her gunners to greater action. But the siege artillery had the advantage over the defense because it could concentrate upon one section of the castle; this was the tactic Cesare adopted. Time was running short for him. Rumors abounded that Ludovico Sforza had raised an army in Germany and was advancing to the relief of his capital, and if that proved true then Cesare's troops would immediately be withdrawn for the defense of Milan.

On January 12 an enormous section of the outer wall fell into the moat. Immediately, soldiers embarked on rafts already prepared and crossed the narrow section of moat not bridged by crumbled masonry. Even now the castle should not have fallen. The gap was strongly covered by guns which could have mowed down the defenseless men on the rafts. But someone in the castle neglected to give the order to fire and the breach was taken. By nightfall the fighting, conducted with a terrible savagery, was over and Caterina was prisoner. It proved supremely fortunate for her that, by accident, the man who actually arrested her was a Frenchman. French military law forbade the taking of women as prisoners of war; she was now only a woman under the protection of King Louis, a technicality which ultimately saved her life.

It did not save her from Cesare. His later reputation as a rapist was on a par with that as a poisoner, a stratum of fact raised into a mountain of legend. Some of his legendary exploits would have done credit to Hercules. Cesare defended himself once against a charge of abduction with the comment that he did not usually find women so reluctant that he needed to use force. It was a reasonable remark for he had inherited that charm of his father's which attracted women "as a magnet attracts iron." But Caterina had fallen to Cesare as a spoil of war and her total violation, personal as well as political, would combine pleasure with a political objective—the degradation of an opponent. So at least her late subjects thought, briefly forgetting their own misery while contemplating "the great cruelties inflicted on our unhappy lady, Caterina Sforza, who had such a beautiful body." For the first time ever known, Caterina lost her nerve, shrieking and fighting when, after a brief period of refuge while Cesare and the French captain disputed her possession, she was dragged back to Cesare's quarters. Ungallantly, and probably untruthfully, he boasted in the morning that she had better defended her castle than her person from him.

According to Cesare's brief report of the action, the actual battle for the castle had taken barely half an hour. He confirmed that very heavy losses were inflicted on the garrison. "On Friday the tenth we placed our cannons before the castle and bombarded the wall throughout Saturday. On Sunday we took the castle after a mere half-hour's battle, killing about four hundred of the defenders, capturing Madonna Caterina Sforza together with two of her brothers and a large number of other important people."

The capture of Forli came not a moment too soon. Ten days afterward, Cesare had struck camp and was advancing on his next victim—Pesaro, the state of his ex-brother-in-law Giovanni Sforza. But before he could begin the siege there, certain news came that Ludovico Sforza was indeed marching upon Milan. It promptly became clear how much Cesare's present power was at the mercy of France. The troops under his command were immediately withdrawn and his campaign came instantly to a halt. There was nothing to do but return to Rome and wait.

Apart from a brief visit to his father before the start of the campaign, Cesare had not been in Rome since he had left it for France fourteen months earlier. His entry was accordingly magnificent, a Roman triumph in the old style.

The job of organizing the procession fell to Johannes Burchard—a thankless task, judging by the tightlipped entries in his diary, for the mixed national groups which formed Cesare's command jostled for precedence and even fought among themselves. Alexander had also ordered all the cardinals, together with their households, to ride out and welcome his duke, and there was trouble between them and the attending ambassadors of foreign powers.

But at last the ceremony was straightened out, and at midday on Wednesday, February 26 Cesare entered the city he had left as an unfrocked cardinal. He did not repeat his mistake at Chinon and appear in ostentatious personal splendor. He was dressed simply, almost severely, in black. Black, too, was the costume of the hundred men who formed his personal bodyguard, their somber dress accentuating their master's eminence among the blaze of color that was the costume of all other men. Gossip later spread that Caterina was in the procession, bound with golden chains. But Burchard knew nothing of this, and Alexander would not have been foolish enough to display so prominently a prisoner in whom the French were already showing a lively interest. Caterina was discreetly hustled away and established comfortably enough in the beautiful little Belvedere palace in the Vatican gardens. Only later, when it was necessary to break her spirit in order to sign away her rights, was she transferred to the dungeons of Sant' Angelo.

The procession continued on to the Vatican, and there Alexander received his son in the chamber called Pappagalio. What passed between father and son remains a secret. Though Burchard strained, he could hear nothing of interest for they spoke in Spanish. But that the relative position of father and son had changed became very obvious during the following months.

Cesare became the effective lord of Rome: the arbiter of the ancient city, the controller of the temporal papacy. The edicts which governed the city went out on his approval or at his direct instigation. The creation of cardinals was at his disposal. He made this clear when nine new members were added to the Sacred College, contributing between them more than 120,000 ducats, which immediately entered his war chest via the papal treasury. Smoothly he addressed the College, expressing the pious hope that the cardinals were content with their new brethren whose presence—and cash—were vital to his enterprises. The Venetian ambassador sent off a highly critical report of the occasion. "Today there was a consistory but instead of the four new cardinals that were expected and as the pope had said, nine were nominated. Most of them are men of doubtful reputation; all have paid handsomely for their elevation —some twenty thousand ducats and more—so that from 120,000 to 130,000 ducats have been collected. Alexander VI is showing to the world that the amount of a pope's income is just what he chooses." [49]

Alexander later indirectly confirmed that it was Cesare, not he, who was responsible. A disappointed courtier protested because he had not been placed on the list of nominations. Cesare had drawn up the list, Alexander replied, with what seemed to be a hint of wryness, of apology. It had nothing to do with him.

What means Cesare employed to gain ascendancy over the tough old man was never certain. Initially, Cesare's power sprang from his father's overweening pride and love of family. In a matter of weeks Cesare had done more for that family than his dead brother Juan had accomplished in years: the state of Caterina Sforza was now, for all practical purposes, a Borgia appanage. Cesare had amply justified his choice of career and Alexander could deny nothing to a son who was manifestly bringing such glory to the Borgia name. It was natural, too, that a vigorous and intelligent young man of twenty-four should shoulder increasingly the burdens of an old man. Alexander by no means abdicated power in his son's favor. It was he who planned the overall strategy, sometimes even in opposition to Cesare's desires, and it was usually the young man who gave way, if with a bad grace. But to most observers it appeared that Duke Valentino was now the head of the Borgia clan, directing it toward a still secret goal.

During that glorious spring and early summer of 1500 when Rome was filled with the chatter of every tongue in Europe, when the great city became again a cosmopolitan center, Cesare Borgia emerged at last into full public view. Yet it was a deceptive publicity, concealing probably more than it revealed. The man seemed to move behind a veil, never quite in focus. No writer, except the Florentine diplomat Niccolo Machiavelli, ever reported any direct speech of his. Information was always at second or third hand, the writer retailing what someone else had told him that Cesare had said. Every man who knew him—and they included such as Machiavelli and the Venetian ambassadors, men experienced to the last degree in the art of character assessment—agreed that his ability to disguise his thoughts and control his emotions amounted to the inhuman. He had made a fool of himself in France by reacting openly; he never did that again. It was impossible to know whether he was in a towering rage or gloating with satisfaction; he appeared exactly the same whether he was on the brink of triumph or facing disaster. In this he differed totally from his father, who reacted impulsively, extravagantly, to the vagaries of fortune—crying or laughing or raging as the occasion demanded. Cesare listened, said nothing, and acted. No one ever knew for certain where he was, or where he was likely to appear. He made a fetish out of mystery, frequently going about masked, or traveling at night when everyone else was in bed. He was helped here by his curious personal timetable. "He goes to bed between three and five o'clock in the morning, his dawn occurs at one o'clock in the afternoon, 2 P.M. is his sunrise and he gets up at 3 P.M. Immediately on arising he sits down to breakfast and while there attends to business affairs."

Despite his slim and elegant figure he was immensely strong. Once, he concluded a bullfight by beheading the animal with one single, terrible blow of the sword. During the months of campaign he would while away an occasional hour by making a tour of the villages, in disguise and with only a handful of personal friends, challenging village champions to boxing or wrestling bouts—which invariably he won, to the dismay and shame of his bull-like opponents. He was also extraordinarily handsome—far more so than even his attractive father had been at the same age. Not one of Cesare's alleged portraits can be linked to him with absolute certainty, but they bear a close enough resemblance to each other to allow the reasonable assumption that they were painted from an authentic original, if not from life. Only the supposed portrait by Raphael shows something of the evil figure of legend. Here the watchful eyes are cold, the beautiful, full mouth cruel; the whole appearance having a coiled, cobralike tension. But the other portraits show a curiously sensitive, thoughtful face —that by Giorgione in particular could be the portrait of a saint or some great national hero who had deliberately given his life for a high ideal.

The portraits are utterly at variance with legend; but so too are some of the precisely written descriptions of the man recorded by those who knew him personally. Pandolfo Collenuccio, the humanist scholar who was so fascinated by his irregular hours, went on to say, "He is considered brave, strong and generous and it is said he sets great store by straightforward men. He is terrible in revenge—so many tell me. In my opinion, he is a man of strong good sense, thirsting for greatness and fame."

Machiavelli thought much the same, "This duke is a man of splendor and magnificence. He has great confidence in himself, treating the greatest enterprise as though it were a small thing. In his search for glory he will deny himself rest, treating fatigue and peril alike with contempt." [50] Even Guicciardini, who pursued the entire Borgia clan with an unwearying malevolence, could not wholly ignore these favorable opinions of intelligent men and grudgingly allowed that Cesare, at least, possessed gifts of administration.

The contrasting contemporary opinions of Cesare Borgia, opinions which saw him alternatively as a blood-maddened fiend and as a level-headed, vigorous man can be explained and reconciled in simple clinical terms. He was suffering from an advanced form of syphilis, contracted on his first visit to Naples in 1497. The disease achieved epidemic proportions at the turn of the century and was viewed with a horror exacerbated by its mysterious nature.

The Italians, believing that the French had brought it into Italy on their first invasion in 1494, called it the "French disease": the French, equally as convinced that they had contracted it in Naples, called it the "Neapolitan disease." Guicciardini classed it with the other great catastrophes that had struck Italy during the closing years of that century. "This distemper, either quite new or never before known in our hemisphere, has made for a number of years such a havoc that it deserves to be mentioned as a fatal calamity." He cleared the French of the charge of having brought it into Italy: "It was conveyed, via Spain to Naples, from those islands which, about this time, were discovered by Christopher Columbus. Nature has been indulgent to the inhabitants of those islands in providing an easy remedy for it by drinking the juice of a noble wood which grows among them; they are easily cured." [51] Quinine, that "noble wood," seemed to be considerably less efficient among Europeans than among Caribbeans and the unfortunate sufferer was usually condemned to a treatment that was painful, disgusting and all too often fatal in itself. Alexander's physician, Caspare Torella, for two months studied the disease at close quarters—its prevalence among the Borgia was remarkably high—and analysed its components without undue squeamishness. But it was not until a generation later that the poetic physician, Girolamo Fracostoro, named the disease in a poem written in the classical manner and "syphilis" at last entered the European vocabulary.

The first visitation of the disease had affected Cesare very badly in Naples, confining him to bed for over six weeks at a period of intense political activity. But though Burchard mentioned the fact, he gave no hint as to its cause, for Burchard, like the rest of Europe, was unaware that a new scourge was moving through the continent.

Throughout Cesare's life its effect upon him would rise and fall, compelling him at times to withdraw into total privacy. In the beginning its sores seemed to have affected only his groin but later the disfigurement spread to his face, and the masks he wore—sometimes sinister, more often incongruously carnival—were intended as much to hide the dreadful ravages as to confer mystery upon him. Whether raging or quiescent, the disease must have had a profound effect upon a handsome man who was otherwise so attractive to women, and accounts reasonably enough for the bursts of near fiendish cruelty of which he was capable.

Apart from the effect that syphilis had upon him, Cesare was, by nature, impatient and totally intolerant. Here, again, he differed profoundly from his father. Alexander could act terribly against those who traduced his children or who stood in his political path, but he seemed indifferent to the vicious attacks made on him personally. He pointed out the difference between himself and his son to the Venetian ambassador, who had come to plead for the life of a Venetian condemned to death by Cesare for circulating a scurrilous pamphlet. "The duke is a good-natured man, but cannot tolerate insults. I have often told him that Rome is a free city and that everyone may speak and write as he pleases. Evil is often spoken of me but I let it pass. The duke replied to me 'It may be true that Rome is accustomed to speak and write as it pleases—but I will teach people to take care.' " The Venetian pamphleteer ended in the Tiber, as condemned. Another man, a drunken masquerader, lost his hand and tongue for mocking Cesare.

To Cesare, the halt in the Romagna campaign caused by the withdrawal of the French troops was no more than an irritating delay—one which ultimately proved valuable. Successes had piled up with an almost embarrassing swiftness, and during the nine months Cesare remained in Rome he and his father were able to catch up with themselves and plan ahead. Alexander had been very caustic about Ludovico's return. "The French certainly know how to take things," he remarked to the French ambassador, "but they are not so good at keeping them." Then in April came the news that Ludovico, the "fox of Milan," had doubled on his last tracks. He was captured and taken to a prison in France, there to spin out the remaining ten years of his life in despair. Ascanio Sforza, too, was thrown into prison and shortly afterward French envoys came to Rome anxious to refurbish the Borgia alliance. Louis would again put his troops at Cesare's disposal, provided that the Borgia assisted him in the forthcoming dismemberment of Naples.

The French proposals created a certain embarrassment for both Cesare and his father. Lucrezia's second husband, Alfonso, the duke of Bisceglie, was a Neapolitan and even then present in Rome. In the past it had been a simple matter to break Lucrezia's fragile betrothals or marriage vows as politics required. But here, unexpectedly, Borgia policy suddenly met an unbreakable barrier—the will of the pretty, shallow, complaisant daughter of Alexander himself. Lucrezia was deeply in love with her husband; moreover, she was now the mother of a six-month-old boy, Rodrigo. Maternal pride and wifely love combined to present a formidable obstacle to the plans of her brother, and presumably of her father. But the obstacle did not halt Cesare.

Lucrezia

10

Here in her tomb lies Lucrezia by name, Thais in fact
Daughter, bride and daughter-in-law of Alexander

"*She is of incontestable beauty* and her manners add to
her charm. She seems so gifted that we cannot, and
should not, suspect her of unseemly behavior. Apart
from her perfect grace in all things, her modest affability
and propriety, she is a Catholic and shows she fears
God." [52]

Jacopo Sanazzaro wrote the mock epitaph. He was a
Neapolitan, exiled as a result of Alexander's policies and
in revenge lashed back with this venom-filled indictment.
The sober, considered assessment, written in 1501, was
the work of the ambassador of the duke of Ferrara,
specifically charged to find out everything, good or bad,
about the girl chosen as wife to the heir of the
dukedom. The epitaph was obviously the product of
bitter political hatred, but it swiftly made the rounds, for

Sanazzaro was a poet of distinction and his neat, precise Latin couplet was highly quotable. The ambassador's assessment was of no interest to anybody outside the bridegroom's family, and the report therefore entered the secret archives of Ferrara and stayed there. As far as the general public was concerned, Lucrezia stood convicted as the incestuous partner of her father and brothers.

Lucrezia was not quite fourteen when she was first married and not quite eighteen when she was divorced. It was during those four years of marriage with Giovanni Sforza—specifically during the tortuous negotiations that at length produced her divorce—that the charge of incest was first whispered, and then shouted. And the maker of that charge was her husband himself. Giovanni Sforza cut a poor figure from any angle. His splendid relatives Ascanio, Ludovico and Caterina, looked down on him as a provincial; he was a soldier without troops and a husband without a wife. But he was also deserving of some sympathy, caught up as he was in the powerful centripetal currents of Borgia family love.

Law and custom dictated that Giovanni should have taken his bride to Pesaro, his home. He and Lucrezia did live together there for a short period but it was an unhappy experiment. The dreary little town on the Adriatic, set between two sad hills and entirely involved in fishing, was a poor place to bring a young girl who had spent all her life at the glittering center of affairs. There was a handsome new palace and a red brick fort in the standard Romagnese design, but not much else. Any other bride would have been obliged to accept the limitations and settle down to create her own pattern of life, but always pulling at Lucrezia was the knowledge that her own lively family was together in Rome, pursuing their fascinating occupations, the center of attraction and gaiety—and waiting for her eagerly should she decide to return. So she did. Giovanni Sforza began to drift into the background, and her own life-pattern became ever more inextricably intertwined with those of her father and brothers.

Although the Borgia had been in Italy for over sixty years and despite the fact that Lucrezia and her brothers had all been born in Rome, the family was essentially, intensely Spanish. All Lucrezia's ladies-in-waiting, like all her brother's lieutenants, were Spanish. The Borgia spoke Spanish, dressed in the Spanish manner, rode like Spaniards, ate like Spaniards. Above all, their fierce family loyalty was characteristic of Spain, not of Italy. Italians looked upon dynastic interrelationships coolly, treating them as useful political alliances. In Spain—still a frontier state with an alien, resourceful, fierce enemy on her very doorstep—the blood-tie was something sacred, transcending all other considerations. In this more primitive, tribal society a man or woman of necessity owed loyalty first to the clan, whatever that clan might do to him or her.

Like the rest of the family, Lucrezia had little time for her younger brother Joffre. Soft-hearted and generous as she was, she could occasionally feel a fleeting sense of pity and was prepared to defend him, if not very enthusiastically, in the family councils. She was on far better terms with Joffre's notorious wife Sancia, even though Lucrezia must have known that the Neapolitan beauty was continually cuckolding Joffre and that the catholicity of Sancia's favors spelled danger and disgrace for the family. But she, like Lucrezia, was young, vivacious, fond of clothes, singing and dancing.

Lucrezia's relationship with Alexander was more that of brother and sister than father and daughter. Apart from the solemn ceremonials of state and Church, Alexander much preferred informality in his human contacts and Lucrezia responded warmly, joyously. He adored his lively, pretty daughter, smiled benignly at her teasing, laughed his splendid, full-bodied laughter at the sparkling wit of her conversation. Although no great scholar himself, he had made sure that his only daughter had a good education in the new learning. Her Latin and Greek, he admitted, were never very good but she spoke Italian, Spanish and French like a native, and was even capable of writing poems in the three languages. Socially, she would have been an asset in any company; small wonder, then, that Alexander, with his pride and delight in family, should want her near him as often and as long as possible. So great was his pride in her that, on one extraordinary occasion, he even made Lucrezia a kind of deputy pope, turning over all the business affairs to her when he had to be absent from Rome for two or three weeks. Burchard recorded this remarkable essay in Church government with his usual impassivity. No member of the Sacred College protested; even the old cardinal of Lisbon, to whom she turned for advice on a difficult matter, seemed more than happy to discuss state affairs with a pretty young woman, garnishing the dullness of politics with an obscene joke according to Burchard. "I can write very well," Lucrezia announced proudly. "Ah, but where is your pen?" he retorted roguishly. She looked at him blankly for a moment, and then "saw that he was joking, and she laughed and thus their conference had a fit ending."

Apart from the unusually deep love that Alexander

bore his daughter, and the fact that it lay within his power to make her an unusually wealthy woman, there was nothing extraordinary about their relationship. In all matters that affected the family as a whole, he behaved toward her exactly as any other dynastic head would toward a marriageable daughter, arranging her betrothals and marriages on strictly political grounds, irrespective of what she might feel or wish. It was only in Lucrezia's relationship with her brothers that there is some ambiguity, something to give color to, if not make credible, the charge of an illicit relationship. As far as Juan Borgia was concerned, that relationship undoubtedly sprang from nothing more than the powerful Spanish bond of blood, raised to a potent degree by the hero-worship any normal young girl would hold for a glamorous older brother. But an analysis of the attraction that Cesare held for Lucrezia leads straight into the very heart of the Borgia enigma.

There was, to begin with, something of a mutual rejection between the two. At times Cesare seemed to go out of his way, if not to degrade her, at least to lead her into degrading situations. There was, in particular, the notorious contest held before the Borgia family when fifty Vatican servants coupled with fifty Roman prostitutes for prizes—an event arranged by Cesare for Lucrezia's entertainment. On another occasion she stood by his side on one of the Vatican's balconies while he shot down unarmed criminals running around terrified in the courtyard below. Was her presence at these and other debaucheries voluntary or forced? No one knew; it was simply reported that Donna Lucrezia took part—as spectator if nothing else—in activities which surprised the by no means impressionable Romans. On her part Lucrezia seemed, in the early years, to treat her brother with a reserve tinged with fear. This was the period when he cast aside his incongruous priest's robes and passionately threw himself into the business of carving himself a princedom. If anybody in Rome suspected Cesare of the murder of Juan in the summer of 1497, that person was his sister.

The fear never wholly left her but it gave an added excitement, an additional color, to the limitless admiration with which she came to regard her eldest brother after Juan's death. The mutual antagonism receded, giving way to a very close, intuitive relationship. Lucrezia, indeed, seems to have been the only person with whom Cesare established any real contact, the only person who could penetrate the façade of polished charm with which he faced the world. And when circumstances forced them to live in different parts of Italy, repeatedly during his whirlwind campaigns he would suddenly descend upon her, riding perhaps scores of miles to spend an hour or so with her. His affection did not prevent him from resenting the favors their father showered upon her, but that resentment sprang from the knowledge that the immense revenues granted her were necessarily diverted from Cesare—and he needed money for his vast schemes. For her part Lucrezia became his most loyal and constant ally. When later, as duchess of Ferrara, she bore a stillborn child and collapsed both mentally and physically, it was Cesare alone who could rally her. The doctors reported that they had attempted to bleed her but she had stubbornly refused. Cesare arrived suddenly at the palace and persuaded her to allow the operation. "We bled madonna on the right foot. It was exceedingly difficult to accomplish, and we could not have done it but for the duke, who held her foot—he made her laugh and cheered her greatly."

It was against this formidable rivalry that Giovanni Sforza, her lackluster first husband, had to fight. The marriage got off to a bad start with Lucrezia impatiently returning to Rome, but worse was to follow. Giovanni had been chosen as husband solely because he was related to the powerful Sforza family of Milan, but when Ludovico Sforza deliberately brought about that invasion of Italy which nearly toppled the pope off his throne, Giovanni's position became intolerable. In a moving letter to Ludovico, he spelled out what it was like to be trapped between conflicting loyalties. Gone now was his glittering future as the pope's son-in-law. "My lord, if I had foreseen in what position I would be placed I would have sooner eaten the straw under my body than have entered into such an agreement. Do not, I beg you, desert me but give me help, favor and advice."

Ludovico Sforza had his own problems, and without compunction left his wretched kinsman to make what he could of his situation. But although Giovanni did not know it, even had the Sforza of Milan remained the Borgia's most loyal ally, the Borgia—and Cesare in particular—had already decided that Lucrezia was wasted on Giovanni. Cesare began a campaign of naked intimidation. Lucrezia either assisted him or, more likely, merely stood by and watched, for she had no feeling for the man she had been forced to marry. Giovanni hurriedly left Rome and the marriage was over, for all practical purposes.

It was Lucrezia's misfortune to have married a stubborn, if weak man. Any smart husband would have recognized the realities of the situation, sold his agreement for the best price he could get and consented to divorce on almost any terms. Giovanni Sforza declined to act sensibly. Instead, he pestered Ludovico and all who would listen

with his wrongs and maintained his demand that Lucrezia
should join him in Pesaro. She had no such intention and
could not have done so even if she had wished, because her
father had appointed a commission to examine the grounds
for her divorce. Alexander remembered that convenient
betrothal of hers to young Gaspare d'Alversa. It had never
been formally dissolved. Therefore, she had been legally
betrothed at the time of her marriage to Sforza; therefore,
that marriage was no marriage. Pleased, Alexander put the
idea before his commission but even his supple lawyers
found they could not stomach this grotesque inversion of
reality. If His Holiness wanted a reasonably legal divorce,
he would have to think again. His Holiness thought again
and came up with the idea that his daughter was still a
virgin after four years of marriage. Giovanni Sforza, it
seemed, was impotent "because of certain physical prac-
tices." Impotence was the perfect grounds for divorce. Not
only did non-consummation mean that there had been, in
fact, no marriage, but it would also leave Lucrezia in the
state she had been before the wedding "and it would therefore be easier to find husbands for her."

What was satisfactory for Lucrezia was, however, considerably less than ideal for her husband, held up thereby
as a stock figure of fun. Giovanni furiously retorted that
their marriage had been consummated at least a thousand
times—an impressive record, considering that they had actually lived together for much less than a thousand days. He
also pointed out that his first wife had died in childbirth, so
how could he possibly be impotent? Alexander stuck grimly
to his intention: he wanted a divorce for Lucrezia and he
wanted her declared *virgo intacta*. Lucrezia had already
obediently signed a declaration which specifically stated

that "after three years of marriage and more she was still without sexual relations and without nuptial intercourse and carnal knowledge, and that she was prepared to swear and submit herself to the examination of midwives." Unless she was to be convicted of perjury, Sforza had to sign a similar declaration.

Giovanni took his troubles to Ludovico but met a sardonic response. The French had left Italy, conditions seemed to have returned to normal, and the last thing Ludovico wanted was to stir up trouble with Alexander. Ludovico seems, indeed, to have found amusement in the situation. He could hardly have taken seriously his own proposal that Giovanni and Lucrezia give a demonstration before witnesses on neutral territory; or perhaps Giovanni could have some public "tryouts" with selected women in Milan. Goaded, humiliated, half mad between public shame and anger, Giovanni burst out that the true reason why Alexander wanted to get rid of him was so that the father could enjoy his daughter himself. It was the first time Giovanni had made the accusation specific, but he had dropped hints in plenty before—so much so that the ambassador of the marchese of Mantua wrote to his master saying that "Giovanni Sforza had evidently found something in his home which did not please him." The marchese of Mantua was Sforza's kinsman by his first marriage but, like most people who came in contact with the unfortunate Giovanni, he was little disposed to help his relative. The accusation remained where it fell. No one examined it closely, to confirm or deny it. But the charge of incest existed and would grow until at last it threw a monstrous shadow over the entire family.

Alexander, if he heard of Sforza's wild remark, did

nothing about it. Instead, the machinery of divorce ground on and at last Sforza gave in—but bitterly, aware that he had been abandoned by every natural ally. "If His Holiness wants to create his own kind of justice there is nothing I can do about it. Let him do what he wishes—but God watches all things," he wrote. On December 22, 1497 Lucrezia appeared before a formal commission and there heard its solemn sentence. Her marriage with Giovanni Sforza, lord of Pesaro, was at an end on grounds of his inability to consummate it. In the eyes of the law she was *virgo intacta* and therefore free to contract another marriage as a spinster.

At the hearing she was able, fortunately, to follow the eccentric fashions of the day and wear a gown of graceful but voluminous cut, for she was, in fact, six months pregnant. The father, however, was not Giovanni Sforza but a handsome Spanish page of her father's court, the young man called Pedro Calderon whose body was found in the Tiber some six weeks after the divorce hearing.

Despite the impression of gaiety that she conveyed and her somewhat shallow lightheartedness, Lucrezia, like her father, was capable of profound, if very brief, emotions. That year 1497 had been particularly difficult for her. She could hardly have been unaware of the vile rumors speeding around Rome regarding her relationship with her father and brothers. She had no affection for Giovanni Sforza —but he was her husband, and the tactics of her father and brother had placed her in a kind of social limbo, possessing neither the status of a married woman nor the freedom of a maiden. Then in June occurred the murder of her brother Juan, which struck her with particular force. Not only was she attached to the handsome young braggart, there had also been a scheme for Juan to take her with him when he

returned to Spain, that magical land which loomed so large
in the Borgia consciousness. Had she been taken out of
Rome's festering atmosphere, her entire life probably
would have changed. At least she would have been
removed during an embarrassing period. Childish disappointment, deep shock and the long drawn-out, distasteful
business of her divorce helped push Lucrezia into the arms
of Calderon. Since the late spring of that year she had been
living in the convent of San Sisto not far from the Circus
Maximus, where she had withdrawn in an attempt to find
some privacy. Pedro Calderon was one of the frequent
messengers who traveled between the Vatican and the convent and, with the aid of Lucrezia's maid Pantiselia, Pedro's
relationship with Lucrezia passed rapidly from that of servant to lover.

On February 14, 1498, Burchard noted briefly that the
bodies of Calderon and of Pantiselia had been found floating in the Tiber. On March 15 the Ferrarese agent in Venice reported that Lucrezia had had a child—a boy—in
Rome. A year later the Venetian Paolo Cappello arrived in
Rome to assume his post as ambassador and immediately
regaled his senate with a dramatic story of how Cesare,
naked sword in hand, had pursued Calderon through the
Vatican halls. Calderon had taken refuge in the arms of
Alexander but Cesare had stabbed repeatedly, until the
lover's blood, spurting out, had dyed the pontifical robes.
Cappello's story was at least a year old when he picked it
up. Burchard, in his usual tightlipped manner, merely recorded the fact that Calderon's body had been found. All
that was known for certain was that a young man who had
been a close friend of Lucrezia's had been found murdered,
and that a new Borgia baby had appeared on the scene.

Had the story been left at that, it would have been

nothing more than the very common tale of a young girl's indiscretion. Alexander, however, with that fatal desire of his to weave a web of legal protection around his family, was directly responsible for turning that commonplace story into a monstrosity. He wanted to recognize, and so protect, the new Borgia baby, but he also wanted to free Lucrezia of the charge of having given birth to an illegitimate child. He adopted the same device he had used in order to ease Cesare into the Sacred College—the issuing of two bulls, one for public consumption, the other, containing contradictory facts, to remain secret. The public bull stated that the child, baptized Juan, was the son of Cesare Borgia by an unnamed Roman spinster. The secret bull stated that it was not Cesare, but Alexander himself who was the father of the child by the unnamed Roman spinster.

Either of the bulls is puzzling; together they bristle with almost insoluble problems. Presumably Alexander had to name the closest possible blood-relative of Lucrezia in order to give her child maximum protection, to ensure that it was regarded as a member of his own family—his grandchild, as it was. But why, after publicly naming Cesare as the father, did he privately withdraw and name himself? For Cesare, a well-known gallant, to admit the paternity of an illegitimate child would not have been shameful; it was, if anything, a badge of manhood. Possibly, Cesare assented to the public imputation in order to maintain his sister's reputation—and value in the dynastic market—but insisted that the family's own private records should show the true facts. But this, the most likely solution, does not explain why Alexander, in that private record, should name himself as the father. He was faced with a graver embarrassment regarding the identity of the mother; that had to remain a secret. Lucrezia obviously could not be named. A fictitious name would have been swiftly found out, and to arrange for another woman to admit to the child would open the close secrets of the family to an outsider. But the "Roman spinster" began to take on an identity of her own, one which Alexander had certainly not planned. Taking his private declaration at face value, it meant that he dared not name the woman by whom he was supposed to have had another child. Inevitably, the provisions of the bull leaked out and speculations began regarding the identity of this woman who could not be named. Such delicacy was wholly foreign to Alexander's normal practice. Did not all Rome know that Giulia Farnese actually boasted of being the mother of his daughter, even though the father might plausibly have been her husband? And was not Vannozza Catanei publicly recognized as the mother of his second family? Why then, this sudden reticence?

The false and the true parts of the declaration were put together to form a monstrous equation: Pope Alexander dared not name the mother of the child whose paternity he claimed because she was his own daughter. In doubling on his tracks, Alexander had yet again trampled on his own reputation—and blackened his daughter's forever.

But the two bulls with their badly concealed secret and their scandalous results lay in the future. In the summer of 1498 there was only an enigmatic quality about Lucrezia's reputation, the mere shadow of the later cloud, and certainly not sufficient to put off any prospective bridegroom. After her divorce from Giovanni Sforza there were plenty of suitors for her hand. Even a member of the Orsini clan came forward, but he was turned down with the rest. This was the time when Cesare began his own wooing of Carlotta, daughter of the king of Naples, and using Lucrezia as pawn in that direction was an obvious move. Besides Sancia, there was another illegitimate member of the royal house of Naples—Alfonso, her eighteen-year-old brother, a handsome, fair-haired youth with all the charm of his sister and a considerably nicer nature. Sancia was already married to Lucrezia's brother Joffre, and it was a neat move to marry Lucrezia to Alfonso, thus brother and sister marrying brother and sister to tie Borgia and Aragon together in the tightest possible way. The ceremony was designed to ease Cesare into Carlotta's bed and thence on to the throne of Naples itself. It failed in that purpose but, as a byproduct, it provided Lucrezia with a period of brief but profound happiness. She fell genuinely in love, probably for the first and only time in her life. Her handsome, chivalrous young husband returned her love and for perhaps eighteen months she lived a normal life as a happy wife and, later, a proud mother. She and Alfonso lived in or near Rome, for even now Alexander could not bear being parted from her. But for most of that period Alexander and Cesare were concerned with propitiating the king of Naples, and Alfonso was accordingly treated both as visiting royalty and as a dear member of the family. But with the eruption of the second French invasion in Italy the picture changed drastically. Cesare Borgia was now the dear cousin of King Louis; and King Louis had let Europe know that, just as soon as he had settled the Milanese affair, he intended marching south and at last place the crown of Naples on the head of its legitimate owner—himself. Ascanio Sforza, just before escaping from Rome, urgently advised Alfonso to do the same. Alfonso sensibly took the advice; foolishly, however, he listened to his father-in-law's protests and promises and returned after a few weeks' absence. Alfonso and Lucrezia settled down again to their life of blissful domesticity and were in Rome to welcome Cesare when he, too, returned to the city in his triumphant procession after the capture of Forli.

That was in February 1500, and for nearly five months thereafter the Borgia family seemed, outwardly, both unified and amicable. For the first time in many months Alexander had his three children living almost within calling distance. Cesare was now almost openly Sancia's lover, but that did not appear to disturb Joffre. Sancia and Lucrezia were close friends, much as Lucrezia and Giulia had been friends. Alfonso appeared to be on courteous terms with the Borgia brothers and was very much a favorite of his father-in-law's; Alfonso was a happy, attractive young man with a witty tongue and must have reminded Alexander of his own youth.

The brief halcyon period ended the night of July 15. Alfonso had dined with Alexander, Sancia and Lucrezia in an intimate family party in the Borgia Apartments. It was late when he left with a gentleman-in-waiting, Tomaso Albanese, and a young page; and the square outside was in darkness. According to Albanese's later report, they noticed a number of figures huddled on the steps of St. Peter's but paid little attention, for in that jubilee year pilgrims slept almost every night outside the great basilica. The men were halfway across the square, headed for the palace of Santa Maria in Portico, when a group of the supposed pilgrims suddenly hurled themselves upon the three. Alfonso was badly wounded and fell. The page began dragging him back to the Vatican while Albanese fought off the assassins, both men shouting for help. Their cries alerted the Vatican guard within the palace; the great gates were opened and a detachment rushed out. By then the attackers had escaped on horseback, but Albanese had recognized at least one.

Alexander, Lucrezia and Sancia were still conversing over the supper table when the door was thrown open by a captain of the guard who had forgotten his etiquette in his terror. Behind him some of his men were carrying the bleeding Alfonso, and coming into the room, they gently laid him at Alexander's feet. Before Alfonso lost consciousness he raised his head and named his assailant. Lucrezia fainted. Alexander, genuinely horrified, gave immediate orders that Alfonso should be carried at once to one of Alexander's own rooms. These were located deep in the palace, and the palace itself was garrisoned by an army of completely loyal soldiers. He nevertheless ordered that sixteen picked men should be stationed in and outside the room, testimony enough to his fear that the danger to Alfonso came from within the Vatican circle. He also gave the Neapolitan ambassador the news and told him that messengers had already been sent to Naples to bring the king's own physicians to Rome.

The morning brought a spate of rumors. The ambassadors and observers of the Italian powers hurried to the Vatican to glean what information they could from a tight-lipped staff and sent it on to their principals with or without embellishments. The Venetian Cappello was, for once, cautious in his opinion. "It has been spread through Rome that these things happened among the Borgias, for in that palace there are so many hatreds old and new, and so much envy in state—and in other matters—that such scandals must needs occur often."[53] Most were in agreement as to the author of the deed. "It is not known who committed the assassination but it is said to have been perpetrated by the same hand which struck down the duke of Gandia,"[54] Sanuto, the Venetian observer, wrote. The Neapolitan ambassador wrapped his suspicions in a heavy irony. "The originator of the crime is without doubt a man more powerful than Alfonso, although Alfonso is a lord, the nephew of a living king, the son of a dead king, and the son-in-law of the pope."[55]

Alfonso's wife and sister were equally in no doubt that the threat came from inside. From the moment Alfonso was established in a chamber in the Borgia tower, one or the other of the women was permanently at his bedside. They superintended the cooking and serving of his meals personally and watched while a procession of physicians came to Alfonso's bed. Protocol demanded that Cesare should visit, but the women doubled their vigilance while he was in the room. The visit passed without incident, although one of the many observers there heard Cesare mutter something to the effect that what was not achieved at breakfast would be completed at supper. Alexander continued to display the utmost anxiety about Alfonso, solicitously inquiring about his condition, sending him delicacies from his own table, sparing neither trouble nor expense in providing doctors—and guards. But gnawing at him constantly was his knowledge of the identity of the instigator. Cappello tried to pin him down on the fact; volubly, Alexander asserted his belief in Cesare's innocence and then, wearily it seemed, stated that if Cesare had indeed attacked Alfonso, then Alfonso must have brought it on himself.

So matters progressed throughout July. Gradually, Alfonso improved. With Lucrezia he decided that, as soon as he was well enough to travel, he would leave this deathtrap of a palace and return to his father's kingdom, Lucrezia joining him later on. On one occasion, taking the fresh air at the window, he caught sight of Cesare walking in the Vatican garden and shot at him with a crossbow. Or so Cesare said, though it is difficult to imagine how an invalid could find a crossbow in a sickroom or have the strength to wield it. Few were interested enough to ponder the problem; the affair was already subsiding in importance with even Alexander displaying impatience. It was, it seemed, no longer a potential tragedy but merely a scandal, and scandals were commonplace. Then on August 18 Sancia and Lucrezia made a mistake. They allowed themselves to be lured from Alfonso's room, leaving him alone for the first time since the attack. When they returned he was dead —strangled.

What exactly happened during the five minutes or so that Lucrezia and Sancia were absent from the room—and how they came to abandon Alfonso—was the subject of so much contradictory speculation that it seemed as though the murder of the duke of Bisceglie was to be as profound a mystery as the murder of the duke of Gandia. Cappello insisted that Cesare personally did the deed after forcing his way into the room and ordering the women to leave. But Cesare throughout had remained in the background, deliberately working through others. Burchard, normally lucid if laconic, decided upon a discretion so absolute that his testimony was useless. He noted that the dead man's physicians were questioned "but were released since the man who entrusted them with the commission went unpunished—and he was well known." Burchard must have known that Alfonso had been strangled and not poisoned, and no learned physicians were needed to diagnose the cause of Alfonso's livid, swollen face and the terrible marks around the throat.

But there was one man very close to the situation and reasonably unbiased who was determined that the truth should be known, if only privately. He was Raffaele Brandolini, a Florentine scholar and preacher who had been Alfonso's tutor and who lived now in Rome as a close friend of the family. It is unlikely that Lucrezia opened her heart to him, for she was too much of a Borgia to unveil family secrets even under these terrible circumstances. But Sancia was with Lucrezia throughout the final minutes of Alfonso's life, and it was she who told Brandolini what had happened.

Sancia's story was of the classic Italian plot, a wide-ranging, well-planned conspiracy which took every detail into account. On the morning of Alfonso's death a squad of Cesare's soldiers, under the command of his most trusted captain, Michelotto Corella, suddenly marched into the Apartments with the orders to arrest everybody on the grounds of the discovery of an anti-Borgia plot. The guards in and outside Alfonso's chamber were taken away, together with his two personal physicians. Lucrezia and Sancia protested vigorously. Michelotto apologized. He was only acting under orders, he claimed, but perhaps there had been some mistake. The best thing that the two women could do was to go to His Holiness and ask him to override Cesare's orders. Michelotto apparently put on such an apologetic air, as he might well have done before the daughter and daughter-in-law of the pope, that the two women seem to have been entirely deceived. Alexander was less than a minute's walk away in one of the adjoining chambers and, flustered but not really worried, Lucrezia and Sancia hastened to him. As soon as they had gone, Michelotto strangled the almost helpless Alfonso, and when the two women returned with Alexander's orders to free the prisoners, Michelotto woodenly informed them that Alfonso, duke of Bisceglie, had just died of an internal hemorrhage.

Sancia raged, screaming like a savage, tearing her hair and clothes, inveighing against all the Borgia. Lucrezia collapsed, crying silently for hour after hour so that her tears became one of the great legends of Rome. Alfonso was hurried into an obscure grave on that same evening, to the accompaniment only of religious rites and those of the barest minimum necessary, for Alexander, torn between love of his daughter and pride in his son, had chosen the passive way out. The whole affair was to be forgotten.

It is perhaps from this moment that Cesare achieved his final dominance over his father. Cappello, making his report, ended it with a curious phrase, seemingly contradictory but in fact remarkably perspicacious for this very imaginative ambassador. "The pope loves, and has great fear, of his son, the duke." The love Alexander bore for Cesare arose from family vanity; that he felt for Lucrezia was deeply personal. Although the murder of Alfonso of Bisceglie fitted in neatly enough with Alexander's overall plans, it is unlikely that he would willingly have inflicted on Lucrezia such an injury. But once done it was finished, the matter was hushed up and Lucrezia banished, with her tears and protests, to Nepi.

At the end of September, Cesare left Rome to continue his round of conquests and paused to visit Lucrezia. The murder of Alfonso had threatened a relationship which he valued, and he went to Nepi in order to state his side of the case. There had been rumors that Alfonso had intended an attack upon Cesare in order to forestall the attack upon himself, and Borgia apologists skillfully used the rumors as justification for the murder. In whatever manner Cesare argued his case, he succeeded. A few weeks later Lucrezia returned to Rome and happily resumed her old life, the tragedy forgotten and the breach in the Borgia family healed. Meanwhile, Cesare had embarked on that incredible series of campaigns which gave him a dukedom in a few weeks and established his name for all time.

The Prince

11

To the bystander's casual eye, the army which Cesare led from Rome in September 1500 differed little from the hundreds of such groups of armed men which were known to have entered or left the city over the past five hundred years. One's eye still went instinctively to the mounted men—noblemen for the most part, and thus able to afford a splendid show to enhance their already dominant position high on their giant horses. Clad in glittering steel from head to toe, wrapped around with the somber richness of velvet or brocade, their mounts decorated with gems or precious metal, they looked at once invulnerable and the natural lords of the earth. The footsoldiers came behind them, almost as an afterthought, bearing weapons whose design had changed little for perhaps a millennium. Only a professional would have noticed that the number of horsemen was rather smaller in proportion to the footsoldiers, and that the changes in the weapons of the footmen, though superficially slight, were nevertheless curious. Again, there were fewer swordsmen than usual and rather more of those gangling Swiss with the ten-foot-long pikes. The professional's eye would have lighted speculatively upon those horsemen whose horses carried, in addition to the great long-sword, a clumsy contraption of wood and iron about five feet long, for which the term arquebus had recently been coined. He would have been even more interested in the giant versions of the same weapon, the bombards and the cannon, which lumbered along in the rear. But all these changes were only by-products of the greatest evolution of all, one not discernible while the army moved peaceably along its route. The force which Cesare Borgia had assembled to gain himself a principality was a machine aimed at killing and not, as in the past, an organization designed for blackmail.

It was the French who had brought blood back into Italian warfare. For over two hundred years, the endless "wars" between the Italian city-states had been fought by mercenaries. Most had been foreigners—English, German and Hungarian usually—and they had come to Italy to make money and not to defend or enforce some abstract cause. Grouping and regrouping solely in the name of profit, fighting with or against the same men, they had no incentive whatever to put their lives at unnecessary risk; and their wars resembled a game of chess rather than a bloody encounter. Machiavelli, the armchair strategist, scornfully noted a "battle" which dragged on for an entire day and ended with only one casualty—a mercenary who had fallen off his horse and was accidentally trampled in the mud.

The French invasion of 1494 had been politically

inept, arousing the scornful mockery of the Italians. Militarily it shocked them profoundly. While they had been engaging in their mock battles, the French had been put to the ultimate test during their long running war with the English, and emerged victorious. When the French turned those war-polished arms against the Italians, the most sophisticated soldiers in Europe initially reacted like so many savages. The French reputation flashed ahead of them, paralyzing the Italians, so that in Naples, the garrison commander merely surrendered when the French artillery arrived. At Rapallo the defenders actually charged the guns, declaring that the noise frightened only cowards. The French use of artillery was dramatic, awe-inspiring; but just as revolutionary were the tactics of their infantry. In Italy the footsoldier was still despised—infantry was used only passively to break a cavalry charge. But the Swiss and German pikemen in the French army actually went over to the offensive, their dense squares—consisting of many thousands of men—keeping perfect formation as a result of endless drill. The Italians, for once, found themselves learning instead of teaching, but out of necessity they learned well and swiftly, and Cesare Borgia gained the fruit of that bitter lesson.

His bodyguard, some eight hundred strong, was composed exclusively of Spaniards. In part, the choice reflected his personal preference; for like his father, he remained wholly Spanish in outlook, dressing in the Spanish manner, speaking Spanish in preference to Italian, indulging in Spanish recreations. But the choice was also imposed upon him, for the Spaniards were about the most consummate soldiers in all Europe, much less Italy. Like the French they had learned in a hard school, in their case during the long battle with the Moors and, in the manner of soldiers, they had adopted their enemy's more efficient tactics. The Spaniards' cavalry, like the Moors', was lightly armored and incredibly agile. They were the first Christians to abandon the luxury of the heavily armored knight supported by five lightly armed, and expendable, followers. The great Spanish general Gonzalo de Cordoba adopted the Swiss tactics for infantry, supplying them with those deceptively simple pikes, ten feet long, which could create a moving hedge of bristling steel. Gonzalo did more: he was perhaps the first European to recognize the value of portable firearms, and now one Spaniard in six carried an arquebus and was skilled in its devastating use. Common to cavalry and infantry alike was their Spartan lifestyle. They had one main meal a day, eaten toward evening, and its ingredients were those which their ancestors had adopted from the very similar Roman soldiers: chopped onions, garlic, cucumber and chilis mixed with bread crumbs, olive oil and vinegar —a sustaining but pungent meal, which must have added considerably to the prevailing odor of unwashed bodies and reeking leather. Each man carried a leather winebag, containing perhaps half a gallon of harsh wine; and with these elementary requirements they could march or fight for days and weeks and continue long after more sophisticated soldiers would have collapsed from exhaustion.

Pikemen and swordsmen, arquebusiers and halberdiers, crossbowmen and cavalry—each had a part to play in the composite whole of an army, a part that had been brought to a kind of perfection during the long history of warfare. But Cesare's forthcoming campaign was unprecedented. In the past a commander might plan perhaps one major siege, if he had the time, but would base the rest of his campaign on a series of pitched battles. Cesare intended the capture of no less than ten walled cities in a small area and had no desire whatever to seek glory in the open field. His campaign was to be directed against cities, not men; against stone, not flesh. Once entry into a city had been gained, he would need infantry or cavalry to crush the remnants of resistance and thereafter to act as a police force. But before entry was effected their value was limited, a species of threat, no more. It was upon the terrible new weapon, artillery, that he relied for his new type of campaign.

Artillery struck the Italians with an apocalyptic force. It was a weapon invented by demons, not men, Guicciardini protested, and he was echoed by almost every writer. Before the French invasion it had been a clumsy, leisurely weapon. No field commander bothered to use it, and a commander engaged in a siege could never be certain whether it would arrive on time. If it did, the small balls of stone hardly affected the besieged, except for the flying splinters. With the advent of the French, the Italians saw gun carriages for the first time, ingenious contrivances which allowed the monsters to be manipulated with ease and speed. Italians saw especially bred horses drawing the guns at the speed of marching cavalry; even the lumbering ammunition wagons kept abreast of the army, for they were dragged by teams consisting of anything from ten to twenty horses. The Italians observed the effect of iron balls as big as a man's head flattening, not shattering, on impact, so that all the terrible released energy was directed immediately against the target. Above all, the Italians experienced for the first time in history the effect of massed artillery, for the compact army of the French dragged with them far more guns than had existed throughout Italy. The rolling thunder of mass bombardment was to be Cesare Borgia's leitmotif throughout his campaigns, a sound which men remembered long after they had forgotten the conventional details of slaughter.

During the bombardment of Imola, an observer living within the borders of the Florentine state heard it as a continual thunderstorm many miles away. Francesco Sperulo, the poet from Spoleto who wrote an immense epic poem in Latin praising Cesare Borgia, the new prince in Italy, lingered over the effect of artillery with a horrified fascination. The bellow of the explosion, that terrifying "bom-bard," provided an onomatopoetic name for the new monster with which the ancient Latin could just cope. In his verse the "horrendis machina bombis" appeared like some appalling natural force, with destruction falling out of heaven in the form of stone and iron, destroying the innocent and the guilty alike, rendering the coward and the brave man equal. The horror of being pulped to nothingness by an irresistible force unnerved the bravest men, providing Cesare with a potent weapon even before the fire was applied to the first cannon. Later in the campaign, Alexander gleefully described to the Venetian ambassador how the town of Ceri had surrendered without any fighting whatever. "Since Sunday to yesterday more than eight hundred balls had fallen on the city, throwing the soldiers into such fear that they declared their wish to surrender rather than be torn to pieces."

Cesare was fortunate in that, among the crowd of famous condottieri who had flocked to his banner, there was an artillery expert, Vitellozzo Vitelli. A pikeman or a halberdier could be trained in a few days or weeks at most but years of devoted study were needed to master artillery's thousand ramifications. A good artillery captain needed some of the qualifications of an apothecary to determine good gunpowder; of a smith to know the limitations of his weapon; of a cavalryman to get his weapon to the field; and once there he had to take advantage of the terrain in a way which only experience could teach. In all Italy there was probably only one better artilleryman than Vitelli—Alfonso d'Este of Ferrara, who had carried the study so far he was even then engaged in redesigning Ferrara's fortifications to prepare it for the new age. Vitellozzo Vitelli's skill, great in itself, was even more remarkable when his career was compared with that of his brother, Paolo. Paolo was reputedly a greater condottiere than his brother, and that was probably true in terms of the old values. But Paolo's hatred of artillery was extreme, his blindness to its potential so total that he habitually gouged out the eyes of captured gunners, declaring it disgraceful that such cowards should kill brave men from afar. Indirectly, Paolo paid the price of his conservatism. Hired by Florence to attack Pisa, he was defeated by the Pisans' superior skill in artillery and the Florentines hanged him for it. They could not believe that so great a captain could be indifferent to the new and vital craft and so believed that he was betraying them.

Cesare, by hiring Paolo's daringly innovative brother Vitellozzo, had shown at the very beginning of his career that he had abandoned the old forms of warfare and had skill enough to appreciate the skill of practitioners in the new form. The sixteen pieces of artillery under Vitellozzo were probably worth more to Cesare than the five thousand men brought by the other condottieri who now fought under his personal banner of the flame.

The army moved north along the Via Flaminia, another ancient road with a modern surface, but in other ways different from that Roman road down which the army had marched to Forli a year before. From Rome to Orte the Via Flaminia ran straight and flat enough, almost within calling distance of the green, full-bodied Tiber. But at Orte the road branched eastward and entered tortuous, haunted lands eternally echoing the sound of waters and full of ghosts, for these were studded with the cities of the race that had preceded even Rome. The road ran past Narni, past Terni with its thundering waterfalls; past Spoleto, which spread its skirts on the plain but kept its head in the hills. Lucrezia had been regent here for a time and Spoleto was sensibly Borgia in sympathies, but beyond lay less certain regions. The army continued compactly through the plain of Foligno, marching below the skeleton-white cities that clung to the hills on the right—withdrawn, self-sufficient communities which warily regarded the army from the eyeless sockets of gaunt watchtowers as they had regarded the march of a hundred such armies. Beyond the plain the road entered cruel country, winding frenziedly between hills that were impossibly steep for artillery. Vitellozzo remained long enough with the main body to launch a vicious attack upon Fossato, which foolishly had announced its intention of resistance; but after its walls had been pounded to dust and the dead heaped high, he took his precious artillery off to the North. The roads wound more gently here through the duchy of Urbino, passing below Urbino itself, which floated like a mirage on its twin hills. The army's passage caused consternation to the gentle Guidobaldo Montefeltro, lord of Urbino, but on this occasion he was treated chivalrously because Cesare still needed his help, and Vitellozzo had been accordingly warned. Cesare rode with the main body, joining his artillery at last on the Adriatic coast near the little city of Fano. His first and immediate goal was less than ten miles away up the coast road—the city-state of Pesaro, that of his former brother-in-law, Giovanni Sforza. But the artillery was not needed and neither were the soldiers. At news of the advancing army Giovanni Sforza had fled and the Pesarese opened their gates and decorated them to welcome the advent of their new lord.

Among the thousands of people who watched Cesare's entry into Pesaro the afternoon of October 27 was Pandolfo Collenuccio, scholar, poet and diplomat of considerable experience. He had once been a counselor of Giovanni Sforza, who, indeed, had owed much of his success to Collenuccio's skill. But with the usual caprice of the petty tyrant, Sforza had first estranged his counselor, then imprisoned him, and finally Collenuccio had abandoned him and escaped to refuge in Ferrara. He was present now in Pesaro at the urgent request of his new master, the duke of Ferrara, who was anxious to know the qualities and motives of the new lord of Pesaro. A long-standing friendship existed between the house of Este and the Borgia, but that did not reduce the duke's anxiety at having Cesare Borgia as a close neighbor.

Two days after Cesare's entry, Collenuccio wrote to Ferrara a long report which, on the whole, bore encouraging news—but the report did more than convey political information. By now Cesare's legend was achieving its epic proportions, each victim in the trail of broken enemies in his wake contributing to the legend as apologia and revenge. Collenuccio, aware that false information was more

dangerous than none, was concerned to correct the legend
of the invincible monster and, as a competent diplomat,
give his master as accurate an assessment as possible upon
which rational policy could be built. His portrait of Cesare
therefore became a piece of documentary evidence of considerable value.

Collenuccio began by confirming that the citizens of
Pesaro had, indeed, freely conferred their city upon
Cesare. Not only that, but the small city of Fano had also
expressed its desire to be included in the growing state.
Astonishingly, "he refused, but the citizens insisted and the
place [Fano] is his when he wants it." Collenuccio had had
bitter experience of the terror and destruction caused even
by Italian soldiers in a defeated city, and there had also
been disturbing reports of the wanton destruction created
by Cesare's Spanish contingent during their march north.
In Pesaro, however, the mixed national troops under Cesare's command were behaving in an exemplary manner.
More than two thousand men were quartered in Pesaro,
Collenuccio informed his master, "but had done no appre-
ciable damage."

Immediately on Cesare's arrival Collenuccio requested an audience. At 8:00 P.M. Ramiro de Lorqua, Cesare's chief of staff, called on him. De Lorqua had a singularly
evil reputation but on this evening he bore himself with the
politeness of a courtier, asking if Collenuccio was comfortable, saying that he had only to ask for his desires to be
granted.

The following morning a courier arrived bearing gifts
and an apology. The gifts were lavish, reflecting that carefully planned generosity which was swelling Cesare's expenses to eighteen hundred ducats daily. There was a sack

of barley, a cask of wine, a sheep, sixteen capons and hens, two large torches, two bundles of wax candles and two boxes of sweetmeats—enough for Collenuccio to stage his own banquet if he wished. The courier apologized on behalf of his master because the hour of the audience had not yet been fixed. The duke was in one of his periods of retirement, caused by the ravages of the "French disease."

Cesare had installed himself in the same palace where Lucrezia had been brought as a bride nearly six years before, and there Collenuccio was finally summoned. Immediately after the interview he wrote his report, giving an almost word-by-word account while it was still fresh in his mind. The veteran diplomat was deeply impressed by the young man's skill in verbal fencing. Nevertheless, he was convinced that Cesare's protestations of friendship for Ferrara were totally sincere. He saw nothing of the blood-maddened demon of popular mythology; instead, the picture Collenuccio presented his master showed a cool-headed politician, no more anxious to begin an unnecessary war than any other sensible general in a newly established base.

By the end of October, less than four weeks after Cesare had marched out of Rome, the entire coastal stretch of the Romagna was in his hands. The beautiful little city of Cesena had made overtures to him even before his campaign had begun and now welcomed him. Its central position in the province, its castle set high on a craggy spur of the Apennines made it an ideal acquisition for Cesare, and thereafter he used it as his base of operations and planned eventually to make it capital of the province. In Rimini the degenerate descendant of the great Malatesta thought it prudent to sell out rather than test the loyalty of his subjects, and a Borgia garrison marched in to take over. Cesare then turned to the city of Faenza.

During his conversation with Collenuccio he had suddenly remarked, "I don't know what Faenza wants to do. She can give us no more trouble than did the others. Still, she may delay matters." Collenuccio had discreetly replied that greater resistance conferred greater honor on the victor—for he knew, as well as Cesare, that the capture of Faenza would entail rather more than a brave show of arms. The city was virtually a republic. True, there was a lord, young Astorre Manfredi, who was genuinely popular with his subjects. But he was only sixteen and, with common sense unusual in a young despot, he allowed himself to be guided by the council that had run the city since his accession at the age of eleven. Faenza, though outwardly a despotism with the advantages arising from a despot's dynastic connections, also enjoyed a considerable range of self-government which its citizens would be most reluctant to lose.

Cesare's army arrived at the walls of Faenza on November 10. It speaks much for Cesare's confidence in his military ability that twice he started a major campaign at the beginning of winter. But this second time he was less fortunate. The winter of 1500 was far worse even than that of 1499, when his army had had the protection of the city of Forlì while it besieged Caterina's castle. Torrential rain succeeded gales; snow came early and by December the land was in the grip of hard frost. And stubbornly Faenza continued to resist. A well-supplied, well-built walled city with a garrison in good spirits could still wear down even a besieging force supplied with artillery.

Cesare was forced to strike camp before the end of

November. With supplies dwindling and his troops exposed to the savage weather, there was little else he could do. He retired with most of his army down the road to Cesena, but his firm control over much of the Romagna enabled him to mount a rigorous blockade of Faenza. The roads leading to the city were policed, cutting off all supplies. Detachments of rested men took turns in maintaining pressure on the city itself, so that throughout the winter the Faenzans were under continual apprehension that a major attack was imminent.

In March the main body of the army again took up the actual siege. Faenza had now been cut off from the outside world for five months. Supplies were running low, the people were wearied and must have known that there could be only one outcome; but, incredibly, they rallied. The story of the city's last days became a minor epic, the details reiterated in wonderment by writers long accustomed to accepting civic treachery as the norm. Rich Faenzans supplied the poor from their own private stocks of food and lent money free of interest to Astorre to pay the troops. Priests consented to the despoiling of the altars, equably watching the sacred vessels being melted down to provide bullion for the financing of the war against the son of their spiritual overlord. The women themselves actively took part in the defense. Cesare was impressed, declaring that with such troops behind him he could conquer all Italy. He reinforced his admiration by hanging one Bernardo Grammante, a dyer of Faenza who escaped and sought to betray it by pointing out a weak section of the walls. Grammante was executed by Cesare for treachery—but the siege guns were immediately moved up to batter the spot indicated.

They made a breach at last and, after ferocious hand-to-hand fighting, the council informed their lord that further resistance was useless. Astorre agreed, envoys were sent to Cesare, and the fighting ceased. As was his habitual policy in the Romagna, Cesare gave Faenza good terms. "Indulgence for the small people, rigorous control of the great"—this principle was followed in Faenza as elsewhere.

Astorre Manfredi and his illegitimate brother were handed over to Cesare. They cherished, perhaps, optimistic views regarding their future. Cesare treated the Manfredis with the respect due their rank, carried them around with him for a while and then sent them to Rome. They were placed in Castel Sant' Angelo at about the time Caterina Sforza was leaving it. The next that the world knew about the brothers is recorded in Burchard's diary: their bodies had been found floating in the Tiber. Thirty years later Guicciardini used the incident to contribute another odious detail to the Borgia legend. The boys were murdered, he said, "but only after they had sated the lust of a certain person"—the "certain person" presumably being the sexagenarian Alexander.

"In order to preserve a newly acquired state, particular attention should be given to two objectives. In the first place, care should be taken to extinguish the family of the ancient sovereigns; in the second, laws should not be changed nor taxes increased."[56] In Machiavelli's opinion Cesare, in the person of the Prince, acted prudently in having the young Manfredi executed. Further on in that slight, enigmatic treatise, Machiavelli hammered the point home. Discussing whether fortresses are really of service to a prince, he used the case of Caterina Sforza to prove that they were of little value. Fortresses always fell if the attack was determined enough. "When she was attacked by

Cesare Borgia she must doubtless then—though perhaps too late—have become convinced that the best fortress for a prince is found in the people's affection."[57] Caterina was ultimately freed on pressure from the French, because the Borgia had nothing more to fear from her. Caterina's craven sons had signed their inheritance away in exchange for gold or contemptuously bestowed ecclesiastical offices. The Forlivese had not the slightest intention of rebelling on behalf of their deposed mistress, and Caterina could therefore be allowed to end her days in a convent. Similarly, Cesare had nothing to fear from the majority of the dispossessed rulers, and they were allowed to live in exile with what loot they had managed to take with them. Astorre Manfredi, however, was genuinely loved by his people, and they undoubtedly would have risen had there been any hope of effecting his restoration. The better the prince, the more certain his execution if he fell into Borgia hands.

Cesare's moves after the fall of Faenza were swift and widespread. First he marched on Bologna but was forced to swing away due to an unequivocal warning that the city was under the protection of France. He deliberately turned south, almost provocatively entering the hitherto sacrosanct territory of Florence. The Florentine Signoria were faced with three choices: fight, appeal to Louis, or buy Cesare off. They appealed to Louis; meanwhile Cesare's army marched to within six miles of the walls of Florence. A hostile army so close had not been seen in Florence for over a generation, and the Florentines hastily compromised with Cesare. Officially, he was to enter their pay as a condottiere at a salary of thirty-six thousand ducats a year. Both sides knew it was only a paper transaction, that the arms of Cesare Borgia would be wielded only for

Cesare Borgia; but only one side knew that no payment would, in fact, ever be made.

Cesare continued his march through Tuscany, crossing the peninsula at high speed, there to lay siege to the city of Piombino. This marked a dramatic change in his policy, which until now had been concentrated on the eastern coast. Piombino's capture would give him a base from which to launch an attack into the Florentine heartlands, so that eventually a ring could be drawn around the republic. So the Signoria observed with something near despair. But Cesare was still aware of the protecting power of France and moved cautiously. And while Piombino was holding out, Alexander recalled Cesare to Rome, for great events were on the move.

Throughout, King Louis of France had looked upon Naples as his ultimate goal. The capture of Milan, the unleashing of the Borgia—these were only means to that end. But now his courage failed. Over the past centuries army after army had been swallowed in the quicksands of Neapolitan politics, and those which survived fell victim to the treacherous diseases of the south. Louis, doubtful of his ability to succeed where so many others had failed, thought of a compromise: the sharing of both the rewards and the dangers with King Ferdinand of Spain. Louis's idea, in Machiavelli's expert opinion, was the biggest single mistake of his career, and one from which all the long misery of Italy flowed. "If the king of France was powerful enough to invade the Kingdom of Naples, he ought to have done it— but if he was not able he should not have divided the task."[58]

Louis quite lacked Machiavelli's perception. The

Aragonese dynasty which ruled Naples was closely related to the royal house of Spain. Ferdinand of Spain, however, consented to betray his relative, Federigo of Naples; smoothly he agreed that the spoils were to be equally divided between himself and Louis, with Pope Alexander allowed to pick up the scraps on behalf of Cesare. The last was because one formality was needed which only Alexander could sanction: a papal bull to dispossess the Christian king of Naples so that his territory could be divided between the Christian kings of France and Spain. Alexander agreed to provide the bull, but there was some difficulty in supplying a pretext for it. Federigo was a very good king, the best that Naples had had for a long and dismal period, and his personal morals were irreproachable. But he was foolish enough to be on good terms with the Turks —a reasonable policy, considering the trade needs of his kingdom and, too, that other Christian kings made such treaties as need required. But the policy proved fatal to Federigo now. Alexander declared him deposed, on grounds that he was a traitor to Christendom; explicitly blessed the coming rape of Naples as a Crusade; and prepared to place the crown of Naples on Louis's head when required.

In a little over six years' time, Alexander had reversed his policy to benefit his son. In 1494 he had stubbornly resisted French pressure to place that same crown on the head of Louis's predecessor, Charles VIII. No one knew what Alexander's private feelings and fears were at having been forced to this point of no return. Yet there were pickings to be had even in this situation. For Cesare's career it was vital that Louis be kept happy; but additionally, in the south of Italy were the rich holdings of the Colonna and Savelli families, lands which could be used to endow Lucrezia's illegitimate son and Alexander's own child by Giulia Farnese. As a bonus, unimportant but not less sweet, was the avenging of that three-year-old insult flung at the Borgia when Federigo's daughter, Carlotta, had contemptuously rejected Cesare.

Cesare arrived in Rome on June 13, 1501, having left a large detachment of his troops still besieging Piombino. The list of his titles was now impressive, for after the fall of Faenza, Alexander had granted him the style of duke of Romagna in reasonable anticipation of later conquests, and he could call himself "Cesare Borgia of France, Duke of Valentinois, Duke of Romagna, Captain General, Gonfalonier of the Roman Church"—supreme head of the armed Church, entitled to bear among his many banners the big white gonfalon with the golden keys. The French army arrived six days later and camped outside Rome. Burchard made his customary meticulous notes, recording without comment the fact that citizens who had already paid to avoid having soldiers billeted on them were nevertheless forced to take them. He also noted the provisions sent out to the officers of the holy army by the papal commissioners: "150 casks of wine, bread, meat, eggs, cheese, fruit and other necessities, including sixteen specially chosen prostitutes for those particular needs."

The actual Neapolitan campaign was an anticlimax. Treachery hastened the end of the ruling house of Naples, as it had marked the beginning. Federigo had placed two major fortresses into the hands of Their Catholic Majesties' general in Italy, Gonzalo de Cordoba, a man who had served Federigo's family well in the past. But Gonzalo's ultimate loyalty lay with Ferdinand and Isabella and he betrayed Federigo's trust, though regretting it. The speed of the collapse which followed did not, however, prevent that almost ritual blood-sacrifice of Italians which marked every foreign invasion. On this occasion the victim was the city of Capua, and the leaders of the sacrificers were themselves Italian.

Federigo had retreated to the city and the people defended him loyally. Even after five days of continual bombardment the defense remained sturdy, but the inevitable traitor appeared and on July 25, Cesare's troops gained entry through a treacherously opened gate. Afterwards, no one could give any rational explanation for the carnage which followed. Centuries of warfare between roughly equal cities had taught the Italians that massacre of a defeated enemy was a double-edged weapon, certain to turn upon the temporary victors. For over a hundred years intercity wars had been fought by mercenaries, and the defeated paid in gold, not blood. The massacre at Capua was probably due in part to the fact that foreign troops again formed the bulk of Cesare's army, but the Italians joined in with equal ferocity. Women, as usual, suffered the most, with inevitable rape preceding ransom or murder. Thirty of the most beautiful were captured and sent to Rome, Christians sent to the seat of Christendom as though to the court of a pagan prince. A Frenchman, d'Auton, recorded this likely enough incident; it was, almost inevitably, the Italian Guicciardini who elaborated it into the Herculean myth wherein Cesare took the thirty women into his own private harem.

In Rome the success of the holy Crusade was credited almost entirely to Cesare. Burchard heard of the sack of Capua on the following day and that, too, found a place in his diary, written with the same passion he recorded details of etiquette and provisioning. "On the night of July 26 the pope heard of Don Cesare's capture of Capua . . . a triumph which crowned the events of the past ten days. A citizen of Capua, a certain Fabrizio, admitted Don Cesare's soldiers by treachery. They killed him, however, and afterward they killed about three thousand ordinary soldiers and two hundred knights and many citizens and priests as well as monks and nuns in churches and convents. The women were treated most cruelly, and the girls were raped or seized as booty. It is said that about six thousand people were killed." [59]

The Neapolitan campaign, however, was only a sideshow for Cesare. Wisely, he had forgotten the dreams he had once had of wearing that particular crown, for such an ambition would have made him an immediate rival of Louis of France, and even Cesare was aware of their disparate statures. He had placed Louis of France in his debt, more revenue was directed into Borgia coffers—but it was in central Italy that Cesare's interests lay. Northern and southern Italy were frontier states, their possession eternally disputed by giants. Only in the center was there relative freedom to pursue that goal now being slowly revealed: the acquisition of a base upon which Cesare could erect not merely a dukedom but a kingdom. Almost accidentally, and rather as a by-product of his own ravening ambition, Cesare had wandered onto that path which had attracted the noblest of Italians for centuries past and would attract more, hopelessly, for centuries to come: the creation of a united nation ruled by one strong man.

Geographically, the southern approach to his embryonic kingdom in the Romagna was now secure. The landholdings of three great Roman families—Colonna, Savelli and Gaetani, all of whom had been allies of the Borgia— had threatened this approach, but after the destruction of their Neapolitan ally, Alexander was able to confiscate their territories wholesale and distribute them in his immediate family. But the northern approaches to the Romagna were still comparatively vulnerable; there was only the duchy of Ferrara between Cesare and French-held Milan on one side, and Venice on the other. Cesare might have been tempted to launch an attack on Ferrara, but the Este dynasty was far too strongly established there to be frightened away by a show of force; and such an attack would, in any case, have aroused the liveliest fears and resentment in both France and Venice, neither of whom would relish Cesare as an immediate neighbor. Less hazardous and far more profitable in the long run was the tying of Ferrara into the growing Borgia dynasty. And for such a purpose Lucrezia was the ideal link; Alfonso d'Este, the twenty-four-year old heir to the ducal throne, was a widower without children.

Lucrezia
in Ferrara

12

Both Cesare and his father had thought many times
of a matrimonial alliance between the houses of Borgia
and Este. Even while Lucrezia's second husband was still
living—the Alfonso di Aragona whom she loved so
deeply—rumor sped around that such a marriage was
contemplated for her. In November 1500 after his
death, rumor became fact as, for the sixth time in
Lucrezia's life, her father began the preliminary
marriage negotiations for her. The negotiations
immediately encountered the same kind of delays and
obstructions which had so humiliated Cesare during his
own matrimonial essays. King Louis of France wanted
Alfonso d'Este for a French princess—but at the same
time he desperately needed Borgia help in the
Neapolitan Crusade, not so much for Cesare as because
Cesare's father alone had the right of bestowing the
Neapolitan crown. At length deciding in favor of that
splendid crown, Louis withdrew his objections and now

actively urged Duke Ercole to accept the Borgia proposals for his son Alfonso.

Ercole disliked the whole matter and agreed to contemplate it only under pressure from France. He made that point in a glum letter which he wrote to his relative and neighbor, Gonzaga of Mantua, just before the nuptial contract was signed.

> We have informed Your Majesty that we have recently decided, owing to practical considerations, to consent to an alliance between our house and that of His Holiness—in short to the marriage of our eldest son, Alfonso, and the illustrious Lady Lucrezia, sister of the illustrious Duke of Romagna and Valentinois, chiefly because we were urged to consent by His Most Christian Majesty, and on condition that His Holiness would agree to everything stipulated in the marriage contract. Subsequently His Holiness and ourselves came to an agreement, and the Most Christian King persistently urged us to execute the contract.[60]

The duke did not mention in the letter His Holiness's roundabout threat to depose him if he did not give way, but neither did he mention the exorbitant demands he had made in exchange for his consent: a dowry of two hundred thousand ducats, a heavy reduction in the feudal dues he paid to the Church as a papal vicar, and other concessions which, though lesser, strengthened his autonomy, alienated Church rights and property, and aroused the strongest possible objections in the College of Cardinals. There remained only the question of gaining the consent of his son Alfonso, the bridegroom-elect.

Alfonso objected strongly. He may or may not have

had grounds to suspect that Lucrezia's moral character was sullied beyond redemption. The tales of incest and promiscuity were almost certainly the invention of enemies and were certainly irrelevant. Virtue was not the prime consideration in a dynastic bride. But he had excellent grounds to object on the score of personal well-being. Two Spanish noblemen who had believed themselves all but married to this particular bride had found themselves dismissed like stableboys. Her first husband had been divorced to the accompaniment of mocking laughter. Her second had been murdered, almost certainly on her brother's orders. Still, Alfonso's father was now as warmly in favor of the marriage —if there were no just impediments—as he had formerly been opposed to it; and he threatened, if necessary, to marry Lucrezia himself. Sullenly, Alfonso gave in and signed the nuptial contract.

But the contract was only the first stage in negotiations. On September 15, about two weeks after it had been triumphantly carried to Rome, two Ferrarese citizens arrived in its wake. They were Gerardo Saraceni and Ettore Bellingere, jurists and diplomats of experience, charged by Duke Ercole not only to see that all the provisions of the contract were fulfilled, but also to place the bride and her family under the most searching, if discreet, examination. They went about their task for nearly four months, keeping their master minutely informed of their activities, and at the end of it their opinion of the bride herself was a glowing testimony to her good sense and virtue. Not only were they enthusiastic about Lucrezia as the future duchess of Ferrara but they also reported that she was already "a good Ferrarese," doing all in her power to bring the negotiations to a successful conclusion. She regarded Rome as a prison, they reported, and looked on this marriage as a heaven-sent opportunity to lead her own life outside her father's and her brother's ambitions.

The ambassadors had need of Lucrezia's goodwill. Immediately after the contract had been signed, Alexander called a full consistory and there boasted of the signal honor being done the Roman papacy by this marriage between the houses of Borgia and Este. But afterward, among the endless legal and financial conferences, he grew exceedingly restless and short-tempered when he realized the full extent of Duke Ercole's demands. The noble duke of Ferrara was behaving like a merchant, Alexander stormed. He had already given way in the matter of feudal dues—and in the face of strong opposition from his own Curia. He had granted the high dignity of archpriest of St. Peter's to the bridgeroom's brother—and still Ercole was not satisfied. There was the squalid business about the dowry money. Ercole had no intention of accepting paper promises; he wanted the precious metal itself, all two hundred thousand ducats of it—and large ducats at that, not the "chamber" ducats which the papal Camera usually employed when paying out. The eagle-eyed Ferrarese treasurers who watched the counting had further cause for complaint regarding the excessive number of worn and even false coins that had somehow got into the enormous pile. They insisted that counting thereafter should occur only in daylight, and five consecutive days of counting passed before at last they accepted the amount as exact.

Meanwhile, there were other more delicate problems to be faced and solved. Living with Lucrezia in Rome was her much-loved son by her late husband, the little boy Rodrigo, not yet one year old. The resident Ferrarese ambassador called on her and raised the problem of the child's future. "As her son was present I asked her, in such a way that she could not mistake my meaning, what was to be done with him. She replied 'He will remain in Rome and will have an allowance of fifteen thousand ducats.' " The child would have been an embarrassment in Ferrara, and very possibly in some danger. In Rome he was treated as a member of the house of Borgia and of Aragon. With distress, but firmly and without having to be prompted by her future father-in-law, she had decided to be parted from the little boy for his own good.

More embarrassing than the child Rodrigo was the ex-husband Giovanni Sforza. He had been living in Ferrara ever since Cesare had chased him out of Pesaro. Alexander now forcefully made it plain to Gerardo that he did not want Lucrezia and her ex-husband to meet, and the ambassador dutifully informed his master of His Holiness's objections, toning down the bluntness.

> As His Holiness desires to take all the proper precautions to prevent the occurrence of anything that might be unpleasant to Your Excellency, to Don Alfonso, and especially to the duchess and also to himself, he has asked us to write to Your Excellency and request that you see to it that the Lord Giovanni of Pesaro shall not be in Ferrara at the time of the marriage festivities. For although his divorce from the above-named illustrious lady was absolutely legal and according to prescribed form, as the records of the proceedings clearly show he himself fully consenting to it, he may nevertheless still harbor some resentment.[62]

Ercole might have reflected that Alexander seemed to be protesting just a little too much, but Ercole had no desire to be caught in the kind of scandal that Giovanni Sforza could precipitate, and the beleaguered ex-lord of Pesaro found one more asylum closed to him.

At last the tedious negotiations were completed, the money counted, delicate questions of etiquette settled and the escort chosen. The escort was military as well as ceremonial, for the bride was carrying, on her back as well as in her coffers, an incredible wealth of precious raiment and metals. Isabella d'Este, Alfonso's sister and also the marchesa of Mantua, was specifically interested in Lucrezia's trousseau for she looked upon the bride as a rival come to challenge her hitherto uncontested role as arbiter of feminine fashion in Lombardy. Isabella was so eaten up with curiosity and envy that she despatched a personal envoy down to Rome, charged with no other duty but to report on Lucrezia and her slowly amassed trousseau. "I will follow the most excellent lady Lucrezia as a shadow follows the body and where the eyes fail to reach I shall go with my nose," the envoy promised, and faithfully kept it. He, too, seems to have fallen for Lucrezia's charms and made no secret of the matter even though the marchesa was regarding the bride with a distinctly frosty eye. "She is a charming and a very graceful lady," he wrote.

> She is seldom seen in public, being preoccupied in preparations for her departure. But on Sunday, the Feast of St. Stephen, I went to see her later in the evening and found her sitting near the bed with ten maids of honor and twenty other ladies wearing handkerchiefs on their heads after the Roman fashion. They soon began to dance and madonna danced very gracefully and well with Don Ferrante [Alfonso's brother]. She wore a camorra of black velvet trimmed with gold fringe, with narrow sleeves slashed to show her

white linen chemise, a vest of black velvet richly embroidered in colors, a gold-striped veil and a green silk cap with a ruby clasp on her head. Her maids of honor have not yet got their wedding dresses. Our own ladies are quite their equal in looks and in everything else. But two or three of them are decidedly graceful—one from Valencia dances well; another called Angela is very charming.

Turning away from his fashion reporting, the enamored envoy gave the marchesa a summary of what Lucrezia was bringing Alfonso.

It is said that more gold has been prepared and sold in six months than has been used in the past two years. The number of horses and persons the pope will place at his daughter's disposal will amount to a thousand. There will be two hundred carriages—among them some of French make, if there is time—and with these will come the escort which will take her.[63]

On the evening of December 30, 1501, Lucrezia led a wedding procession, for the second time, down the corridors of the Vatican to a chamber where her father sat enthroned. On the first occasion she had been little more than a child, blindly obedient, now she was an experienced woman of twenty-one, able to handle with expert flair her stiff, sumptuous wedding dress. She wore a robe of gold brocade with sleeves so long they trailed upon the floor, and whose immense train of crimson velvet was carried by ten maids of honor. Her hair was caught up in a heavy gold net; pearls, rubies and emeralds flashed on her neck and bare shoulders. The bridegroom was not present, his place being taken by his brother Ferrante. But the bridegroom's family had sent Lucrezia even more jewels to compensate, perhaps, for his absence. After the rings had been exchanged, Ferrante presented a heavy casket of jewels to the bride. Alexander's face lit up with delight as the lid was opening, and the completion of the ceremony was delayed while he fingered the heavy rings and buckles and necklaces. Lovingly he drew through his plump fingers the immense pearl necklace which had belonged to the bridegroom's mother, and he remarked that young Ferrante's courteous manner had doubled the value of the gifts, affecting to ignore the clause in the contract which thriftily stipulated that the jewels were to be returned to the Este if the marriage should be dissolved.

Johannes Burchard had learned his lesson, and this time there were no ceremonial improprieties to mar the occasion. Afterward Cesare and Lucrezia danced "with a rare grace" for their father's entertainment, beginning the wedding festivities which again went on far into the night. Cesare played a leading role in the continuous carnival with which all Rome was regaled during the following week. New Year's Day was greeted with an allegorical procession which paid not very subtle tribute to him as a new Julius Caesar; he displayed his grace and skill as a horseman in an elaborately staged bullfight in front of St. Peter's; and he both organized and acted in a number of masques, magnificently staged in the Vatican, whose general theme was how fortunate the Este were to be united with the Borgia. Lucrezia watched them from her favorite and favored position, a cushion on the floor beside her father's throne, for during those last days of their life together Alexander was reluctant to let her go far from him.

On January 6, the day set for her departure, Lucrezia

took her leave from her father in the room called Pappagallo. Cesare joined them after a few moments, warmly dressed, for he was accompanying his sister on the first part of the journey. The courtiers drew aside, and the three Borgia conversed closely together in Spanish, that language which set them apart and made them a unit of their own. Then Alexander embraced his daughter and, as she drew away, called after her in Italian, and in a loud voice for all to hear, that she was to be of good cheer for he granted her, before she could ask, everything she could possibly want. He hastened to a window and looked down into the piazza where the bridal procession was gathering under a thin powdering of snow and remained there until the procession had wound its way out of sight, headed north toward Ferrara. He and Lucrezia never saw each other again.

Some three weeks later, while Lucrezia was approaching the end of her journey, the Este were gathering in Ferrara to greet, with very mixed feelings, the latest addition to the family.

Duke Ercole could, on the whole, congratulate himself for making the very best out of what could have been a most unpleasant situation. He had established, to his own satisfaction, that the gossip regarding Lucrezia's personal morals was just rumor. Less satisfactory had been his agents' inquiries into the Borgia ancestry. "We made a thorough investigation, but although we finally succeeded in ascertaining that the house is one of the oldest and noblest in Spain, we did not discover that its founders ever did anything very remarkable, perhaps because life in that country is quiet and uneventful. Whatever there is worthy of note dates from the time of Pope Calixtus."

It was not difficult to read between the lines of that report. It concerned the family of a girl who would one day be duchess of Ferrara, and the writers had no intention of finding themselves in a dungeon tomorrow because of an indiscreet letter today. But the agents had also been specifically ordered to report on the family for the present duke's guidance. The result was a courtier's admixture of flattery and tongue-in-cheek condescension, which could be read either way; but summed up in a phrase: the Borgia were parvenue as far as Italy was concerned. As for Spain, Ercole echoed his agents' condescension. They were both Italians and Italians habitually termed as "barbarian" all northerners, whether they came from beyond the Alps or behind the Pyrenees. The French might, on occasion, be regarded as a species of honorary Latin, but the information that Lucrezia's family was "one of the oldest and noblest in Spain" left Ercole quite unmoved. As far as Italians were concerned, the average Spanish nobleman was merely a soldier —or bandit—turned farmer. And as for the phrase "from the time of Pope Calixtus"—the writers made it seem as though the old lawyer had been coeval with Charlemagne himself, instead of having flourished barely forty years earlier. The Este, by contrast, had been rooted in Ferrara for over three hundred years. Nevertheless, the Borgia had arrived and, like all parvenues, were willing to pay heavily for the privilege of uniting themselves with a family of ancient lineage. Thus Ercole comfortably reflected, basking in the praise of his subjects who hoped, with some reason, that they would benefit from the pope's overweening love for his daughter—if only through a reduction of taxes.

Ercole's son Alfonso, the reluctant bridegroom, now

accepted his role with an amiable enough resignation. Alfonso's objection had been partly based on habit. As a matter of principle he opposed anything his father wanted. Alfonso had been reluctant, also, to change his comfortably squalid habits and adapt himself again to even a sketchy domestic life. Ever since the death of his previous wife he had been free to pursue his two great interests with a minimum of outside interference. He knew nothing and cared less about art and letters, leaving all that to his blue-stocking sister, Isabella, and his more cultured brothers. Whores and guns—these were Alfonso's real delight. The first had given him a disease, the second a nationwide fame as an artilleryman. To be fair, his preference for paid sex stemmed directly from his passion for the properties of gunpowder. He could not be bothered with the traditional chase; the silken dalliance with promises and tantrums took up time which could be more profitably spent in the foundry or on the testing field. He paid for the woman he wanted and went on his way, deeply engrossed in technical problems; his preferred companions were men skilled in casting bronze or who knew how to lay a gun. But now that his marriage with Lucrezia was settled, Alfonso accepted it equably enough. As heir to the dukedom he obviously had to marry and beget a son, and there was a certain attraction in a bride whose brother had the right attitude toward artillery.

Alfonso's sister Isabella had come to Ferrara especially for the wedding, though it meant leaving her husband, the marchese, behind in Mantua. He had wanted to come too, but her father had talked him out of it, pointing out how dangerous it would be to leave his state unattended while Cesare Borgia was still prowling, looking for new conquests. Duke Ercole had no illusions whatever about the family with whom he was uniting his own.

Isabella had her own problems. She had come to Ferrara at her father's request to preside over the wedding festivities, but she was also consumed with curiosity about Lucrezia. Isabella's man in Rome had kept her closely informed about Lucrezia's preparations, but his letters had only whetted Isabella's appetite. As the marchesa of Mantua, in Lombardy she was the undisputed arbiter of fashion and all cultural matters; now she was to be challenged on her own ground by a woman who not only seemed to be her equal in matters of costume and taste but had the immense and unfair advantage of being His Holiness's beloved daughter. Restlessly Isabella toured Ferrara, looking at the spectacles prepared along Lucrezia's processional route; discussing their details in her brisk, mannish way with the artisans responsible; conferring with her father—criticizing, suggesting, encouraging, threatening. The honor of the house of Este bore heavily upon her. Two of her brothers—the witty Ferrante and the elegant Cardinal Ippolito —were traveling up from Rome with the bridal party; her father meant well but, she considered, was old-fashioned in his tastes; Alfonso was a liability. Bitterly, now, Isabella missed her sister, the beautiful, witty Beatrice, dead these five years, but whose brief rule in Milan was still remembered in Lombardy as the epitome of elegance. Together, the Este sisters could have presented a formidable front to the Spanish invasion coming up now from the south.

Normally, the trip from Rome to Ferrara could have been comfortably accomplished in a week. But most of Lucrezia's journey ran through cities that either now belonged to her brother or were in close alliance with him, and each city thought it advisable to entertain his sister royally. Still, the Ferrarese envoy, who was traveling with the party and kept Duke Ercole closely informed of its movements, also believed that Lucrezia was genuinely popular on her own account. Her father's anxious love followed her every step of the way, the envoy reported. "His Holiness is so concerned for her majesty that he demands daily and even hourly reports of her journey, and she is required to write him with her own hand from every city regarding her health. This confirms the statement frequently made to Your Excellency—that His Holiness loves her more than any other person of his blood." [64]

But there was another reason for the slowness of the journey, which the envoy shrewdly noted. "She does not wish to be worn out when she reaches Ferrara." Lucrezia was as anxious as Isabella to make a good impression, and overnight stops were extended into days to allow Lucrezia to rest and refurbish her appearance. At Faenza it was solemnly announced that the entire cortège would spend Friday at Imola in order that "madonna could wash her hair"; she had apparently not been able to do so for the past eight days and as a result was suffering from a headache. Some two hundred people in the party therefore idled away another twenty-four hours while Lucrezia's hairdresser carefully dismantled his last creation, discreetly restored the golden glory of her hair with special bleaches, and created another confection with pearls and feathers.

Unexpectedly, Alfonso joined the bridal party while it was still enroute to Ferrara, and Lucrezia met her third husband for the first time. The burly, heavily bearded young man was no courtier, but he seems to have gone out of his way to put his bride at ease. He remained only a couple of hours with her and then galloped off as unceremoniously as he had arrived, but the meeting gave Lucrezia confidence to face the rest of the Estes. The last part of the journey was to be by boat. She and Isabella met on a barge some five miles ouside Ferrara and exchanged cool compliments.

A mile or so upstream on the Po the barge pulled into a dock where Duke Ercole was waiting with his court, and after warmly greeting Lucrezia—who insisted on kissing his hand—he conducted her on board the great state barge. It was a happy party, Isabella wrote to her husband that evening. Her father and brother were much taken by Lucrezia's Spanish clowns, roaring with laughter at their quips and antics. Lucrezia, seated between the French and Venetian ambassadors, conducted herself modestly; it was impossible to associate this quiet-spoken girl "who is not beautiful but sweet and attractive in appearance" with the monster of the Roman legend. Conversation sparkled, wine flowed in abundance, warming the gray February afternoon; and along the river bank the thundering of gun salutes alternated with the shrilling of trumpets.

The welcoming party left Lucrezia at Casale, just outside the city, and returned for her the following morning for the state entry. Ercole, thrifty rather than miserly, financed the grandest, most elaborate pageant Ferrara had seen. Isabella minutely described it for her husband, keeping a sharp eye on its central figure.

The bride was mounted on a roan mule with velvet trappings covered with gold lace and fastened with nails of beaten gold. She wore a cloth-of-gold camorra with purple satin stripes and flowing sleeves after the French fashion,

and a sbernia of wrought gold, open on one side and lined
with ermine as were her sleeves. Around her throat was the
necklace which belonged to my mother—of blessed memory. On her head was the jewelled cap which my lord father
sent to her in Rome, together with the necklace. Six of Don
Alfonso's chamberlains, all wearing fine gold chains, held
the reins.[65]

The learned doctors of the university held a great canopy
over Lucrezia's head and next to her rode the French ambassador. He was there at her specific request, for her father had wished to honor the king of France for bringing
about this highly desirable marriage.

Outside the palace two rope dancers swept down from
the dizzy heights of the towers and, as they struck the
ground before the bride, trumpets shrilled again and the
doors of all the dungeons were opened, releasing the prisoners. Now it was Isabella's turn to take a leading role.
Dressed in her favorite, somewhat startling gown of gold
cloth embroidered with musical notes, the marchesa descended the great steps of the palace and conducted
Lucrezia within, the whole company following into the
enormous hall. There the scholars and poets took over,
each spinning his literary fancy. The oddest, perhaps, was
that of the aged pedant Prisciano, who affected to find a
Biblical precedent for Lucrezia's existence. St. Peter, it
seemed, had also had a daughter; so the current occupant
of Peter's throne was therefore to be doubly praised and
congratulated.

The celebrations continued for eight days. For eight
days the plays of Plautus were performed to a somewhat
restive audience which did not wholly share Duke Ercole's

idea of entertainment; there were ballets, allegories, balls and banquets. But despite Ercole's well-meaning efforts there was a stiffness, a certain lack of ease about the celebrations. Certainly Isabella thought so. "Don Alfonso and the bride slept together last night but we did not pay them the usual morning visit because, to say the truth, this is a very cold wedding." The coldness undoubtedly arose out of the antagonism between the bride and her influential sister-in-law, the rest of the court choosing sides. Isabella deliberately set out to win the French ambassador away from Lucrezia, inviting him to a private party with her husband's beautiful sister, the duchess of Urbino, singing to him and bestowing her own perfumed gloves upon him. The canny Frenchman ate the meal, listened to the songs, took the gloves and, while swearing undying fealty to Isabella d'Este Gonzaga, made certain that Lucrezia Borgia d'Este was informed of the party. Undoubtedly, Isabella was irked that, now, not she but her brother's wife set the pace of the court. "Yesterday we all stayed in our rooms till five o'clock because Madonna Lucrezia chooses to spend all those hours in dressing so that she may outshine the duchess of Urbino and myself in the eyes of the world." [66]

Shrove Tuesday was the last day of the festivities and was marked with an orgy of present-giving. Ercole bestowed even more jewels upon Lucrezia. The French ambassador, perhaps bearing in mind her semi-sacerdotal nature, presented Lucrezia with a golden rosary, each bead of which contained priceless perfume. Somewhat enigmatically, he gave Alfonso a golden shield with a representation of Mary Magdalen upon it. The two Venetian ambassadors stripped themselves of the heavy velvet and ermine cloaks they had worn all week and laid them at the bride's feet, "upon which everyone who was present burst out laughing," noted Isabella's lady-in-waiting. Elaborate compliments were exchanged, and the same lady-in-waiting informed Isabella's husband that the marchesa had again shone, remarking cattily that "although Donna Lucrezia has had more husbands than either your wife or your sister, she could not attain by a long way the wisdom of their answers."

By February 10 Ferrara had resumed its workaday self. The temporary stages were dismantled; the acrobats, musicians, and actors paid and dismissed. Isabella left for Venice, accompanied by the duchess of Urbino; Alfonso went on a brief tour of the state; the ambassadors of the foreign powers paid their respects and departed. Everyone was leaving Ferrara—except the Spanish contingent. Lucrezia, it seemed, was reluctant to dismiss her friends and embark yet again on the cold water of matrimony more or less alone. Adriana da Mila, grown stouter and more discreet with the years, still flustered around her; the lighthearted Angela Borgia, Lucrezia's cousin, seemed determined to make Ferrara her own home, an aim apparently shared by Orsina Orsini. Duke Ercole began dropping heavy hints and went on from that to outright complaints to his ambassador in Rome. "These women by remaining here cause a large number of other persons, men as well as women, to linger, for all wish to depart at the same time and it is a great burden and causes heavy expenses. The retinue of these ladies, taken into consideration with the other people, numbers not far from 450 persons and 350 horses." [67]

The ambassador somewhat reluctantly passed on his master's complaint to the pope. Alexander was not disposed to be sympathetic. He had already received complaints from Lucrezia that Duke Ercole was proving miserly in the matter of an allowance. Now Ercole took charge of the housing situation, stipulating the number of servants and ladies-in-waiting which he felt were sufficient for even such an exalted daughter-in-law as Lucrezia. She protested indignantly, but he stuck grimly to his intention, dismissing outright all other servants and dependents and making it plain to the rest that the Este hospitality was at an end. Alfonso took no part in the argument between his wife and father. He had regularly done his duty as a husband and saw no reason to put himself out further. In mid-March, just six weeks after the wedding, the ducal doctors announced that an heir to the throne was on the way. Ercole rejoiced exceedingly, but refused to relent regarding either the number of servants allowed or the amount of the allowance paid to Lucrezia.

The Duke
of Romagna

13

Some sixty miles from where Lucrezia was warily
settling herself into a new life in Ferrara, her brother
Cesare was laying the foundations of a new court.

Cesena was far less impressive than Ferrara. There
were no great palaces, no elegant summer villas, no
canals crowded with prosperous shipping. The river
which pierced it was of little commercial value, a roaring
torrent in winter and a ravine in summer. There was a
cathedral, still unfinished after more than a hundred
years of labor; a beautiful library; a sprinkling of
churches; an ancient monastery just outside the city
walls and little else. It was a city by courtesy in a land
where all urban communities were called cities. If
elsewhere in Europe, it would perhaps be dismissed
simply as a country town.

But though it could not seriously compare with
Ferrara, more than four times its size and the seat of a
long-established dukedom, Cesena was by no means

negligible. Its site was pleasing. It was a city of the plain which enjoyed all the advantages of a hill town, for it nestled in the rounded foot hills of the Apennines in a remarkably fruitful area. The hills, clothed in vineyards, swept down to luxuriant orchards of apples, apricots and peaches, and the little city was set like a gem among the fruit trees. The great Via Emilia swept through, and from it branched other roads which could take the traveler north into the Lombard plain or south, deep into the heart of the Apennines and on to Rome. Cesena's position was the reason why Cesare chose it as his headquarters, despite its somewhat provincial nature. Over the next two years he was to add far more impressive cities to his dukedom, but Cesena, so conveniently placed, remained his capital; and its red brick castle, perched on a spur of the Apennines, became his court. The castle was built for durability rather than elegance, but it suited his purposes well enough. Towering high above the cypresses and vineyards, it looked directly down into the heart of the city, and there was ample room for his large, permanent bodyguard in the generous circuit of its walls.

Cesare habitually worked on an ad hoc basis, grasping opportunity as it occurred rather than planning meticulously ahead. The administrative machinery of his dukedom, therefore, either was spontaneously evolved to meet immediate needs, or consisted merely of existing administrations adapted to meet his particular purpose. Such an organization might have lasted indefinitely, the fact that some of its components continued to function after his sudden fall arguing that they worked efficiently enough for local needs. But the system was not put to the ultimate test of time, because less than four years elapsed between

Cesare's appearance on the political stage and the ruin following his father's death.

The court which grew up around Cesare was also evolved on an ad hoc basis, but it more clearly reflected his personality and his goal. Essentially, it was the court of a nomadic chieftain. Again, given time, he might have created in Cesena a cultural heritage the equal of Rimini and Urbino which, in their time, had been established by similar men and means. But in the brief, action-packed years of Cesare's ascendancy, he needed a weapon which could strike at any point and distance rather than the settled court of the Renaissance prince.

At the heart of Cesare's court, forming a kind of steel core, were the men who had identified themselves from the beginning of his career. They were soldiers, not politicians, and most were Spaniards. Apart from the strong tie of blood that led him to place confidence in them, he could count upon their support to a high degree because they were aliens among a people who feared and hated them. Three achieved a kind of immortality, the pale reflection of their master's: Michelotto Corella, the murderer of Lucrezia's beloved Alfonso of Bisceglie; Sebastione Pinzone and Ramiro de Lorqua. Lorqua, noted for his cruelty even in that band of cruel men, was made governor of the dukedom of Romagna with his headquarters in Cesena. He had powers second only to Cesare. Corella was Cesare's right-hand man, his friend—insofar as any man could claim friendship with him—his general and executioner. Most murders by obvious violence were those of Corella's staging. Sebastione Pinzone, a more shadowy figure, was commonly referred to as the duke's poisoner, an appellation arising more probably from his secretive methods than from any particular skill he may have had with poisoning.

The legend of the Borgia poison was one of the clan's more potent weapons. "Ha bevuto"—"he has drunk"—was the customary laconic phrase to describe the sudden death of any enemy, and many friends, of the clan, the unspoken implication being that the Borgia magic potion had been administered. Fantastic accounts developed around the origins and use of the poison. Some claimed that it was administered to a bear which was then suspended upside down and the venom-laden vomit carefully collected. Others referred simply to a "certain white powder," presumably a preparation of arsenic. But chemically speaking none of the crude poisons then available could have had the selective qualities attributed to the Borgia poison—the ability to strike down a particular victim at any distance of space or time belonged strictly to mythology. Cesare certainly preferred the far more certain method of dagger or cord, and those assassinations for which his father might have been responsible could have come about naturally enough from the appalling conditions in the Sant' Angelo dungeons. But poison fascinated the Italian mind, with its preference for the devious and the secretive; so the Borgia, to match the rest of their reputation, were accordingly invested with an almost magical power in the art of poisoning.

On the fringe of the inner core of Spanish confidants was the usual colorful, evanescent court of poets and artists, diplomats, writers and professional courtiers who would be attracted to any rising man. Cesare shared the prevailing Renaissance pretensions to universal culture. At Cesena he was building up a superb library, largely furnished by robbery. He patronized sculptors and painters—

mandatory for any prince who desired to pass as civilized, but a patronage which he exercised with discernment. Scholars gravitated to his court—but not many and few very great scholars, if for no better reason than that the restless, peripatetic nature of the court was hardly conducive to learning. This accounted, too, for the curiously shadowy picture posterity received of Cesare himself. Humanist scholars were a sedentary breed, preferring the comforts of the city to the rigors of campaigns and whirlwind rides across half of Italy. Thus, reports of the duke's activities tended to be transmitted by illiterate or inarticulate men more accustomed to using a sword than a pen and were picked up at second or even third hand by those who would eventually record them in permanent form.

Cesare himself seems to have had small interest in the current passion for the classics. Despite his ecclesiastic training he had little knowledge of Latin. Italian he spoke when he had to; Spanish continued to be his preferred tongue among intimates.

But if scholars received little encouragement from him, architects and engineers were certain of lucrative employment. Bridges, roads, water supplies, forts—these were the nerves and sinews of his dukedom and their maintenance was vital. It was as engineer that Leonardo da Vinci entered Cesare's service sometime following the year 1500. After the fall of Milan and the destruction of his patron Ludovico Sforza, Leonardo sought another purchaser for his more marketable talents and found immediate employment with Cesare. Da Vinci's tasks were the repair of the siege-battered fortresses in the Romagna and the establishment of fortifications for the siege of Piombino. Throughout, he maintained his voluminous notebook, recording what his selective, inquisitive eye had rested upon. That eye must have regarded Cesare Borgia scores of times, but the duke of Romagna and his frenetic activities were, it seems, of no interest whatever to da Vinci. On the day when the murdered bodies of Astorre Manfredi and his brother were found in the Tiber, da Vinci recorded "In Romagna they use carts with four wheels, the two in front are small, the rear ones are large—which is an absurd construction according to the law of physics." The Manfredi murder precipitated a wave of speculation—but not in the notebook of Leonardo da Vinci.

The third group of men which formed Cesare's court were the condottieri—territorial lords who had placed their swords at his disposal for a limited period and a fixed sum; wolves temporarily harnessed by a great wolf—the men who fought his wars.

Apart from a doubtful incident at Capua when Cesare reportedly led the cavalry charge which broke the Colonna, there is only one recorded incident of Cesare actually fighting on a battlefield, and that was the skirmish in which he was killed. His major military talent lay in his ability to move with incredible speed, appearing before the walls of a town when his victims believed he was miles away. But even this was merely the necessary adjunct to a political talent, his ability to deceive the victim as to his intentions. The impassivity he adopted was perhaps his most valuable political weapon. "He turned the art of war into the art of deceit—and thereafter all others copied him," was the judgment of a Perugian diplomat. Cesare had little knowledge of conventional warfare because he had little use for it. He possessed the one ability vital for a military commander, that of controlling men in the mass. Behind

Cesare's easily assumed charm lay a genuinely terrifying personality which seemed to exert an almost hypnotic influence capable of halting even the most predatory thief. On one occasion a group of Cesare's men panicked while crossing a river. The officers tried in vain to restore order; the chaos worsened; there was danger that hundreds might drown. The panic stopped, abruptly, when the duke rode his horse to the riverbank and sat totally silent, looking down on his men.

Ordinarily after the capture of a city, there would ensue two or three days of wild disorder while the victorious army plundered and murdered. It was the men's expected right, and any attempt to deprive them of it would usually lead to immediate mutiny. In the cities that Cesare captured, order prevailed within hours of the surrender— if it suited him.

But though his military talents were adequate for the civic dominance which was his objective, Cesare was hampered by lack of men. True, he had the troops lent him by Louis, but they possessed the weakness of all auxiliaries, as Machiavelli noted. "When defeated, the prince suffers the consequences; when victorious he lies at the mercy of such armies."[68] At the beginning of his career Cesare had no territorial troops of his own; he therefore had to employ those of other Italian lords—and the lords themselves.

An ample pool of men upon which he could draw existed, for the trade of condottiere had long since passed into native Italian hands after its domination by foreigners for nearly a century. A local lordling, gathering together a few hundred mercenaries, would march out and offer his sword to the highest bidder. The chances of his being killed in battle were now somewhat higher than in the past, but the rewards still appeared to be immense. Cesare's difficulty lay neither in acquiring nor controlling the men themselves but in exerting his authority over their leaders, each of whom saw himself as an independent power and was merely using Cesare as a stepping stone to greater things.

His artilleryman, Vitellozzo Vitelli, had an additional and, in Italian eyes, honorable motive for joining Cesare. Vitellozzo wanted to revenge himself on the Florentines for their execution of his brother Paolo—a desire which was to place Cesare in considerable danger. His other condottieri were more of the ordinary type. Among them were members of the Orsini clan, Paolo and Francesco. The latter had no little opinion of himself; he had come forward and offered himself as a bridegroom for Lucrezia when she was in between husbands. The twists and turns of Alexander's policy had temporarily brought Borgia and Orsini together in an effort to break the hold of the Colonna in Rome and the Orsini now, foolishly, tended to regard themselves as being in a special relationship with the Borgia.

Cesare imposed good government on the captured cities of the Romagna. It was true enough that his leniency and justice were only means to an end, that if it suited his tactics he would as willingly obliterate a city as reform its government. But for the inarticulate mass of the people, the anonymous citizens who remained mostly indifferent to whose banner it was that happened to float over their fortress, the Borgia rule was the best they had known within living memory. Under that rule roads and bridges were repaired and, above all, policed. The bandits who had long infested the area, taking advantage of the fragmentation of power, were ruthlessly exterminated. In the cities themselves price regulations were established, controlling the cost of living. Justice was again available to all. It could still be manipulated in the prince's interest, but that interest was no longer petty, prepared to starve a province to furnish a mistress's bedchamber. Again, Cesare was fortunate in the enormous power that backed him. Amply supplied with funds drawn from the papacy itself, he could afford to be generous and not only refrain from increasing the burden on his new subjects but, in certain cases, actually reduce taxation.

It was this aspect of his career that attracted the attention of the Florentine secretary of state, Niccolo Machiavelli, and for a time persuaded him that here was the messiah come to save Italy from herself. The Romagna could not have been better designed as a working model to demonstrate the evils that had afflicted Italy since the fall of the Roman Empire. Here was shown in miniature the results of the continual fragmentation of power—minor lordlings with high titles uneasily tyrannizing minute states, compromising with and against each other solely to maintain their sterile power. In the ensuing chaos foreign nations could invade and force their will unchecked. "If Italy must be under the sway of a despot, let it be an Italian despot" was the burden of Machiavelli's argument. In that context the aggrandizement of the Borgia seemed a small price to pay.

That conflict should eventually arise between such men as the condottieri and their temporary overlord was inevitable, and the first indications of trouble appeared when Cesare was absent on the Neapolitan campaign. Vitellozzo Vitelli went off on a freebooting expedition of his own; he crossed into the Florentine state and successfully produced a rebellion in the subject city of Arezzo. Florence immediately protested to Louis of France that Cesare was violating her territory—a reasonable protest, for a condottiere was assumed to be acting under the orders of his principal. On the previous occasion when Cesare had threatened Florentine safety, King Louis's reaction had been unequivocal. "We have twice told our captains in Italy that if Valentino should threaten either Bologna or Florence, they were to attack him without warning." The promise was now fulfilled and French troops began to march toward Arezzo.

Meanwhile, Cesare had returned to the Romagna. The news from Tuscany caused him some perplexity. In principle he had no objection to harassing Florence; sooner or later a clash between himself and the republic was inevitable. But that must come only when he was prepared for it. His condottieri were threatening his vital relationship with France—but on the other hand he had no intention of going to war against his own hired soldiers to protect Florence. In the situation, he temporized, sending an urgent message to Florence requesting that they despatch an envoy with whom he could discuss the matter.

The Florentine Signoria were still suspiciously debating the request when Cesare, the object of those justifed suspicions, executed the neatest piece of treachery that even he had yet achieved, gaining thereby the entire duchy of Urbino without the loss of a man.

Guidobaldo Montefeltro, duke of Urbino, had good reason to suppose himself secure in his beautiful home in the hills. He was not merely a paper ally of the Borgia but a fighting partner. When Cesare himself was a seventeen-year-old cardinal, Montefeltro had fought in the disastrous expedition against the Orsini, bearing the brunt of the fighting and ending imprisoned. He seems to have held no grudge for Alexander, for letting him languish in prison instead of paying his ransom and was now actually a member of the Borgia matrimonial network. Montefeltro's wife was the sister-in-law of Isabella d'Este—and Isabella d'Este was now the sister-in-law of Lucrezia. Cesare, throughout his Romagna campaign, had been careful to treat Guidobaldo with the greatest respect and later with that familiar affection due even distant relatives by marriage. Hence, when Guidobaldo received requests for supplies and troops to reinforce Cesare's he was ready to oblige. Cesare told him he was marching to attack Camerino and asked for one thousand men—a substantial part of Urbino's defense. But Guidobaldo, anxious to maintain his good relations with the Borgia, sent them off. Any doubts he quieted with the knowledge that Cesare was far away, and if danger threatened there would be ample time to call out the militia remaining.

Guidobaldo was at supper three nights later when news was brought that Cesare, traveling with his phenomenal speed, had entered the duchy in the south; simultaneously, two other groups were advancing from the north and east: a total of some six thousand men were converging upon Urbino itself—an Urbino denuded of troops.

Guidobaldo had no other choice but to flee. He was a brave man, and also that rarity, a good Romagnol prince. Urbino, set high on its steep hill and with massive retaining walls, could have held out for some time. His people would have fought for him. But he saw little point in subjecting them to the horrors of street warfare merely to delay the inevitable for a week or two. He escaped, making his way

with considerable difficulty through a countryside swarming with enemy soldiers, and ultimately reached the protection of his brother-in-law's court at Mantua. From there he
wrote a pathetic letter to Cardinal Giuliano della Rovere,
begging him to inform King Louis of the incredible treachery. "I cannot understand why I have been so treated, for
I have always sought to please both the Pope and Duke
Valentino. Indeed, two Spanish noblemen came to me
from His Holiness, bearing a letter in which His Holiness
assured me that always he had held me to be a good son
of the Holy See and therefore asked me to aid the Duke in
his enterprise." Guidobaldo was particularly indignant at
the rumor that his own people had rebelled. "They say that
Valentino claims that my people drove me out. I swear,
they wept when they heard of my plight."[69]

Giuliano della Rovere stored the treachery in his memory for attention when the time was more propitious. There
was nothing he could do about it now, for Cesare and the
Borgia were too high in the esteem of the French king.
There came, too, another piece of news which told della
Rovere, if he needed telling, that Italians were their own
worst enemies—that he who could exploit their callousness
to each other's sufferings might yet indeed make himself
master of the country. Isabella d'Este, marchesa of Mantua,
sister-in-law of the deposed Guidobaldo, hastened to contact his despoiler—not to protest and threaten Cesare with
vengeance but to make a request. In the priceless art collection in the palace of Urbino was a beautiful piece of marble
statuary which she had long coveted. Would the duke of
Romagna be so graciously pleased as to. . . . Cesare acceded
to the request, promptly despatching the statue to her and
receiving, in equally graceful return, a collection of one
hundred fantastic carnival masks for his special delight.

A few hours after Guidobaldo had fled Urbino, Cesare was installed in his place, that beautiful palace of the Montefeltri which had been a cradle for the infant culture of the Renaissance. And it was there that the Florentine embassy waited upon him at two o'clock on the morning of June 25, 1502.

The leader of the embassy was an ecclesiastic, Francesco Soderini, bishop of Volterra. His secretary was a pale young bureaucrat of thirty-three, Niccolo Machiavelli, now meeting for the first time the man whose name had predominated in so many anxious debates of the Signoria. Soderini did the talking but it was from the secretary's letters that the Florentine Signoria—and posterity—gained an insight into the character and possible motives of the duke of Romagna. That night Machiavelli wrote his first, necessarily hurried assessment of Cesare Borgia, one intended as political guidance for embassy principals and yet ending as a glowing tribute. "His soldiers love him and he has chosen the best in Italy. Good fortune follows him. Altogether he is a successful man, and one to be feared."[70]

The first embassy ended inconclusively, as Cesare intended. He had opened it with a sweeping, almost petulant attack upon the Florentine Signoria itself. He did not approve of it, he declared, and if the Florentines sincerely wanted his friendship they would have to change their method of government. The attack invited, and received, a retort that the Florentines had no intention of meddling with their constitution in order to please Cesare Borgia. Soderini then swung over to the direct attack himself. If Valentino was really anxious for Florentine friendship he would order Vitelli to surrender Arezzo. Cesare riposted with a skillful two-pronged return. He had no control over

Vitelli, who was carrying out a private vendetta—with King Louis's consent and encouragement.

The reply alarmed Soderini. Louis might, indeed, be engaged in double-dealing; the whole pattern of Florentine alliances might have changed within the past few days—or hours. It was well known that Cesare had means of gaining swift, accurate information denied others. The duke pressed home his advantage, knowing that it might very well prove possible to wring concessions from Florence during this period of doubt. He gave the Signoria exactly four days to decide whether they would have him for friend or enemy, and permitted Machiavelli to depart immediately with his message. Soderini remained with Cesare.

Louis had his own problems, for the neat carving up of the Neapolitan state between himself and Spain had not gone according to plan. Spain's demands were increasing, as Machiavelli had foreseen, and a full-scale war between the French and Spanish armies in southern Italy was threatening. Louis apparently was to be forced to choose between Florence and Cesare Borgia, between the wealthy Tuscan bankers and the descendant of a Spanish house who might suddenly remember blood ties and throw in his lot with Spain. Louis temporized too. The army group enroute to Arezzo continued its march and hurled itself upon Vitellozzo Vitelli's company, thus demonstrating that France was honoring its promise. But simultaneously, French ambassadors hastened to Florence and to Cesare urging each to give concessions to the other. The king himself was coming into Italy at the head of a large army when he would, in person, smooth out the differences between his ill-assorted allies.

Cesare decided he had pushed his defiance of France

about as far as he safely could, and accordingly ordered Vitelli to agree to an immediate armistice and withdraw from Tuscany. He backed up the order with the threat that, should Vitelli not immediately obey, his own city of Città di Castello would be sacked. Vitelli obeyed, but reluctantly and in fury, his attitude an ominous and accurate index to the state of mind of his fellow condottieri.

King Louis of France entered Italy in July 1502, committed to that war with Spain which brought misery to a generation of Italians. Thirty years later Spain would emerge triumphant in the shattered land that had been the battleground for the two superstates.

Left to himself, Louis probably would have devoted his limited talents to France rather than dissipate them in yet another ill-starred Italian expedition. An easy-going, self-indulgent man, he was guided onto that disastrous path by his highly capable minister, George d'Amboise, to whom Cesare had brought a cardinal's hat on his visit to France four years earlier. D'Amboise wished to wear nothing less than the papal tiara, an ornament which seemed now the property and gift of the Borgia family, and he proved to be Cesare's most valuable ally at the royal court of France.

Immediately upon Louis's arrival in Italy, the victims and enemies of Cesare hastened to Louis to lay their interminable, and justified, complaints and protests before the only man who could exert some influence. The complaints grew steadily, accurately charting Cesare's expanding power in central Italy. The Varano family, late lords of Camerino, were the latest victims, bearing the tale of yet another Romagnol city which had fallen to the Borgia onslaught. Its head, old Julius Cesare Varano, had achieved power in the normal Romagnol fashion—his specific crime, fratricide—but now that he was a dishonored corpse and his sons the helpless prisoners of the duke of Romagna, old Varano's crimes were forgotten and his blood turned into good propaganda. The Malatesta had been driven out of Rimini, where the banners of the bull and the flame now waved. In Bologna the Bentivogli family were looking over their shoulder and making prudent overtures to the enraged Vitellozzo Vitelli. Even the Orsini admitted to unease: clearly, their temporary usefulness to Alexander was over and their territories ripe for invading. Rumors abounded, fed by the hopes of frightened men. It was said that the king had come to Italy especially to chastize his insolent protégé; he feared the growing might of Cesare; Cesare would be taken back in chains to France.

In August, Cesare visited Louis in Milan; and Louis, instead of arresting him, seems to have gone out of his way to make it known that the duke was his very good friend. In public, before the affronted eyes of those who had hoped to see the Borgia pride laid low, the king of France threw his arms around Cesare's neck, addressing him not merely as ally but as cousin and most dear kinsman. The two spoke at length privately. Details of their conversation remained secret but the result was soon only too obvious: Cesare was given a free hand to settle his difficulties in central Italy.

Of those the most pressing was the disaffection rapidly spreading through his condottieri. Each of them was a territorial lord in his own right, and therefore each had links with at least one family which knew themselves to be threatened by Cesare. Word rapidly spread that Louis had withdrawn his protection from Bologna and, so it was said, had actually lent Cesare troops to smash the Orsini. A spur of fear superceded the constant motive of ambition, and the condottieri moved in mutual self-defense.

For the first time in his career, Cesare was outpaced by events—the deceiver for once deceived. In October 1502, a few weeks after his return from Milan, the condottieri revolted in the state of Urbino and arranged for the return of Guidobaldo. As soon as their base was secured in his state, they arranged an impressive conference in which all holding grievances against Cesare could concert their actions. The conference took place in Orsini territory, where the victims of Cesare rubbed shoulders with the men who had wrought their destruction in his name. Cardinal Orsini presided with his kinsmen Paolo and Francesco Orsini. Petrucci came from Siena, Baglioni from Perugia, Vitelli from Città di Castello, Montefeltro from Urbino. Oliverotto da Fermo also was present. He held no particular grudge against his employer, the duke, but attended on the sound principle of seeking safety with the majority.

Cesare was at Imola when news of the conference broke. His inner core of Spanish followers remained loyal as ever, but the troops at his command were outnumbered by those the condottieri could raise. Pressured by need, he stepped up recruitment of mercenaries but increased, too, the recruitment of soldiers from his own territories in Romagna. It was a wise move, Machiavelli judged—compared with veteran mercenaries, the native militia were raw recruits but they were far more dependable. Thereafter Cesare steadily increased the ratio of native to mercenary troops. By October he had some six thousand men under arms with the promise of more military aid from Louis. But even graver than the immediate military danger from his rebellious condottieri was the political threat from Florence. Would the Signoria make common cause with those rebels to eradicate the prime source of trouble?

Again Cesare sent to Florence, urgently requesting that an ambassador armed with full powers be attached to his court. The Signoria were just as anxious to know what was happening in the Romagna but they cannily decided to send, not an ambassador, but an envoy. An ambassador could be maneuvered into a position where he might make damaging concessions; an envoy without powers preserved all the observational value of an ambassador without the weakness. The Signoria sent Niccolo Machiavelli with strict instructions to admit nothing, promise nothing, concede nothing. He was to observe Cesare until the situation cleared.

Machiavelli arrived at Imola on October 7. Thereafter he remained with Cesare almost continually until the end of that year, 1502, observing him at close quarters as he felt his way through the perilous, swiftly changing conditions that followed the revolt, and recording his observations with the detachment of an anthropologist. Later, he drew heavily on the experience of these three months to create his enduring portrait of a universal prince.

Cesare, despite his imminent danger, appeared to be in an optimistic, expansive mood. Even when he learned that the faithful Michelotto Corella had been heavily defeated in the first trial of arms with the rebels, and barely escaped with his life, Cesare seemed undismayed. Doubtless he was concerned to put a bold face on the matter in front of Machiavelli, knowing that the Florentine Signoria were being kept closely informed of his reactions. But Machiavelli was convinced that, all evidence to the contrary, Cesare was still in control of events. He warned Machiavelli that the condottieri were no friends of the republic, and the Signoria would do well to enter into an alliance with him while they still had the opportunity. "Secretary, I know who are my friends—and who are my enemies. I am taking you into my confidence. Tell your masters that I wish to count them as friends—if they show themselves as such."[71]

Machiavelli soon learned the reasons for Cesare's confidence. Inevitably, the condottieri had sought to draw Venice into their plans. The Venetians had at first seemed interested, even encouraging; but on learning that Cesare still enjoyed the support of Louis, the Venetians disentangled themselves. Dismay struck the rebels; the more timorous began scrambling back to solid ground. Still in his remarkably frank mood, Cesare told Machiavelli of the latest moves. "They have begun to be friends again, writing pretty letters. Paolo [Orsini] is coming today and the cardinal comes tomorrow. In this way they believe they can trick me. But I tell you, I am merely playing with them. I listen to all they have to say, and take my own time."

By the end of October the revolt was at an end. The conspirators had found that it needed skill of a very high order to weld into one the conflicting ambitions of a group of independent men, each of whom was aware that his colleagues would betray him at a moment's notice for the sake of immediate gain. Paolo Orsini's mission to Cesare had been undertaken on behalf of Paolo's colleagues, but even he had made it known that he would be ready to make a separate peace. Cesare accepted the overtures from the rebels, and Machiavelli obediently passed on the details of the peace treaty to Florence. Cesare would renew the engagements of the condottieri, on condition that Pesaro and Urbino were returned to him. The condottieri cheerfully assented to the abandoning of Giovanni Sforza, who had been reinstated in Pesaro, and Guidobaldo Montefeltro, who had at least deserved to be restored in Urbino. Machiavelli was at first surprised at the ease with which the treaty was completed; it seemed unlikely that such deep and bitter animosity could be smoothed over. But he later came to the correct conclusion that both parties were merely maneuvering for a better position—the condottieri in order to launch an attack from more solid ground, Cesare with the intention of removing his enemies one by one. An accident, however, enabled him to remove them all in one operation, that which Machiavelli called the "beautiful deception" of Sinigaglia.

On December 10 Cesare left Imola, still accompanied by Machiavelli, to join the attack on Sinigaglia, a small city on the Adriatic coast. The force at the duke's immediate disposal was impressive, for in addition to the draftees and mercenaries was a large contingent of French auxiliaries who were later dismissed. The French were hardly needed, for the condottieri, anxious to reinstate themselves in Cesare's good graces, already were vigorously assaulting Sinigaglia while he made his leisurely journey across the Romagna. Machiavelli asked discreet questions of all who would answer and came to the opinion that Cesare's dismissal of the French auxiliaries was part of some stratagem to lull the condottieri into a feeling of security.

The company halted at Cesena, and Cesare was immediately inundated with complaints against his governor, Ramiro de Lorqua. The Spaniard had ruled energetically in Cesare's name, but simultaneously had indulged in an orgy of cruelty surpassing that of the most depraved Romagnol tyrants. One of the many tales told against him was of how he had thrust a clumsy page boy into the fire, pressing him down with a foot while the boy burned alive.

Cesare was indifferent to the cruelty as such. Nevertheless, de Lorqua's habits had seriously undermined Borgia control in the areas he governed, for the Romagnols had accepted Cesare's rule only because it delivered them from the arbitrary cruelty of their own lords. There was, too, the matter of a serious deficiency in the supplies which had been sent to Cesena to ward off famine. De Lorqua was summoned from Pesaro where he had gone on a visit, to account for his stewardship. The accounting was deemed inadequate. On the morning of December 26 the Cesenese found a carefully arranged tableau in the marketplace below the castle: the headless corpse of de Lorqua still clad in its Christmas finery, his fierce head itself displayed on a pike and, near it, a bloodstained cutlass.

The body was still in the marketplace when Cesare left the city shortly afterward. At Fano, Vitellozzo Vitelli was waiting for him with the news that Sinigaglia had fallen but that the governor in the castle had refused to surrender the keys to anyone except Cesare himself. Cesare confirmed that he was marching on to the city and requested Vitellozzo and his fellow condottieri to remain in Sinigaglia. Almost as an afterthought Cesare sent orders that they should remove their troops from the city, giving as reason the fact that his own troops would have to be quartered there.

As soon as Vitellozzo had left, Cesare told eight of his most loyal captains the plan he had in mind. The army was to march to within five miles of Sinigaglia, and from that point a detachment of two hundred lances was to ride for-

ward under the command of Michelotto Corella. Cesare
would follow immediately with the rest of the army. As
soon as they met the four condottieri—the two Orsini,
Vitellozzo and Oliverotto da Fermo—the eight captains
were to move forward and, two with each condottiere, accompany them back to the city. Care was to be taken not
to arouse their suspicions of anything unusual.

The first part of the plan worked smoothly. On the
morning of December 31, Vitellozzo and the two Orsini
rode out of Sinigaglia to meet Cesare, leaving Oliverotto in
the main square with about one thousand men. "Vitellozzo,
who was wearing a cloak without any armor underneath,
appeared melancholy and dejected which surprised those
who knew his normal bearing," Machiavelli learned afterwards.[72] Vitellozzo was, in fact, suspicious and had tried to
talk his colleagues out of the meeting but had been over-
ruled.

Cesare greeted the three men courteously but noticed
immediately that Oliverotto was absent. Cesare made a
slight sign to Michelotto Corella, who hurried into the city
where he found Oliverotto and warned him to move his
men out of Sinigaglia. The reason given was the shortage
of quarters which might produce bad feeling between Oliverotto's men and the newcomers. Corella also pointed out
that Cesare would take it very badly if Oliverotto did not
come out to pay his respects. Oliverotto did as he was
advised, dismissed his men and joined his colleagues.

Machiavelli did not arrive in Sinigaglia from Fano until
four o'clock in the afternoon, at least two hours after
Cesare's plot against the condottieri had been brought to
its conclusion. But he had a long interview with the duke
at six o'clock and from what Cesare then told him, and from

information gleaned around the city, Machiavelli was able to build a very clear picture of what had happened. Vitellozzo Vitelli alone had held any suspicion. He had been reluctant to go to Fano, to disperse his troops, to enter Sinigaglia accompanied only by Cesare's bodyguard. But Paolo Orsini, a boastful, empty-headed young man, had assured him Cesare was only too anxious to make amends for the past. Even then, Vitelli was unconvinced. "I have a conviction that if I go with you I go to my death," he said to Orsini. "But seeing that you are resolved to take the chance of fortune, whether it be to live or to die, I am ready to face it with you and with the others to whom destiny has linked us." He paid the penalty for violating the prime canon of a condottiere's code by placing comradeship above self-interest.

The whole party—condottieri and their still courteous guards—reached the palace. The condottieri wanted to disperse but Cesare pressed them to enter on the excuse that he wanted to hold an urgent staff conference, the first he had been able to have since the rebellion. They agreed and, talking amicably, the party entered. The doors closed behind them, Cesare walked away, and his bodyguard hurled themselves upon the startled condottieri. Paolo Orsini cried out to Cesare, begging him to keep his word. Vitellozzo Vitelli was the only one not totally taken by surprise, and he managed to kill one of his attackers but was swiftly disarmed with the rest. Immediately afterward the rest of the army galloped into the city and, at its head, Cesare scoured the place and suppressed the incipient uprising. Sinigaglia was firmly in Cesare's hands by the time Machiavelli arrived, and shortly afterward he was summoned to his interview with the duke. "His face lit up with delight at his success. He bade me rejoice with him at the happy event, reminding me that he had given me a hint of it at Fano the night before. He then went on to urge me to represent to you that Florence had the best of reasons for rejoicing with him in what had befallen her bitterest foes."

Cesare demanded that Florence should show gratitude by refusing to give sanctuary to the refugee Guidobaldo Montefeltro. Writing again on that same night of December 31, Machiavelli told the Signoria, "The city is still being sacked. I am in the greatest difficulties—it may not be possible to find a messenger to deliver this letter. Tomorrow I shall send more news. However, I think it unlikely that they [the condottieri] will be alive by morning."[73]

Paolo and Francesco Orsini survived that night; their powerful kinsman, the cardinal, was in Rome and Cesare was uncertain of the reactions if the Orsini were executed immediately. But Vitellozzo and Oliverotto were strangled "in the Spanish manner," seated back to back. Oliverotto died badly, crying for mercy and attempting to throw the blame on Vitellozzo. Vitellozzo died as he had lived— gravely, lamenting only that he had not heeded his own instincts and begging Cesare to persuade Alexander to grant him indulgence for his sins.

In Rome, Alexander adopted a simplified form of his son's stratagem to capture Cardinal Orsini. The cardinal was invited to the Vatican, where he was arrested and taken to Sant' Angelo where he died shortly afterward, probably by poison. His possessions were confiscated, his household evicted. His mother, who had lived with him, "was driven out of her home with her serving maids. No one would give them shelter, for all were afraid, and they wandered through the streets of Rome." Thus the Orsini brothers in

Cesare's hands were deprived of what little protection they had enjoyed, and they were strangled as soon as Cesare knew it was safe to do so.

On January 10 Machiavelli took his leave of Cesare; the Signoria had decided that their interests, at this critical juncture, should be represented by a man of greater weight. Cesare maintained his curious frankness with the Florentine to the last, treating him to a summary of his immediate future policy and giving him, too, an insight into how he and his father worked together.

> My enemies are either dead, or my prisoners or are fugitives. Even if they stand their ground they, nonetheless, consciously await their fate. Chief among these last is Pandolpho Petrucci. Petrucci must go. He is at once too astute, too rich, too strongly posted in his city of Siena to be left there with impunity. If possible I aim at securing his person and, to this end, His Holiness is plying him with pleasant phrases while behind that screen I push forward toward his capital. I know that I should not be allowed by that shopkeeper, the king of France, to keep Siena for myself. But I must secure myself against its present lord.[74]

He urged the Florentines to join him in the attack which would eliminate an enemy as dangerous to themselves as to himself. Machiavelli promised to pass on the request and departed, full of thought.

"The dragon that devours lesser serpents": such was the opinion of those who watched the events in central Italy. The deadly swiftness and efficiency with which a group of dangerous men had been eliminated as though they were inexperienced boys completed the legend of

Cesare's invincibility. The Vitelli family abandoned their state of Città di Castello, Petrucci fled Siena, Baglioni from Perugia. Cesare's march south from the Romagna to Rome was less a military campaign than a hunting expedition, with frightened men running for cover as soon as his now formidable army appeared. City after city in the Papal States fell, or hastened to accept him, so that within a month of the coup d'état in Sinigaglia, the greater part of the states was under his firm control. There was a brief rebellion from the few surviving barons in the south, hereditary enemies combining in desperation to save what they could. They achieved little enough, saving their lives but not their possessions.

Cesare came to Rome to confer with his father, almost certainly because of the growing disagreement between them. Alexander was alarmed at the sudden, tumultuous nature of Cesare's successes, and complained bitterly that he knew nothing of what his son was doing until it was done. That ignorance he was able to use as a political tool, in effect shrugging his shoulders when complaints were laid before him and continuing secretly to forward Cesare's projects—but with increasing unwillingness. He even confided to Giustinian, the new Venetian ambassador, that it was time that they began to think about poor Italy. His old desires for a Spanish alliance again came to the fore, now that the French were obviously making very heavy weather with their Neapolitan campaign. "If the French court can do nothing better than look on whilst its armies are scattered and captured—if, in a word, its policy is to get us to do its work for it, then we must consider where we stand. It is clearly the Divine will that Spain should emerge victorious. Who are we that we should try and withstand the decree of heaven?"[74] But he had too long left matters in Cesare's hands, and Cesare still needed France; so the French alliance continued.

Cesare kept himself secluded that summer of 1503. "He is known to be in Rome but very few people see him," Giustinian reported. "The pope does not refer to him and so I shall pretend ignorance unless he mentions it. The duke's actions are incomprehensible to everyone." His actions would not, perhaps, have mystified his physician for that summer Cesare's syphilitic rashes were at their most disfiguring. He always affected an element of mystery but, at this period, he seemed almost pathologically reluctant to be seen either unmasked or in daylight. Rome again knew a reign of terror—not now of political assassinations but the fear of a macabre unknown. Rome had always been dangerous at night but now few ventured out after sunset, so terrible was the fear of encountering a gang of veteran killers led by a fantastical masked man who would murder and mutilate with total impunity.

But in that summer of 1503 Cesare was also at the zenith of his career. Louis of France had become a colleague, not a master. The French had been badly defeated in the Kingdom of Naples, and now Louis needed Cesare more than Cesare needed him. The Papal States were virtually Cesare's personal possession, and the other neighboring states were either allied with him or afraid, so that his influence was strong in central Italy. Alexander even considered erecting a monarchy on the foundation of the Papal States so that his son could be styled king. That plan foundered on French opposition but there was another and, in the long run, an even better plan—the passing of the tiara to Cesare. Alexander made that suggestion explicit when wooing the Venetians. "After my death either he, or you, shall have the crown." All things seemed possible in that muggy, sultry summer. Alexander, though in his early seventies, still enjoyed remarkably good health and could reasonably look forward to living most of another decade—more than long enough to allow Cesare to exploit his position under the continuing power of the keys.

On the evening of August 11, 1503, the eleventh anniversary of Alexander's accession to the throne, Antonio Giustinian settled to his almost daily task of despatch writing. "Today was celebrated the occasion of his election—but His Holiness was not his usual jovial self when he left the chapel but seemed depressed in spirits and disturbed in mind."[75] Giustinian laid Alexander's unusual low spirits to his preoccupation regarding the French; others, if they noticed at all, merely assumed that he was physically out of sorts. August was a terrible month to be in Rome, particularly this unusually hot one which had already produced a minor malaria epidemic. On August 1 Alexander's loyal cousin, Cardinal Juan Borgia, had died. "August is a bad month for stout people," Alexander had observed glumly as he watched the funeral cortège from the Vatican window, but he himself seemed unaffected by the weather.

On August 12 both Alexander and Cesare fell suddenly, dangerously sick. On August 18 Alexander was dead and Cesare was battling for his life.

The suddenness of the disease, its astonishing coincidence, and the fact that it struck father and son when Cesare was at the very peak of his career threw an almost superstitious fear into the observers. It seemed as though they had witnessed the direct intervention of Divine justice.

At the time no one suggested poison. The Ferrarese ambassador spoke the thoughts of most when he remarked that no one was surprised, for almost everyone in Rome was sick "because of the bad condition of the air." But the legend which grew around the Borgia and Alexander in particular could not be contented with such a commonplace explanation. It had so happened that on August 5, both Alexander and Cesare had dined with a certain Cardinal Adriano Corneto in his vineyard outside Rome. It was very probable that both Borgia contracted malaria then, for the banquet was *al fresco* and Corneto, too, fell ill. Nevertheless, legend seized upon the occasion and twisted it during the months that followed. Alexander and Cesare were supposed to have planned the death of Corneto by poison; the poisoned flagon was accidentally switched and father and son at last fell victim to their own crime. The fact that nearly two weeks passed between the alleged poisoning and the day when both Borgia became sick was conveniently ignored by those with a taste for melodrama and the contemplation of Divine retribution.

Alexander seems to have given himself up from the moment that malaria struck him, for though he lingered for six days, he was maintained in rigorous seclusion. Not once did he ask after Cesare; not once did he refer to Lucrezia, his most beloved child; not once did he refer to his possible successor or the state of affairs in the outside world. "The palace was in total confusion and each sought to save his own, and in great secrecy."[75] Extreme Unction was administered at the hour of vespers on August 18, and Alexander died not long afterward in prayer and penitence, some said, though others claimed he called upon the devil. His body, rendered rapidly horrific by malaria and the climatic conditions, became the temporary property of the man who had so often tended it ceremonially. Johannes Burchard did what he could to give the corpse decent shelter in a palace that seemed to have gone mad with fear and hatred—at one period the body was left unattended for hours after the papal guards had attacked the priests surrounding it—and on August 19 what remained of Pope Alexander VI was buried.

Thirty years later Francesco Guicciardini pronounced his epitaph, savaging the memory of the man, enshrining as indestructible truth every vile story that political enmity had coined. Disarmingly, he admitted that Alexander "was a man of the utmost power and of great judgment and spirit, as his actions and behavior showed." But then, seeming to lose control of his pen, Guicciardini rushed on to create that portrait which was to pass as the final truth. "There were in him and in full measure, all vices both of flesh and spirit. He was most sensual toward both sexes, keeping public women and boys, but more especially women. And so far did he exceed all measures that public opinion judged that he knew Madonna Lucrezia, his own daughter. He was exceedingly avaricious . . . he caused by poison the death of many cardinals and prelates, even among his intimates . . . his cruelty was great . . . there was in him no religion nor keeping of his troth . . . no care for justice. In one word, he was more evil and more lucky than ever for many ages peradventure had been any pope before."[77]

It was probably through the golden pen of Francesco Guicciardini, first of the great Italian historians, that the Borgia legend rooted itself. For that pen transmuted into permanency the scandals which, generated in the spontaneous hatred of battle or minted for the purposes of propaganda, would otherwise have proved evanescent, fading with the events that had provoked them. The clearest possible example of that process was the sequence whereby Cesare and his brother Juan were turned into rivals for their sister Lucrezia's sexual favors. Machiavelli, writing about a year after Juan's murder, recorded simply that it had taken place and wisely refrained from speculating as to motive. Some years later, however, when he was working his notes into a more permanent form, he altered his cautious statement and gave gossip the status of historical record. "At the time it was not known who did it but later it was said that it was the cardinal of Valenza [Cesare] who was the author of this murder, either through envy—or on account of Madonna Lucrezia." Busy tongues had obviously turned the rivalry of Cesare and Juan for their sister-in-law Sancia into an incestuous rivalry for Lucrezia, and Machiavelli, without troubling to track down the source of his story, added it to the store of Borgia scandal—though with that saving phrase "it is said." Even now, the story would probably have been dismissed by posterity for Machiavelli's works, despite their manifest genius, are as manifestly infused with polemics. But when Guicciardini took the tale over and enshrined it in his great history of Italy —that monumental work which sought to unify the fragmented story of the nation—salacious gossip became lapidary fact. Guicciardini's sober, lucid account in his sober lucid history bears no indication whatsoever of the tortuous evolution of the story; speculation finally disappears and it is presented as just one more example of Borgia depravity which scarcely needs even a passing comment. Accurately, Guicciardini summarizes Alexander's hopes and plans for

Juan, and then goes on to describe how Cesare, filled with hatred and jealousy of his brother "and besides, at his having a greater share in the affection of Madonna Lucrezia, their common sister, incited by lust and ambitions—powerful incentives to the commission of any shocking piece of villainy" planned the murder of Juan.

Guicciardini and his friend and fellow-citizen Machiavelli between them fixed the Borgia permanently in the historic framework of their day. But while the disreputable, lecherous Niccolo Machiavelli concentrated on the political significance of the family, the elegant, successful, ice-cold Francesco Guicciardini seems fascinated to the point of obsession with the supposed sexual criminality of the family. It was he who recorded as fact the pure mythology of how Cesare took thirty women from Capua for his harem: it was he who recorded as fact the vicious, but transient Roman gossip of the supposed relationship between Alexander and his daughter. His pen faltered a little when it came to record the story of how Alexander, in his seventies, was supposed to have raped the Manfredi boys before having them executed: they were executed "after having satisfied the lust of someone" he recorded with unwonted delicacy. But nowhere else did he show such restraint toward the Borgia. Other men were to commit even more salacious gossip to paper, but these were far lesser writers. In his *History* Guicciardini had created a medium that would survive the centuries, and through it was transmitted the portrait of Alexander Borgia not simply as a sinful man, but as a monster breaking every canon of sane and civilized conduct. Long after Guicciardini's reasons for creating such a caricature were forgotten, the caricature itself remained, obscuring what might have been the true picture of the man.

The Fall of Cesare Borgia

14

Immediately on news of the death of Alexander, three columns of troops began converging on Rome. From the south came the Spaniards of Gonzalo de Cordoba, Their Catholic Majesties' general in Italy; from the north came the French of King Louis; and from the northeast marched a powerful contingent of Cesare's own troops, summoned to the city by his lieutenant, Michelotto Corella. In addition to the usual anarchy following a pope's death, it seemed that Rome was to become the battleground between three armies, each intent upon securing their master's hold over the city so that a pope favorable to his interest would be elected. Cesare himself was in a sickroom above the Borgia Apartments in the Vatican, his confident world suddenly in a shambles. "He told me himself that he had foreseen every obstacle that could arise on the death of his father and had prepared adequate remedies. But he could not foresee that, at the time of his father's death, his own life would be in such imminent hazard,"[78] Machiavelli reported later. The effect of malaria, in conjunction with the syphilis that was probably approaching its tertiary stage, nearly killed Cesare outright. His physicians adopted an extreme remedy, plunging him up to the neck in a tub of ice-cold water. It might have temporarily reduced the fever, but it had an appalling effect on his body for the skin peeled off over large areas, so that it was torment for him to bear even the lightest touch of garments. Half delirious from pain and fever, so debilitated he had to be carried like a child, he was forced to rely utterly on the loyalty of his staff. They gave unstintingly; otherwise he would not have survived among his resurgent enemies. About an hour after Alexander had died in the room below, Corella demanded the keys of his private treasury and later that evening brought to Cesare one hundred thousand ducats in coin together with a large quantity of precious plate and gems. Now that the immediate link with the papal treasury had been cut, money was going to be in very short supply.

On the day of Alexander's funeral, a deputation from the College of Cardinals waited upon Antonio Giustinian, the Venetian ambassador. Tongue-in-cheek he noted how they flattered both him and his government grotesquely and then came to the object of their visit: would he go to Cesare and ask him to remove his troops so that a free conclave could be held? "It seemed to me that this was no office of mine, as I had no instructions. However, at their earnest persuasion and thinking it would redound to the credit of our government, I went." Outside Cesare's apartment he found "a crowd of his cardinals—whom he treats as chaplains—and with the sweetest words in the world they told me that they desired only that a good pope should be elected by the will of God, complaining how the College suspected both them and the duke." Returning hypocrisy with hypocrisy, Giustinian made his way through the group and entered the sickroom. Cesare had obviously made an attempt to look alert. "I found him in bed, somewhat pale but not all that bad as far as I could see." Giustinian passed on his government's formal condolences and then raised the question of the presence of Cesare's troops in the city. As he expected, Cesare gave him only "good words" and Giustinian was obliged to report to the college that he had been unable to accomplish anything.[79] But it was obvious that to hold a conclave while Cesare himself was still in the city would be impossible; and after a week's hard bargaining he agreed to withdraw, on condition that he be recognized as captain-general of the Church—at least until the identity of the new pope was known—and that neither the Spanish nor the French troops, nor the troops of Orsini and Colonna be allowed in the city. On September 2 his artillery rumbled out of Rome and shortly afterward he followed it, borne on a litter, and took up his position in Nepi.

The conclave met on September 16. Giuliano della Rovere was there, confident of his chances now that his bitterest enemy was dead. Ambitious, too, was Ascanio Sforza, especially released from prison by Louis to cast his vote for the French faction, but intent now—and too late —on his own cause. Once again, the conclave came to a deadlock. The three opposing forces—Spanish, French and Italian—were almost equal and out of their deadlock arose the usual compromise, the election of an aging man. Francesco Piccolomini, nephew of the long-dead Pius II, emerged as pope and in memory of his uncle took the style of Pius III. Cesare was satisfied. He had, indeed, ordered his Spanish allies in the College to vote for Piccolomini on the theory that the next best thing to a Spanish pope was an aged and infirm man who would enter upon his pontificate under a sense of gratitude. Pius acknowledged the debt by confirming Cesare as captain-general, and on October 2 Cesare returned triumphantly to Rome, bringing with him his mother Vannozza and his brother Joffre. The Borgia luck seemed to be holding.

Pius III was a gentle, kind old man full of good intentions but sadly aware that his health and strength would hardly allow him to begin the massive task of reform after the Borgia rule. Giustinian visited him a few days after his election and found him in bed, his legs being bad. They talked about Cesare, and Pius told him how the palace had been stripped bare even of its furnishings. Furniture would have to be borrowed to make it habitable. "And he lamented that he had found the Apostolic Camera burdened with debt, without any credit whatever, and he added 'I don't wish the duke any harm, because it is the duty of the pope to have love for all. But he will come to a bad end by God's judgment, that I can see.' "[80] Cesare certainly had nothing to fear from the old man, and if Pius had lived for even a few months there is little doubt but that Borgia rule would have been re-established in the Romagna. But fate, which had already dealt Cesare one melodramatic blow, now struck him again. The coronation ceremonies of October 8 undermined Pius's already feeble constitution; on the thirteenth he grew mortally ill and on the eighteenth he was dead. Cesare, who had returned to Rome, attempted to leave before it proved a trap, but outside the city a detachment of the Orsini fell upon him and forced him back into the city. Cesare took up his quarters in Sant' Angelo, taking with him Lucrezia's little son Rodrigo and the boy, Juan, who was publicly stated to be his own son, and there again awaited the turn of events. But matters now were far graver. The hereditary rivals, Colonna and Orsini, had actually made an alliance, so great was their hatred of their mutual enemy. The Romagna, which had been held together largely by the force of Cesare's own personality, began to disintegrate. Some of the cities remained loyal, but in Pesaro and Urbino, in Rimini and Faenza the lords returned. Worse still, Venetian troops began moving across the frontier. His own troops began to disperse. The hard core remained, as ever, loyal; but the nationalistic stresses at work in the mixed army under his command began to break it asunder in his absence, with the French and Spaniards drifting toward the main armies of their fellow nationals in Italy.

But "the duke, who still occupies quarters in the Castel Sant' Angelo, is in greater hope than ever of doing great things, for he believes that a pope favorable to him will be elected,"[81] Machiavelli reported. He had arrived in Rome on October 27, despatched there by his government to keep track of the bewildering events. He remained there until the spring of 1504; and so was able to chart, almost hourly, Cesare's fall into the abyss just as he had been able to plot his rise to supreme power. Astonishingly, Machiavelli found Cesare pinning his hopes on the election of Giuliano della Rovere, Alexander's bitterest enemy. "No one can be unaware of the natural hate which [della Rovere] bears him, for he could not so readily forget the exile in which he has been kept for ten years. The duke, on the other hand, allows himself to be guided by a blind confidence. He imagines that the word of others is more sincere than his own had been."

Cesare was not blindly confident; he was taking a calculated risk. The unpredictable currents that could sweep a man into the supreme office had abruptly altered in favor of della Rovere. On October 29, two days before the conclave opened, betting in the city had given him a sixty per cent chance while Ascanio Sforza, the nearest rival, had a mere eight per cent. The night before the conclave, betting in della Rovere's favor had soared to ninety per cent, and even before the conclave opened, the rest of the Sacred College were already scrambling for his favors. He who had so piously protested the simony which had disgraced Alexander's election, now liberally distributed favors, whether in promises of hard cash or benefices. He was all the more generous in that, as Machiavelli later observed, "this pope settles his debts in the best of all ways—he wipes them out with the cotton-wool of his inkwell." But despite the high percentage in his favor, della Rovere badly needed the votes of the eleven Spanish cardinals who formed Cesare's following in the Sacred College to make up the necessary two-thirds. They could not hope to elect one of their own, for it would be a very long time before Italy would again stomach a Spanish pope; but they could block the chances of another man. Della Rovere swallowed his pride and went to see Cesare personally. In return for the Spanish votes, he swore that if elected pope he would not merely confirm Cesare in his office of captain-general but would do all in his power to re-establish him in his dukedom. Accepting, Cesare instructed his cardinals to vote for the man who had been the bitterest, most consistent enemy of his house. With the certain backing of the Spanish group, della Rovere's election was assured. The conclave itself was a mere formality, lasting little more than an hour, and at the end Cardinal Giuliano della Rovere emerged as Pope Julius II.

He could not have chosen a better name. Indeed, his fellow-Genoese boasted that he more closely resembled some antique emperor than a pope. All Italians would remember him as the "Papa Terribile"—the "awesome pope"—who, in a tempestuous pontificate, reshaped the face of the country and made Rome a wonder of the Renaissance world. They witnessed again the change that came upon a man with the winning of the tiara. The devious bureaucrat, who had sulked ten years under the protection of the French disappeared and in his place emerged one of the greatest of Italian generals. The good looks of his youth had gone but the introspection remained and deepened; the white-bearded, powerful face, when seen in repose seemed that of an Old Testament prophet. But periods of repose were rare; men felt they were in the presence of a briefly dormant volcano.

> He has not the patience to listen quietly to what you say to him, and to take men as he finds them. But those who know how to manage him, and whom he trusts, say that his will is good. No one has any influence over him and he consults few, or none. . . . It is almost impossible to describe how strong and violent and difficult to manage he is. In body and soul he has the nature of a giant. Everything about him is on a magnified scale . . . there is nothing in him that is small or meanly selfish.[82]

He was also, from his point of view, an honest man. The purchase of votes at an election was an accepted common-

place, the means whereby he took a short-cut to one great
goal: the restoration to the Church of the things of the
Church. And that included, pre-eminently, those states of
the Church at present forming part of the dukedom of
Cesare Borgia.

Initially, the new pope gave every indication of intend-
ing to honor his promise to Cesare. A brief was sent to
Florence ordering the Florentines to give the duke of
Romagna free passage through their state so that he could
return to the Romagna, and Cesare himself was given a
pressing invitation to leave his cramped quarters in Sant'
Angelo and resume residence in the Vatican. Rome was
agog with rumors regarding the relationship between the
two men and what Cesare's intentions were. Machiavelli
summarized the position for his government.

> The pope has promised everything asked of him—but the
> difficulty will be in making him keep this promise. As for the
> Duke of Valentinois, it is said that he [Julius] has promised
> to reinstate him in the Duchy of Romagna, and as a pledge
> has yielded him the port of Ostia, where the Duke has two
> ships and some troops. The Duke occupies an apartment,
> known as the Nuove Stanze, in the palace, living there with
> about forty of his old servants. No one knows whether or
> not he intends to stay. Some believe that he will go to
> Genoa, where he has deposited the great part of his money,
> and that from there he will proceed to Lombardy to raise
> troops and march on Romagna. He seems in a position to
> do this for he still has two hundred thousand ducats or
> more, most of it invested with Genoese merchants. Others
> say he will not leave Rome but is waiting there for the
> pope's coronation when, as he was promised, he will be
> proclaimed gonfalonier of the Church and so be enabled to
> recover his dukedom.

Julius may well have intended to keep his word, in letter and spirit. He was, above all else, a realist and it was clear to him that were Cesare removed, a vacuum of power would be created in the Romagna—and that vacuum would be filled immediately by Venice, no more friendly toward the Holy See as a temporal power than any other Italian state and considerably more capable of causing harm. Already Faenza and Rimini were under direct Venetian influence. Forli, too, had fallen. The Romagna, in Cesare's absence, was breaking down into its component parts, which were again being dominated by separate lords. Julius wanted the return of the Papal States in their entirety, and if he could have trusted Cesare to act as a loyal vicar of the Church, then Cesare would certainly have been reinstated. But no man who knew Cesare Borgia could possibly believe he would remain contented for long in a subordinate position. "Aut Caesar, aut nihil" was the motto displayed on his sword; Julius would have been remarkably naïve not to have taken the boast at its face value. He was statesman enough to realize that Venice, in the long run, represented a far more serious threat to the Papal States than did Cesare; but ten years' exile, ten years spent brooding about the Borgia, seemed to have temporarily blinded Julius to that worse threat. Only a week after Machiavelli reported that Cesare seemed about to recoup all he had lost, Julius summoned the Venetian ambassador to discuss Venetian interests in the Romagna. "We want the States to return to the Church," he said firmly. "It is Our intention to recover that which Our predecessors have so malevolently alienated." Outrageously, he flattered the Venetians "with sweet and loving words," then turned to the question of Cesare. "We made promise of certain things to the Duke, but we intended by that merely a guarantee of his personal

safety and the possession of his moveable property—
wealth which, after all, he merely stole from its rightful
owners."[83]

Cesare as yet knew nothing of this change of attitude.
Machiavelli visited him on November 8, the first time the
two had met since January when Cesare, in his towering
confidence, had graciously invited the Florentines to share
in his conquest of Italy. Machiavelli found him now cursing
Florence, for the Florentines, as skilled at scenting weakness as the Venetians, had not only declined to provide him
a safe conduct but had actually participated in the attack on
Forli. "In words full of venom and passion," he predicted
the immediate ruin of Florence now that the republic's
protectors, the French, were running from the Spaniards,
"and he would laugh at it. And he declared that never again
would he be mocked by you." Machiavelli held his tongue
and, as he expected, Cesare had changed his position again
a few days later. "It is best, he says, to let bygones be
bygones, to think no more about the past, but only of the
common benefit, to act in such a way that the Venetians are
prevented from becoming masters of the Romagna. He
added that the Pope was ready to help him." The cold eye
of the Florentine envoy noted that the young man had
begun to crumble, swinging from one extreme of policy
and of mood to the other.

On the night of November 18 Cesare unobtrusively
left Rome with a small escort and arrived safely at Ostia,
where he boarded one of the galleys waiting for him. It was
believed he might sail up the coast to Genoa, but he was
still in a state of acute indecision waiting, perhaps, for
Julius to exert his full authority and, with that powerful
backing, hurl out the invaders in the Romagna. Julius did,
indeed, come to a decision but it was not what Cesare

hoped or expected. The pope had now grasped the essentials of the situation: the Venetians were flooding into the states but most of the strongpoints were in the hands of Cesare's troops. Acting with his usual violent impetuosity, Julius sent a peremptory order to Cesare at Ostia that Cesare should immediately disclose the passwords so that papal troops could enter the strongpoints and take over the defense. Cesare refused—and, Machiavelli believed, thereby destroyed himself. An outright refusal was the one thing that Julius II could never tolerate. "The rumor is going about that the duke was thrown into the Tiber on orders from above. I cannot confirm or deny it. What I do think is that if it is not done yet it will be."

It was not done because Julius still needed the essential passwords. Without them, the meager forces at his disposal would have been forced to fight on two fronts—holding off the Venetians with one hand while attempting to dislodge Cesare's garrisons from their well-fortified positions with the other. Reacting promptly to Cesare's refusal, Julius despatched a strong guard to Ostia with orders to bring Cesare back to Rome, by force if necessary. The farce of negotiations between equals was at an end; Cesare was to be imprisoned until he obeyed. He was dragged off the galley in Ostia, and on that same day Michelotto Corella was defeated by two of his master's former condottieri. Julius immediately demanded that Corella be handed over to papal custody "to be questioned about the deaths of many persons, the most important of whom are the duke of Gandia, the lord of Camerino and his two sons —who had their throats cut, the lord of Faenza and his brother, Duke Alfonso of Bisceglie, the lord of Sermoneta, the archbishop of Cagli. . . ."[84]

Cesare's arrest marked the moment of his final decline

In Rome, Giustinian showed the decisive change in public opinion by refusing to call upon Cesare, although Cesare urgently requested him to do so, and Julius would not have forbidden it. It was a mean-spirited action but it showed, at least, that the Venetian ambassador was thoroughly in tune with his surroundings. Swiftly, word spread through Rome that Cesare's iron will was now broken, that he, the man who had once looked upon either triumph or disaster with the same apparent indifference, was now a weeping wreck, full of self-pity and apologies. "It seems to me that, little by little, this duke of ours is sliding into his grave," Machiavelli reported with clinical detachment. There was report of a poignant interview between Cesare and one of his victims, Guidobaldo Montefeltro, where Cesare fell on his knees, groveling, begging for pardon, promising to return the art treasures he had stolen from Urbino. Julius, whether by accident or design, confined Cesare in the same room in the Torre Borgia where Lucrezia's second husband, Alfonso, had been murdered by Michelotto Corella. Cesare, it was stated, wept and protested and had to be dragged in. It is probable that his total collapse could mostly be attributed to the effects of his recent serious illness but, in the cold eyes of Renaissance diplomats, the effect was the same. It was during these days that Machiavelli revised his opinion of the man he had once thought might be the leader of a united Italy. In his eyes there had been two Cesares. The splendid Duke Valentino would be enshrined for all time as "The Prince"—but the cowering, chattering invalid was fit only for a gallery of second-rate failures.

Under the shock of imprisonment Cesare's will to resist ended and, obediently, he dictated the passwords to the papal commissioners. But now both he and Julius met an

unexpected obstacle, the stubborn loyalty of Cesare's en-
trenched commanders in the Romagna. Anticipating what
indeed happened, Julius had insisted that one of Cesare's
personal servants should accompany the papal commissioners when they went to demand the surrender of the
fortress in Cesena. The man, Pedro d'Oviedo, was known to
be loyal to Cesare but the Spanish governor of the castle
hanged him as a traitor. The governor's misplaced loyalty,
and the loyalty of others like him, condemned Cesare to
another four months' imprisonment. He pleaded his help-
lessness in the matter but Julius was not convinced. The
most he would do was allow Cesare to take up residence in
Ostia under strong guard, and there he remained throughout February and March while the Spanish cardinals in
Rome urged his case with the pope. It was not until April
12 that the major strongpoints were yielded, and Cesare
immediately demanded his release. A week later he sailed
south to Naples.

On December 28 had been fought the battle of the
Garigliano in which the Spaniards finally crushed the
power of France in the south of Italy. Henceforth, the Kingdom of Naples was a Spanish possession and, in seeking
refuge there, Cesare was virtually severing himself from his
long and profitable association with Louis of France. Exactly why Cesare made the choice can only be conjectured,
for by leaving Rome he moved out of the orbit of the
ambassadors and observers who hitherto had recorded his
activities almost by the hour. He was probably influenced
by the fact that members of the Borgia family had sought
refuge in Naples from the moment it was known that Julius
was hostile to him. Cesare, ever an opportunist, may have
acknowledged the long dormant ties with Spain because

Spain was now in ascendancy. But he was ignorant of his standing at the court of Spain. Even while he was imprisoned in Ostia, Ferdinand and Isabella had written their ambassador in Rome, telling him that "Their Majesties have strictly directed Gonzalo to aid the pope in recovering Imola, Forli and Cesena to the Church, seeing that they hold the interests of the pope even above their own." Such an act was, perhaps, only incidentally hostile to Cesare, a mere by-product of the desire of Their Catholic Majesties to make peace with Julius in order to consolidate their gains in southern Italy. But Cesare had forgotten, or chose to ignore the fact, that Isabella of Spain had a personal dislike for him, a dislike continually fueled by the hatred that his brother's widow, Maria Enriquez, had held against him ever since Juan's murder. That was made plain in the dispatch sent in the name of both monarchs to their ambassador just four days after Cesare had arrived in Naples.

> This journey of the duke we regard with deep displeasure, and not for political reasons alone. For, as you know, we hold the man in deep abhorrence for the gravity of his crimes, and we have no desire whatever that a man of such repute should be considered as in our service, even though he came to us laden with fortresses, with men and with money. We have written to the duke of Terranova [Gonzalo] that he send the duke to us, providing two galleys for the voyage, so that he cannot escape elsewhere. Or Gonzalo may send him to the emperor, or to France to join his wife.[85]

Unaware of the new storm building around him, Cesare seems to have regained his old confidence on setting foot in Naples. The night after his arrival he dined with

Sancia. She had escaped from Rome at about the time he was first imprisoned, with the aid of an old enemy of his, Prosper Colonna, and had become Colonna's mistress in Naples. The fascination that Cesare held for Sancia seems to have been undiminished by his recent troubles, and bygones were apparently to become bygones. Joffre, too, was in Naples but that marriage was over for all practical purposes.

Cesare resumed his old life with joy, throwing himself into the business of raising troops. Sooner or later the Spanish must continue the advance to the north, and it seemed to him axiomatic that Gonzalo de Cordoba would include him in any such undertaking. And once in the north, with a Spanish contingent behind him, there would be nothing to prevent his marching into the Romagna, scattering his enemies and reigning once again as Cesare Borgia of France. So for three weeks of a beautiful Neapolitan spring, his life was full, happy and hopeful, alternating between the barrack yard, the ballroom and the bedroom. Perhaps a little coldness existed between himself and Gonzalo—no longer a general but now the Spanish viceroy in Italy, indication not only of his status but of Spain's in Italy. Gonzalo proved oddly reluctant to provide funds for troops, seemed curiously lukewarm about the prospect of attaching the famous Cesare Borgia to his staff. But Cesare, if he thought about this at all, put it down simply to the long-held dislike the Spaniard seemed to have for the Borgia.

By the third week of May, Cesare had made full preparations for an independent advance to the north. Throughout the weeks Gonzalo had stood aside, watching. In his files were explicit instructions from his queen that Cesare

Borgia should not be allowed to participate in any military operations in Italy, either independently or as part of a major Spanish campaign. But viewed from another angle, Cesare, a fellow-Spaniard, had sought refuge in territories under Gonzalo's command. The Spanish cardinals who had negotiated this asylum for Cesare were certainly under the impression that Gonzalo had given his word that Cesare would not be molested. Later there were to be bitter accusations of treachery on the part of Gonzalo, but even had he provided Cesare with a safe-conduct, it was limited strictly to the Kingdom of Naples. And now that Cesare had made it obvious he intended throwing all north Italy into uproar, thereby embroiling the Catholic monarchs with the formidable Julius II, there was but one path Gonzalo de Cordoba could follow.

On June 1 Francesco Pandolfini, Florentine ambassador in Naples, told his government what had happened.

On Monday [May 26], Valentino requested an interview with the grand captain to discuss his still uncertain affairs. He had already prepared the artillery and had ordered wines, bread, and other things necessary for the expedition. In the evening he had his interview, lasting two hours, and was dismissed. Accompanying him was Niugno del Campo, castellan of the Castel Nuovo, and when the duke turned to descend, Niugno stopped him, saying "Signore, your way lies here," and took him into a room in the Torre dell'Oro. It was a beautiful and an honorable room but on Tuesday morning they transferred him to another tower and placed him in a room which was also very beautiful but was very strong with the windows protected by iron. It is called the "oven," and various important people have been imprisoned there at one time or another. He is there now, with two of his servants. The grand captain refuses to talk with him.

> I have not found a single man in the city who does not praise the deed—truly, it is pleasing to all.

A Florentine diplomat was, as usual, very well informed and a later, Spanish source confirmed the main details of Pandolfini's story—with one dramatic addition: Cesare's cry of despair when he learned that he had been outwitted. "When the duke heard this he gave a great cry saying 'Santa Maria, I am betrayed. With me only has my Lord Gonzalo dealt cruelly; to all other but me he has shown mercy.' "[86]

Committed to the distasteful task, Gonzalo now acted openly on the pope's behalf to assuage Julius's justified suspicions that the Spaniards in Naples had given shelter to his most dangerous enemy. The fortress in Forli still obstinately held out under its Borgia Spanish commandant, Gonzalo de Mirafonte, and papal forces had proved inadequate to dislodge him. De Cordoba, acting now as viceroy, threatened Mirafonte with the confiscation of his Spanish estates if he did not at once give up the castle. Faced with this extreme penalty and knowing Cesare was now effectively removed from the Italian field of action, Mirafonte surrendered. But he did it proudly, marching out under the Borgia standard, the last captain ever to do so, and was saluted by all Italy as a brave man and most loyal soldier. Thus, Cesare lost his last foothold in Italy; and ten days later he was sent in a galley to Spain, landing in Valencia whence his great-uncle, Alonso de Borja, had departed seventy-two years earlier to found the Borgia fortunes in Italy.

In October 1504 Lucrezia in Ferrara heard the first news of how her brother was faring in Spain. "The duke of Valentinois's situation does not seem as desperate as is feared. He is shut up with a page in the castle of Seville which, though austere, is immense. He has been given eight servants. The duke's steward, Requesnez, writes that he has spoken to the king about his release. His Majesty said that he did not order his imprisonment but only his transfer to Spain, following certain accusations brought against him by Gonzalo."[87] Superficially, Cesare's imprisonment seemed a formality and probably brief, but almost immediately after that encouraging report came other, more sinister news. "A letter from Spain contradicts what has been reported concerning the release of Valentinois. He is more closely guarded than he was before, for it was discovered that he had attempted an escape." He had, in fact, not only sought escape but had nearly murdered his jailer.

The "castle of Seville" of the Ferrarese ambassador's report was the castle of Chinchilla, a massive structure on a crag some seven hundred feet above the small town of the same name. Ferdinand's leniency, arising from his uncertainty over what to do with his prisoner, had given Cesare a considerable amount of freedom in the castle, and he habitually spent hours on the open balcony of one of the towers. Don Guzman, the castellan, sometimes joined him there, engaging in somewhat embarrassed conversation. The day of the near-murder, Cesare affected an interest in identifying the sites visible from the tower, and Guzman unsuspectingly approached the battlements while they were talking. Cesare grabbed him around the waist, lifted him and attempted to hurl him over the battlements. But Guzman, strong and agile, twisting in Cesare's grasp, wrestled him to the floor. Cesare rose, grinning, and held out his hand, pretending that he had only been engaged in a test of strength. Guzman backed away and immediately complained to Ferdinand. As a result, Cesare was transferred from Chinchilla to the immensely strong palace-fortress of Medina del Campo, the favorite residence of Ferdinand and Isabella. Oddly enough, he was still allowed considerable freedom of movement; one of the reports from Spain stated that "he amuses himself on his balcony by watching the falcons in flight," and the local nobility were allowed remarkably free access to him. One of them, the count of Benevente, succumbed to the famous Borgia charm and became Cesare's devoted friend, arranging supplies of delicacies for him and keeping him in contact with the outside world.

Ferdinand was embarrassed by the presence of his prisoner. His wife Isabella might have had a personal motive in destroying Cesare Borgia; what Ferdinand wanted was to ensure that Borgia did not cause trouble between Spain and the papacy. Throughout, there had been a vagueness regarding Cesare's ultimate destination once in Spanish hands. Ferdinand, personally, would have been only too glad to have seen Cesare shipped off to France or even left in Italy. Isabella had been the one pursuing the vendetta on behalf of Cesare's ex-sister-in-law, Maria Enriquez, the duchess of Gandia. But four months after Cesare arrived in Spain, the great-hearted queen died. Even had he desired, Ferdinand now would not have had time to pursue a family quarrel, for the hard-won unity of Spain was on the brink of dissolution. Isabella's heiress in Castile was the unfortunate girl known as Juana the Mad, and Juana's husband, the duke of Burgundy, was making fantastic claims. Ferdinand also deeply suspected the loyalty of Gonzalo in Italy. Theoretically, Gonzalo was the

viceroy of Their Catholic Majesties; in practice, his loyalty
had been toward Isabella. It seems, and probably was,
mean-minded of Ferdinand to impugn the honor of a man
who had devoted his life to the service of his king and
queen. But Ferdinand may have had justification. In distant
England, King Henry VIII had dropped a word in the ear
of the Spanish ambassador there. "If I were in Ferdinand's
place I would sift the matter to the bottom. I must tell you
that the great captain once made an offer of his service to
me, but although I was at that time not on the best of terms
with King Ferdinand, I did not choose to give him encouragement."[88] Henry's motive in passing on this snippet of
information at this time was suspect, but it did not necessarily affect the truth of the story. Ferdinand concluded he
should go personally to Naples and it occurred to him that
having a soldier of Cesare Borgia's status in his entourage
would be useful if Gonzalo de Cordoba was, in fact, planning to make himself king of Naples. Tentative overtures
were therefore made between the king and the prisoner in
Medina del Campo, directed toward the possibility that
Cesare Borgia might, himself, become Ferdinand's genera-
lissimo in Italy.

But fate, which had already dealt Cesare two heavy
blows through a coincidence of time, now struck him a
third through the coincidence of space. The castle of
Medina del Campo was in Castile, now under the control,
not of Ferdinand, but of his daughter Juana. The sanity of
the new queen of Castile was, even now, balanced on a
razor's edge, and there is no rational answer to why she
took up the vendetta against Cesare Borgia. She may have
wanted to copy her admired and feared mother; her husband may have pushed her into it on the general grounds

of causing Ferdinand as much trouble as possible. On the same day that Ferdinand expressed the wish that the prisoner be released, Cesare was indicted on a charge concerning "the death of the duke of Gandia, his brother, and of Alfonso of Bisceglie, his brother-in-law, with the intention of inflicting on him the punishment of death for these two crimes." Ferdinand was informed that Cesare's case was now sub judice and, accordingly, he sailed for Italy on September 4, 1506, leaving Cesare in the hands of his daughter and son-in-law. Cesare determined to make his escape—and did, six weeks later.

That news struck Italians as a calamity or triumph, according to the hearer's partisanship. Julius was frankly alarmed; Florence and Venice immediately looked to the protection of their frontiers. Both pope and republics were convinced that this incredible man would reappear among them and recreate that which they had now almost totally destroyed. In the Romagna there was open rejoicing, and even in Ferrara the less discreet, or the less fearful, congratulated Lucrezia. Details of the escape entered folklore and made the rounds long after Cesare's death. In the verses of sincere but third-rate poets, the escape inevitably became an heroic tale. A version of it tells how Cesare, "a man expert in many things," prevails upon his guard to bring him gunpowder in a loaf and fire in a reed. With their aid he blows down a section of the wall, swims across the sea to safety, and finds horses waiting which his wife had sent.

The folklore tale was wrong in almost every possible detail, not least that remarkable swim from a castle situated in the heart of Spain. But captured was the essence of an extraordinary story. The prime mover in the escape was the count of Benevente, but the actual details were probably Cesare's, depending as they did on secrecy and conspiracy rather than upon the naked force which Benevente favored. The plan was simple enough. Cesare was lodged in the upper chamber of the big tower called Homenaje; all that was required was a long rope—and the courage to descend it. Benevente sneaked the rope to Cesare by means of a certain Garcia de Mangone, a personal servant of the castellan; it was never established whether Garcia undertook his perilous, ultimately fatal, task through bribery or his admiration for Cesare. The night of October 25, Garcia secured the rope to one of the battlements and began his descent. In the dark it was not until he reached the bottom of the rope that he discovered it was many feet too short. He could not climb back up, for Cesare, hearing sounds that indicated pursuit, had hurriedly begun his own descent. Garcia let go, fell, and broke both his legs. Meanwhile, at the top of the tower the castellan's son had discovered the rope and began to jerk it from side to side, so that Cesare's grip was broken and he, too, fell. Benevente's men were waiting for him at the bottom and, discovering that Cesare, too, had broken bones, hoisted him on horseback and secured him as best they could. Garcia de Mangone was left to his fate, a swift one. He was executed the next day.

What happened to Cesare thereafter was the subject of a searching inquiry ordered in the name of Queen Juana. Cesare apparently hid in one of Benevente's villas for at least a month while his wounds healed. A witness described seeing him in the area late in November, still with his hands bandaged, probably a result of rope burns. At the end of November Cesare began the most hazardous journey of his life—escaping from Spain through a countryside swarming with enemies. In disguise he traveled north to the coast with only two companions. The next that the world heard of him was in the form of an official letter sent out in the queen's name to the governors of all cities in the north of Spain.

> The duke of Valentinois, a prisoner by my command in the fortress of Medina del Campo, has escaped. I am informed that he reached the city of Santander, where he was arrested by the alcalde, but that the latter released him upon receiving gifts from the duke. I wish you to inform us of everything concerning him, and to take possession of the person of the said duke wherever you find him—whether it be in a church, monastery or any privileged place, even though it may be outside your jurisdiction, and having done that keep a close watch on him with a strong guard until further orders. And be it known that if anyone hides him, he will incur the penalty of death."[89]

The alcalde of Santander successfully defended himself against the bribery charge, saving himself from the garrotte and, incidentally, providing a brief but vivid picture of Cesare's movements. On the night of November 29 Cesare's horse had become lame a short distance outside Santander. He sent his two companions ahead to find an inn and to charter a boat that would take them down the coast to Laredo. Still suffering from the escape injuries he limped into town. At the inn he met his companions and the three famished men ate a large meal, including "three chickens and a huge piece of meat." They were still at supper when an officer of the alcalde entered the inn and arrested them. Suspicions had been aroused by the large sum offered for the hire of a boat, an elementary mistake on the part of Cesare's companions which very nearly cost them their freedom. Brought before the alcalde, however, they succeeded in deceiving him with their cover story. They claimed they were wheat merchants, hurrying to take over a cargo of wheat that lay down the coast beyond Laredo and which would spoil if there was any delay. The story seemed to explain they were traveling with the large sum of money found on them and the haste which made them bid above the going rate for hiring a boat. The alcalde let them go.

> Your Majesty may rest assured that if I or any of my officers had known of the escape when I had him in my power, even though he had given us all the treasures imaginable, it would never have entered my head to do anything against Your Majesty. I should certainly not have released the duke if I had known that it was he or if I had even suspected him. But when he was in my hands, I did not know that he had escaped and was not, indeed, even aware of his existence.[90]

On December 3, 1506, Cesare appeared "como un diabolo" in Pampeluna, capital city of his wife's brother, Jean d'Albret, the king of Navarre. The fact that Cesare had chosen—or rather, had been forced to choose—this obscure little court as his asylum was a more exact index to his fallen state than his imprisonment in the royal castle of Medina del Campo. Seven years had passed since Cesare had married Charlotte d'Albret, a time during which he had given her and her family scarcely a thought. There had been a few letters and an expensive gift of sweetmeats and fine wines sent on his behalf from Venice, but that was all. The Easter of 1502 there had been a plan to bring Charlotte and their two-year-old daughter Louise to Italy but that had fallen through, largely because King Louis had seemed reluctant to part with what was, in effect, a hostage. Life for Cesare had been too full, too rich, too triumphant then to trouble much about a grass widow. But during his late imprisonment, Navarre, so conveniently close, had emerged as a potential asylum. Its petty king, Jean, had been only too pleased to consider the overtures and also had probably contributed to Cesare's escape. Yet again Cesare's fame as a general had raised his value—Jean d'Albret was welcoming him as a condottiere, not a prince. The tiny kingdom of Navarre, caught between Castile and France, and existing only precariously as an independent state, was itself split between two warring factions. Cesare's task was to suppress his brother-in-law's enemies at home and afterward, perhaps, defend Navarre from the encroachments of its giant neighbors.

But there was heady talk, too, of supplying Cesare with troops to recommence his conquests. Impoverished Navarre could pay him only a token sum as condottiere, but in Italy and France there were, theoretically, Borgia assets totaling nearly one-half million ducats. Pope Julius had promptly impounded the two hundred thousand ducats which Cesare had banked in Genoa, on the reasonable enough grounds that they had been obtained from, or through, the Holy See. But there was that huge treasure which Michelotto Corella had taken from the Vatican while Alexander lay dying, treasure which included not only gold cups and plates and precious stones but also ceremonial robes of enormous value. Additionally, there were the various precious objects which Cesare had acquired as booty and which were in the safe-keeping of the Este family in

Ferrara, a hoard conservatively estimated at being worth some three hundred thousand ducats. In January 1507 two of Cesare's servants went their separate ways from Navarre in an attempt to realize his assets. His secretary, Federigo, went to Italy, and his steward, Don Jaime de Requesnez, made the shorter journey to Bourges in France, where Louis was seated with his court. In Italy Federigo barely had time to greet Lucrezia in her brother's name before he was arrested on Julius's orders. The Borgia art treasure had, in any case, been seized by Giovanni Bentivoglio, lord of Bologna, and was already the subject of spirited litigation. In France Requesnez became the accidental instrument for the final and formal degradation of his master.

Requesnez could not have approached Louis at a worse time. Gone were the high hopes with which Louis and Cesare had set out to conquer Italy seven years before. Once, the French had all but ruled the peninsula; now they were penned into Lombardy, barely holding on to Milan while the tide of Spanish arms was at its flood. Outwitted by King Ferdinand of Spain, outgeneraled by Gonzalo de Cordoba; betrayed, as Louis thought, by the Italians, he turned, snarling, when Requesnez made his request of money on behalf of the Italo-Spanish duke. Some one hundred thousand ducats were owed Cesare as part of Charlotte's dowry which Louis had royally promised but had never actually paid. There were also the rich revenues from Cesare's dukedom which now would help to re-establish him. Louis declined to pay either. He went further—in one last gesture of spite he revoked the proud title of Cesare Borgia of France, stripped him of the royal arms, and snatched away the dukedom of Valentinois. Louis's reasoning held a modicum of truth, padded out to give grounds for an act which not only placed some salve on his wounds but also saved his treasury an immense sum. "After the decease of the late Pope Alexander, when our people and our army were seeking the recovery of the Kingdom of Naples, he went over to the side of our enemies, serving, favoring, and assisting them at arms and otherwise against ourselves and our said people and army, which resulted to us in great and irrecoverable loss." The uninformed reader of that letter patent might have concluded that Cesare had led an entire army against the French, instead of merely plotting to take a company against the occupiers of the Romagna. But the letter served its purpose. Louis of France had little squeamishness about the propriety of kicking a fallen man.

By the beginning of March 1507, Cesare was a landless, penniless man; at the age of thirty-one he possessed infinitely less than he had at eighteen; and it was with this knowledge that Cesare rode out on what was to be his final foray. The action was unimportant even in the minuscule affairs of Navarre. The castle of Viana, a city on the Navarre-Castile frontier, was held by a rebel lord, Don Juan, count of Beaumont, and it was Cesare's task to capture it. He was well supplied with troops for the troubles in Navarre had attracted the usual free-ranging mercenaries. Under his immediate command he had perhaps one thousand cavalry, five thousand infantry and some artillery pieces. The artillery was far inferior in number and quality to what he had been accustomed to using in Italy but, in the present campaign it should have proved more than sufficient. The castle was expected to fall quickly, for it was badly provisioned.

But Don Juan of Beaumont was a brave, resourceful

man. The castle was separated from the city, which Cesare had taken over as his headquarters, by an area of rough scrubland, and Beaumont decided it would be possible to sneak a convoy of provisions in under cover of darkness. It could have been a foolhardy attempt but, fortunately for Beaumont, a violent storm broke during the night (March 11), and the guards who should have been patroling the city walls sought shelter. Beaumont left the main body of the escort in a ravine some distance from the city and sent on the convoy. It succeeded in entering the castle, but the detachment of soldiers who had accompanied it, on returning collided with a detachment of royalist troops who were marching to Viana as reinforcements. Dawn had not yet broken and in the uncertain light the royalists believed they had been trapped by a major force. The alarm was sounded and confusion swept the city. Cesare leaped out of bed, armed himself hastily with the aid of a young squire, and without giving any orders whatever he, the commander of the garrison, hurled himself on horseback and galloped alone out through the city gate. His horse slipped on the wet pavement as it passed through. He wrenched it upright and "screaming blasphemies," continued his headlong ride into the dawn. To some of the watchers in the city, his horse seemed actually out of control and bolting with him.

Outside the city, Cesare encountered the detachment of Beaumont's men who were returning from the castle, and rapidly killed three of them. The rest retreated and he followed, galloping farther and farther from the city that was his charge and support until at last he came to the ravine where the main part of Beaumont's force was temporarily camped. It is probable that the soldiers in the camp had no idea who he was in the first moments, but reacted instinctively as a screaming, quite berserk horseman erupted in their midst. One man thrust a lance under Cesare's armpit, badly wounding him and tumbling him from his horse. He fought on against an unknown number of men until at last he was killed. A rescue force was now pouring out of the city and, hurriedly, the men in the ravine began to withdraw, taking Cesare's armor with them. As they were retreating they encountered his squire, who had ridden out to search for his master, and showed him the armor. He burst into tears, saying that it was indeed the armor of the duke and, satisfied, they released him and continued on to safety. By now the sun had risen, and those who came out of the city found Cesare's corpse easily enough, naked and covered with twenty-three dreadful wounds.

The testimony as to what happened during that twenty minutes or so between Cesare's exit from the city and death in the ravine was inevitably confused, for that testimony was mostly the accounts of men who had been fighting a figure that was already legendary. But piecing together the evidence provided by the actual killers, by those who had seen Cesare ride out of the city, and by those he had pursued, it appeared to many that Cesare Borgia, late duke of Valentinois, late duke of the Romagna, late captain-general of the Roman Church, had, in effect, committed suicide. Never before had this cold, collected young man been known to scream and curse as he rode into battle. Never before had this superb horseman ever lost control of his mount. Never before had this brilliant general ever committed the elementary error of letting himself be cut off from all lines of support. It may have been that his reason went awry momentarily; that the shame of being outwitted and surprised by an inferior enemy, falling atop all he had experienced during the past four years, culminating with the vicious rejection of Louis of France—released the Spanish bloodlust and so provided a way out of an intolerable situation.

Cesare was buried in Viana in the church of Santa Maria. An epitaph was composed that managed to distill, in part, a truth about its subject:

> *Here, buried in a little earth, lies one who held the world in fear, one who held peace and war in his hands. Oh, you that go in search of things deserving praise, if you would praise the worthiest, then let your journey end here nor trouble to go further.*

But his legend survived and grew, at last disturbing his bones for, two centuries later, the bishop of Calahorra, offended that such a man should lie in such a place, ordered the epitaph destroyed and the bones removed from the church and buried under the road outside.

In Italy the Borgia family survived the catastrophic events that destroyed Cesare but now, without his dynamism, it began to slide into respectable obscurity. The younger brother Joffre remained in Naples; ironically, the flighty Sancia, who had caused so much trouble in Rome, proved barren, and it was through a second wife that Joffre obtained an heir to his modest estates. The mother of the family, Vannozza Catanei, passed her remaining years fighting for her property in the law courts and amassing heavenly credit through pious works. She became something of a tourist attraction in Rome, but conducted herself with immense respectability and in her will left her considerable property to the Church. Giulia Farnese not only survived the loss of her protector, Alexander, but even managed to marry her daughter by him to the nephew of his bitterest enemy, Pope Julius II. In this matter, certainly, Julius was an excellent disciple of Machiavelli's, judging an action solely on the grounds of its expediency.

Lucrezia, too, survived. She had twelve more years remaining, time in which she would provide the last, ironic twist to the legend of her family. The news of her father's death prostrated her, not least because her husband and his family took little trouble to conceal their delight. Her grief was so great that, later, she confided to a friend that she thought she was dying. She dressed in complete black, dressed all her ladies in black, turned her private room into a black, hushed cavern. Pietro Bembo, the sprightly young Venetian poet who was first her admirer and then her lover, left a poignant description of her condition at that time.

> I called upon Your Majesty yesterday partly for the purpose of telling you how great was my grief on account of your loss, and partly to try and console you, for I knew that you were suffering a measureless sorrow. I was able to do neither, for as soon as I saw you in that dark room, in your black gown, lying weeping, I was so overcome by my feelings that I stood still, unable to speak, not knowing what to say. Therefore I departed, completely overcome by the sad sight, mumbling and speechless as you noticed—or might have noticed.[91]

The shock of her father's death was followed not long after by the even more shattering news of the ignominious reversal of her invincible brother's fortunes. Suddenly, the

Borgia family were in very real danger. She in Ferrara and Joffre in Naples were safe enough but scattered throughout Italy—and in Rome particularly—were blood relatives of the clan, who were likely to fall victim to the rage for vengeance against all Borgia. Apart from Cesare on his Roman sickbed, there was her own child, Rodrigo, as well as the mysterious little boy Giovanni in whom she displayed such curious interest. There were also her illegitimate half-brother—Alexander's last child—as well as two of Cesare's bastards, a girl and a boy. Lucrezia did what she could for the defenseless children, arranging their refuge in neutral areas. And under pressure of necessity she became a politician and a military organizer. She knew only too well that neither her husband nor her father-in-law would lift a finger to help Cesare merely because he was her brother; but she was shrewd enough to see that the Este would prefer even the Borgia as neighbors rather than the Venetians who would flood into the Romagna vacuum. Out of her own allowance she financed a troop of one thousand mercenaries, the money intended for perfumes, silks, and fine wines hastily gathered together and used to equip horsemen, crossbowmen and infantry. One of her brother's ex-companions, Pedro Ramirez, was given command. Lucrezia may not have known it at the time but the first opposition he would have encountered were the troops led by Giovanni Sforza, her ex-husband, intent upon reconquering his city of Pesaro. But the clash never occurred. Ramirez was marching toward the Romagna when news came that Cesare had been shipped to Spain, and the now pointless opposition collapsed. Yet she did not give up hope. How could she for whom Cesare had always been the very symbol of triumph? She made use of her father-in-law's ambassadors at the court of France to plead Cesare's cause and received back fair enough words from King Louis. But privately he wrote to Este, telling him not to make so much fuss about a priest's bastard. Finally, it seemed as though her wholly irrational faith in that splendid brother was justified when she heard of his escape. The person who brought her the news was one of Cesare's companions who had accompanied him during that incredible escape across Spain. The man was a priest and his news earned him a lifetime of pampered idleness at the court of Ferrara—that, at least, was what Lucrezia intended for him. But her in-laws thought otherwise and made their own plans.

After Cesare's escape, after that miraculous deliverance, the news of his death came like a ghastly shock in a nightmare. She said nothing at the time but retired immediately to her room, dismissing her attendants and all through that night the awed women heard her repeating, again and again as though in some magical incantation that would roll back the fact of death, the name of her brother.

Afterward there was nothing to be done by, or for the Borgia. Old Duke Ercole died and Lucrezia became duchess of Ferrara. Her husband, the duke, made sure she remained in a more or less continuous state of pregnancy so he could remain with his artillery and whores. He treated her correctly, coldly and gave no overt indication that he was aware of the passionate love affair with Pietro Bembo that filled her life after death had darkened it. Death seemed to move not far from her skirts during these middle years of her Este marriage. The priest who was her special protégé was hacked down by unknown hands; so, too, was Ercole Strozzi, the poet who had praised her and her clan

Why? Perhaps, it was whispered, because he had acted as go-between for Bembo and Lucrezia.

> Ercole Strozzi to whom was given Death
> Because he wrote about Lucrezia Borgia

Such was the couplet whispered widely, and the grimly smiling duke of Ferrara did not trouble to track its source and punish the impious originator.

Her son by her beloved second husband, Alfonso of Bisceglie, also died, to her immense grief. Five of her children by the duke of Ferrara hastened from the cradle to the grave. But two survived and one ascended the ducal throne; so that it was only in Ferrara, and under another name, that some of Alexander's dynastic hopes were fulfilled in Italy. It was in Spain and through the implacable Maria Enriquez of Gandia, the murdered Juan's widow, that the house of Borgia continued in its own right, surviving until the eighteenth century and, incidentally, giving a saint to the Church. The fourth duke of Gandia, better known as St. Francis Borja—he was canonized in 1671—was also the great-grandson of Pope Alexander VI.

Lucrezia died in 1518 in childbirth, shortly before her fortieth birthday. In the last few years of her life, when all else had been eroded, her lovers and her husbands and her family drifting into the past or legend, she turned to religion, not with the ostentation of her mother but with a quiet, deep conviction, nowhere better expressed than in the letter she wrote Pope Leo X a few hours before her death. She knew she was dying and begged his high blessing on her passing—a passing which, she said, she yearned for as a tired person yearns for bed.

In France, Cesare's wife Charlotte retired to a convent and survived her husband by only seven years, dying while still a young woman. Their daughter Louise was twice married, the second time into the Bourbon family, but made no particular mark of her own. The two natural children of Cesare were raised in Ferrara under their Aunt Lucrezia's protection. The girl eventually became an abbess; the boy disappeared—to turn up nearly fifty years later in Paris, asking the king for aid on the grounds that his father Cesare had served France well. They gave the Borgia one hundred ducats and sent him away.

Bibliography

Acton, Lord, "The Borgias and their latest historian." *Historical Essays and Studies.* London, 1907.

Alvisi, E., *Cesare Borgia, duca di Romagna. Notizie e documenti.* Imola, 1878.

Archivio della R. Societa Romana di Storia Patria (ASRP). Rome, 1876.

Archivio Storico Lombardo (ASL). Milan, 1874 seq.

Antonelli, G., *Lucrezia Borgia in Ferrara.* Ferrara, 1897.

Bellonci, Maria, *The Life and Times of Lucrezia Borgia,* trans. by Bernard Wall. London, 1953.

Bernardi, A., *Cronache Forlivesi . . . dal 1476 al 1517;* G. Mazzatinti, ed. Bologna, 1895.

Beuf, C., *Cesare Borgia, the Machiavellian Prince.* Toronto, 1942.

Bisticci, Vespasiano da, *Lives of Illustrious Men of the 15th Century,* trans. by William George and Emily Waters. London, 1926.

Branca Tedallini, Sebastiano di, "Diario Romano dal Maggio 1485 al 6 Giugno 1524." *Rerum Italicarum Scriptores* N.S. XXIII, 1907.

Breisach, Ernst, *Caterina Sforza, a Renaissance Virago.* London, 1967.

Brezzi, P., "La politica di Callisto III: equilibrio italiano e difesa dell Europa all meta del secolo XV." *Studi romani*, VII, 1959.

Burchard, John, *Diarium 1483–1506*, L. Thuasne, ed. 3 vols. Paris, 1883. The period 1483–1492 translated with notes and appendices by A.H. Matthew, London, 1910. Selection relative to the Borgia trans. by Geoffrey Parker *At the court of the Borgia*, London, 1963.

Cartwright, Julia, *Isabella d'Este, Marchioness of Mantua 1474–1539.* 2 vols. London, 1903.

Catalano, M., *Lucrezia Borgia, duchessa di Ferrara.* Ferrara, 1920.

Cellini, B., *Autobiography,* trans. by J.A. Symonds. London, 1896.

Comines, Philip de, *Historical memoirs.* London, 1817.

Conti, Sigismondo dei, *Le Storie de suoi tempi dal 1475 al 1510.* 2 vols. Rome, 1883.

Corio, B., *Storia di Milano.* 3 vols. Milan, 1855–57.

D'Auton, Jean, *Chroniques de Louis XII.* 4 vols. Paris, 1889.

Delaborde, H.F., *L'Expedition de Charles VIII en Italie: Histoire diplomatique et militaire.* Paris, 1888.

De Roo, P., *Materials for a History of Pope Alexander VI, His Relatives and His Times.* Bruges, 1924.

Ehrle, F., and Stevenson, H., *Les Fresques du Pinturrichio dans les Salles Borgia au Vatican.* Rome, 1898.

Fabroni, A.L., *Laurentii Medicei Magnifici vita.* Pisa, 1784.

Feliciangeli, B., *Un episodio nel nepotismo borgiano: il matrimonio di Lucrezia Borgia con Giovanni Sforza.* Turin, 1901.

Firnus, Michaelis, *Historia nova Alexandri VI ab Innocenti VIII obitu.* Rome, 1493.

Ferrua, A., "Ritrovamento dell epitaffio di Vannozza Catteaneo. *ASRP*, lxxi, 1948.

Gandini, L.A., "Lucrezia Borgia nell'imminenza delle sue nozze con Alfonso d'Este." *AMR*, 1920.

Garnett, R., "Contemporary poems on Caesar Borgia." *English Historical Review*, Vol. 1, 1886.

———"A Laureate of Caesar Borgia." Ibid., 1902.

Gaspare da Verona, "Le vite di Paolo II." *Rerum Italicarum Scriptores*, XVI.

Giustinian, A., *Dispacci*, Pasquale Villari, ed. 3 vols. Florence, 1886.

Gregorovius, Ferdinand, *History of the City of Rome in the Middle Ages*, trans. by Annie Hamilton. Vols. VII–VIII. London, 1909.

———*Lucretia Borgia: According to Original Documents and Correspondence of Her Day*, trans. by John Leslie Garnet. London, 1903.

Guicciardini, Francesco, *The history of Italy*, trans. by Austin Parke Goddard. London, 1763.

Infessura, Stefano, *Diario della citta di Roma*. Rome, 1890.

Jacopo dal Volterra, "Diario romano 1479–1484," E. Carusi, ed. *Rerum Italicarum Scriptores*, N.S. xxiii, Pt. iii.

Leonetti, A., "Papa Alessandro VI." secondo documenti e carteggi del tempo. Bologna, 1880. *Lerreve di Principi*. Venice, 1562.

Luzio, A., "Isabella d'Este e i Borgia. *Archivio storico lombardo*, xli–xliii, 1914–15.

Machiavelli, Niccolo, *The History of Florence and the Affairs of Italy, The Prince, Murder of Vitellozzo*. London, Bohn Library, 1847.

———, *Opera*, vols. 3 & 4, *Le legazioni e commissarie*, L. Passerini, and G. Milanesi, eds. Rome, 1875.

———*The Discourses*, trans. by L.J. Walker. London, 1950.

Mallett, Michael, *The Borgias: The Rise and Fall of a Renaissance Dynasty*. London, 1969.

Matarozzo, F., "Cronaca della citta di Perugia dal 1492 al 1503," A. Fabretti, ed. *Archivio storico italiano*, xvi, 1851.

Mathew, A.H., *Life and Times of Rodrigo Borgia, Pope Alexander VI*. London, 1912.

Menotti, M., *Documenti inediti sulla famiglia e la corte di Alessandro VI.* Rome, 1917.

Miron, E.L., *Duchesse Derelict: A Study of the Life and Times of Charlotte d'Albret.* London, n.d.

Müntz, E., *Les arts à la cour des papes pendant le XVe et XVIe siècle.* Paris, 1878.

Negri, P., "La missione di Pandolfo Collenuccio a Papa Alessandro VI (1494–98)." *ASRP,* XXXIII, 1916.

Paschini, P., *Roma nel Rinascimento.* Bologna, 1946.

Pastor, Ludwig, *The history of the Popes from the close of the Middle Ages,* Frederick Ignatius Antrobus, ed. Vol. 2, Vols. 5–6. London, 1891, 1898.

Pepe, G., *La politica dei Borgia.* Naples, 1946.

Pius II (Aeneas Sylvius Piccolomini), *The Commentaries,* abridgement trans. by Florence A. Gragg. London, 1960.

Picotti, G.B., *Nuovi studi e documenti intorno a Papa Alessandro.* Rome, 1951.

Priuli, G., "I Diari." *Rerum Italicarum Scriptores,* XXIV, 3, Città di Castello, 1921–41.

Raynaldus, *Annales ecclesiastici.* Lucca, 1738 seq.

Rerum Italicarum Scriptores. Milan 1723–51. New series, Città ₫ Castello, 1900 seq.

Ricci, Corrado, *Pintoricchio: His Life, Work and Time,* trans ence Simmonds. London, 1902.

Rodocanachi. E., *Le Chateau Saint-Ange.* Paris, 1₵

Sacerdote, G., *La vita di Cesare Borgia.* Milan

Sanuto, Marino, *I Diarii.* Venice, 1879 se₵

———, *La spedizione di Carlo VIII in Italia.* Ven...e, 1873.

Saxl, F., *The Appartamento Borgia* (Lectures). London, 1957.

Schulz, J., "Pinturrichio and the Revival of Antiquity." *Journal of the Warburg Courtauld Institute,* XXV, 1962.

Soranzo, G., *Studi intorno a Papa Alessandro VI.* Milan, 1950.

Notes

1 Vespasiano, p. 134.
2 Piccolomini, Chapter 4, p. 132.
3 Ibid., p. 135.
4 Raynaldus, An. 1460, p. 31.
5 Piccolomini, Chapter 4, p. 141.
6 The whole letter in Pastor,
   Volume V, pp. 366–367.
7 Sigismondo, Volume II, p. 53.
8 Guasti, p. 475.
9 Fabronius, Volume II, pp.
   308–312.
10 Machiavelli, Op. III, p. 21.
11 Jacopo, p. 130.
12 Sigismondo, Volume II, p. 45.
13 Burchard (Matthews translation),
   App., ii.
14 Ibid.
15 Pastor, Volume V, 237.
16 Burchard, op. cit., App. 5.
17 Guicciardini, Volume I, Chapter
   III.
18 Ibid.
19 Corio, Chapter I, pp. 464–466.
20 Quoted in Gregorovius, *Lucretia*,
   p. 29.
21 Brognolo's despatch in Pastor,
   Volume V, Doc. 18.
22 *Lettere*, 31.
23 Quoted in Villari, Volume II,
   pp. 165–66.
24 Gherardi, pp. 183, 194.
25 Cellini, p. 93.
26 Quoted in Antonelli, p. 160.
27 Cellini, p. 199.
28 Burchard, An. 1488.
29 Ibid., An. 1503.
30 Pastor, Volume V, p. 233.
31 Quoted in Gregorovius, *Lucretia*,
   p. 57.
32 Antonelli, p. 34.
33 Despatch quoted in
   Gregorovius, *Lucrezia*, p. 89.
34 Burchard (Matthews translation),
   App. 5.

35 *Lettere*, 33.
36 Corio, Volume VII, Chapter I, p. 458.
37 Comines, Chapter IV, p. 323.
38 Ibid., p. 330.
39 Guicciardini, Volume I, Chapter II.
40 Despatch in Gregorovius, *Lucretia*, p. 89.
41 Comines, Chapter V, p. 339.
42 Ibid., p. 342.
43 Brown, Volume I, p. 74.
44 Sanuto, Volume I, p. 988.
45 Ibid., p. 859.
46 Quoted in Miron, p. 132.
47 Machiavelli, Op. III, p. 143.
48 Sanuto, Volume I, p. 876.
49 Giustinian, Volume II, pp. 29–30.
50 Machiavelli, Op. IV, p. 201.
51 Giustinian, Volume I, p. 232.
52 Cf. Lucas's despatch quoted in Gregorovius, *Lucretia*, p. 137.
53 Sanuto, Volume II, p. 330.
54 Ibid.
55 Pastor, Volume, p. 349.
56 Machiavelli, Op. II, p. 132.
57 Ibid.
58 Ibid., p. 154.
59 Burchard, An. 1501.
60 Ercole's letter in Gregorovius, *Lucrezia*, p. 120.
61 Despatch in ibid., 210.
62 Despatch in ibid., 250.
63 Ibid., p. 279.
64 Quoted in Gregorovius, *Lucretia*, p. 80.
65 *Lettere*, p. 143.
66 Ibid., p. 229.
67 Quoted in Gregorovius, *Lucretia*, p. 87.
68 Machiavelli, Op. III, p. 273.
69 *Lettere*, p. 84.
70 Machiavelli, Op. IV, p. 15.
71 Ibid., p. 25.
72 Ibid., p. 30.
73 Ibid., p. 35.
74 Giustinian, Volume II, p. 46.
75 Ibid., p. 50.
76 Ibid., Volume I, p. 31.
77 Guicciardini, Volume II, p. 34.
78 Machiavelli, Op. IV, p. 39.
79 Giustinian, Volume II, p. 33.
80 Ibid., p. 38.
81 Machiavelli, Op. IV, pp. 58ff.
82 Sanuto, Volume X, p. 73.
83 Giustinian, Volume II, p. 65.
84 Sanuto, Volume IV, p. 330.
85 Giustinian, Volume II, App. Doc. 15.
86 Ibid., Doc. II.
87 Quoted in Gregorovius, *Lucretia*, p. 235.
88 Prescott, p. 340, n. 3.
89 Zurita, p. 230.
90 Ibid., p. 241.
91 Quoted in Gregorovius, *Lucretia*, p. 116.

Index

Alain, Cardinal (Avignon), 6, 8

Albanese, Tomaso, 219–220

Albret, Alain d', 179–180

Albret, Charlotte d', 179–182, 320–321, 322, 331

Albret, Jean d', 320–322

Alfonso I, King of Naples (V of Aragon), xvii, xviii, xxix, 112, 113

Alfonso II, King of Naples, 111, 112, 114, 115–118, 123, 126, 129, 137, 138–139

Allegre, Yves d', 133

Alexander VI, Pope, 20, 48–91; and Cesare (French dukedom), 162–185; and Cesare (rise of), 142–161 passim; and Cesare (Romagna), 187, 192, 195–204 passim, 231, 239–246 passim, 275, 276, 288–292; and children, 92–118 passim; death of, 267, 292–298, 321, 323, 327; descendants of, 330; and French invasion, 124–141 passim; and Lucrezia, 205, 207, 208–209, 219–224 passim, 247–264 passim; mistresses of (see: Catanei, Vannozza; Farnese, Giulia). See also Borgia, Rodrigo

Alversa, Gaspare d', 101, 102–103, 212

Amboise, Georges d', 279

Angevin dynasty (France), 111, 116, 182–183

Anne of Brittany, 161, 173–174

Apostles, The (Pinturicchio), 76

Aragon: and Castile, 18–21; and Naples, xvii, 111–113, 242 (see also Naples). See also: Carlotta of Aragon; Ferdinand, King

Aragona, Alfonso d', Duke of Bisceglie, viii, 112, 158–159, 184, 204, 218–225, 247, 249, 250, 267, 308, 330

Aragona, Isabella d', 112, 119, 122–124, 131

Aragona, Rodrigo Borgia d', viii, 204, 250–251, 301, 328, 330

Aragona, Sancia d', viii, 111, 115, 116, 117–118, 124, 153–154, 156, 157–158, 184, 207, 218–224 passim, 295, 311, 326

Arignano, Domenico d', 33, 34, 96, 164

Arrezzo (Romagnol city), xi, 274, 277–278

Artillery (weapons), 230–232, 257, 323

Augustus (Roman Emperor), xiii

Auton, d' (Frenchman), 244

Baglioni family (Perugia), 281, 290
Bajacet, Sultan, 88, 107, 108
Barbo, Pietro, 6, 13, 16. *See also* Paul II, Pope
Battistina (Innocent VIII's granddaughter), 103–104
Beaumont, Don Juan, 323–325
Bedding ceremony, 106
Behaim, Lorenz, 27
Bellingere, Ettore, 249–250
Bembo, Pietro, 327, 329–330
Beneimbene, Camillo, 27, 32–33, 104
Benevente, Count of (Spain), 315, 318
Bentivogli family (Bologna), 280
Bentivoglio, Giovanni, 322
Bernaldez (Spanish chronicler), 108–109
Bessarion, Cardinal (Greece), 5
Bisticci, Vespasiano da, xxii–xxiii
Boccaccio, Andrea, 97–98, 104–106, 109
Bologna (Romagnol city), 192, 194, 240, 274, 280
Borgia, Alonso, xvi–xx, 313. *See also* Calixtus III, Pope
Borgia, Angela, 263
Borgia, Cesare, viii, 33, 37–39, 40, 67, 69, 79, 91, 93–98, 100, 101, 106–107, 115, 117, 128, 129, 135, 138; children of, 182, 321, 328, 331; death of, 270, 323–326, 329; fall of, 297–331; and French dukedom, 162–185; illnesses of (*see:* Malaria; Syphilis); and Lucrezia, 209–211, 216–225 passim, 247–264 passim; marriage of, 179–182 (*see also* Albret, Charlotte d'); rise of, 142–161; and Romagna, 184–185, 186–204, 226–246, 265–296 (*see also* Romagna)
Borgia, Cardinal Francesco, 62, 182
Borgia, Gerolama, viii, 36–37, 95
Borgia, Isabella (Alexander VI's daughter), viii, 36–37, 95
Borgia, Isabella (Alexander VI's mother), xxiv
Borgia, Joffre, viii, 33, 34, 37–39, 40, 79, 98, 111, 112, 115, 116–118, 124, 153–154, 155, 157, 158, 162, 184, 207, 218, 219, 300, 311, 326, 328; wife of (*see* Aragona, Sancia d')

Borgia, Juan, viii, 33, 37–39, 40, 69, 79, 96, 97, 98, 103, 106–111, 116–117, 142, 143–144, 146–147, 163, 166, 199, 209; murder of, 147–157, 160, 162, 167, 176, 178, 184, 210, 214–215, 221, 222, 295–296, 310; son of (*see* Borgia, Juan II); wife of (*see* Enriquez, Maria)
Borgia, Juan II, viii, 146, 155, 156, 330
Borgia, Juan/Giovanni (Lucrezia's illegitimate son), 215–217, 243, 301, 328
Borgia, Louise, viii, 182, 321, 331
Borgia, Lucrezia, viii, 33, 35, 37–39, 40, 78–79, 90–91, 98–106, 109, 111, 112, 115, 124, 153, 158, 162, 184, 204, 205–225, 233, 236, 243, 272, 293, 294, 322, 327–331; children of, 330 (*see also:* Aragona, Rodrigo Borgia d'; Borgia, Juan); and Ferrara, 246, 247–264, 313–314, 317, 330; husbands of (*see:* Aragona, Alfonso d'; Este, Alfonso d'; Sforza, Giovanni); incest legend and, 206, 213, 249, 294–296
Borgia, Luis, 6
Borgia, Pedro (Alexander VI's brother), xxiv–xxix passim
Borgia, Pedro (Alexander VI's son), viii, 36–37, 95, 108
Borgia, Rodrigo, xxiv–xxx, 6–9; as Vice-Chancellor, 9–21 passim, 23–47 passim. *See also* Alexander VI, Pope
Borgia, Rodrigo (son of Alexander VI), viii, 328
Borgia-Lanzo, Cardinal Juan, 147–148, 292
Borgia/Orsini, Laura, viii, 42, 99, 217, 243, 327
Borja, St. Francis, 330
Bourbon family (France), 331
Brandolini, Raffaele, 223
Briçonnet (Charles VIII's adviser), 126, 137, 138
Brotherhood of Prayer and Death, xiii–xiv
Burchard, Johannes, 50–51, 87–91, 103–104, 106, 115, 117–118, 134–135, 136–137, 145–146, 148, 149,

150, 165–166, 197, 202, 208, 215, 222–223, 239, 243, 244–245, 254, 294

Calandrini, Cardinal (Bologna), 6, 7
Calderon, Pedro, 214, 215
Calixtus III, Pope, xx–xxx, 3, 9, 10, 16, 17, 29, 39, 62, 76, 255, 256. *See also* Borgia, Alonso
Campo, Niugno del, 312
Canale, Carlo, 35, 107
Canale, Ottaviano, 33, 34
Cappello, Paolo, 215, 220–221, 222, 225
Capua (Romagnol city), 244–245, 270, 296
Cardinals, College of, xvii, xix–xx, 3–9, 29–30, 46, 47, 50–54, 126–127, 198, 298–300, 302–303
Carlotta of Aragon (princess of Naples), 158–161, 163, 173–175, 176, 218, 243
Castel Sant' Angelo, 45, 80, 81–86, 128–129, 135–136, 176, 189, 197, 239, 268, 288, 301, 304
Castile: and Aragon, 18–21. *See also:* Isabella, Queen of Spain; Juana the Mad
Castro, Giovanni di, 64–65
Catanei, Vannozza, viii, 33–39, 40, 41, 96, 98, 103–104, 107, 111, 128, 136, 147, 148, 153, 217, 300, 326–327, 330; children of (*see:* Borgia—Cesare, Juan, Joffre, *and* Lucrezia; Canale, Ottaviano)
Catherine of Alexandria, St. (Disputation of), 77–79, 80
Cellini, Benvenuto, 75, 85
Cesena (Romagnol city), 265–266, 267, 268, 284–285, 309, 310
Charles VIII, King of France, 116, 124–126, 129–141 passim, 143, 144, 161, 167, 242. *See also* France
Cibo, Battista, 46–47. *See also* Innocent VIII, Pope
Cloaca Maxima (Rome), 23
Collenuccio, Pandolfo, 201, 234–236, 237
Colonna, Prosper, 311
Colonna family (Rome), xiv, 6, 242–

243, 246, 270, 272, 299, 301
Columbus, Christopher, 202
Comines, Philip de, 121, 125–126, 136, 138, 139–140, 161
Condottieri (mercenary leaders), 28, 182; and Cesare (in Romagna), 231–232, 240, 270–272, 273–274, 279, 280–290, 307
Constantinople, Turkish conquest of (1453), xx
Cordoba, Gonzalo de, 144–146, 229, 243–244, 297, 310, 311–312, 313, 314, 315–316, 322
Corella, Michelotto, 223–224, 267, 282, 286, 297, 298, 307, 308, 321
Corio, Bernadino, 53, 56–57, 58
Corneto, Cardinal Adriano, 293
Corpus Christi pageants, 11
Croce, Giorgio di, 35
Crusades: Calixtus III and, xxi, xxii, xxiii, xxviii; financing of, 66; Pius II and, 11; Sixtus IV and, 18

Dante Alighieri, xxvi
Diocletian (Roman Emperor), 35, 147
Doria family (Rome), xii

England: and Crusade (last), as nation-state, xvi
Enriquez, King (Castile), 18–21
Enriquez, Maria, 108–111, 156–157, 176, 310, 315, 330
Este, Alfonso d', viii, 112, 232, 246, 247–264 passim, 327, 328, 329–330
Este, Beatrice d', 112, 121–122, 123, 258
Este, Ercole d', 112, 114, 248–264 passim, 328–329
Este, Ferrante d', 252, 253–254, 258
Este, Cardinal Ippolito d', 258
Este, Isabella d', 112, 252–253, 257–263, 275, 276
Este family (Ferrara), 191, 234, 246, 256, 321–322
Estouteville, Cardinal (Rouen), 6–9, 12, 24, 32

Fabrizio (citizen of Capua), 245
Faenza (Romagnol city), 237–240, 243, 301, 305

Fano (Romagnol city), 235
Farnese, Cardinal Alessandro, 40, 129, 132, 136
Farnese, Angelo, 105
Farnese, Giulia, viii, 39–42, 80, 90, 91, 98–100, 103, 104, 105, 129, 132–134, 135, 136, 217, 219, 327; daughter of (*see* Borgia/Orsini, Laura)
Federigo (Cesare's secretary), 322
Federigo, King of Naples, 112, 147, 155–156, 158–160, 242–244
Ferdinand, King of Spain, 92, 93, 108–109, 114, 137, 144–146, 164, 178, 310, 312, 314–317, 322; marriage of, 18–21; and Naples, 241–242, 243–244 (*see also* Naples—Spain vs.). *See also:* Cordoba, Gonzalo de; Spain
Fermo, Oliverotto da, 281, 286–288
Ferno, Michael, 57–58
Ferrante, King of Naples, 54–55, 92–93, 111, 112, 113–115, 122, 123, 124, 139
Ferrantino, King of Naples, 112, 139, 141, 146–147, 158
Ferrara (duchy): Lucrezia and, 246, 247–264, 313, 314, 317, 330; and Romagna, 232, 234, 236, 246. *See also* Este family
Ferrari (datary), 72–73
Feudalism, xiii, 185
Florence (city-state), xi–xii, xiv, xvi, 23, 65, 119, 190, 192, 232; Cesare and, 274, 277–279, 281–283, 288, 289; and French invasion, 132; and Romagna, 190, 191, 240–241, 306, 317; slavery in, 26
Forli (Romagnol city), 31, 86, 187, 188, 189, 190, 192, 193–196, 219, 233, 237, 240, 305, 310, 313. *See also* Sforza, Caterina (of Forli)
Fornovo, battle of, 141, 142
Foscari, Marco, 123
Fossato (Romagnol city), 233
Fracostoro, Girolamo, 202
France, xvi; Angevin dynasty of, 111, 116, 182–183; Cesare's dukedom in, 162–185, ·322–323; and Florence, 132, 306; invasions of Italy, 115–117, 119–141 passim, 218, 227–228, 230; and Milan (*see* Milan); and Na-

ples (*see* Naples); and Romagna, 191, 193, 240, 241–242, 243; vs. Spain, 278–279, 290, 309, 322. *See also:* Charles VIII; Louis XII
Franciscan order, 30

Gaetani family (Rome), 246
Garcia (Cesare's personal envoy), 180–181
Garigliano, battle of, 309
Gaspar (chamberlain), 72–73
Genoa (city), xii, 23
Germany, and last Crusade, xxi
Giorgio (witness to Juan Borgia's murder), 149–150
Giorgione (painter), 201
Giovio, Palo, 119
Giustinian, Antonio, 290, 291, 292, 298–299, 300, 308
Gonzaga, Francesco, 114
Gonzaga family (Mantua), 191, 248. *See also* Este, Isabella d' (marchesa of Mantua)
Grammante, Bernardo, 238
Granada, Spanish conquest of, 15
Guicciardini, Francesco, 50, 54, 129, 201, 202, 294–296, 230, 239, 244
Gutteri, Bernard, 91
Guzman (Cesare's jailer in Spain), 314–315

Hadrian (Roman Emperor), 81–82
Henry VIII, King of England, 316
Holy Angel Castle. *See* Castel Sant' Angelo

Imola (Romagnol city), 31, 186, 187, 188, 190, 192–193, 231, 310
Incest legend. *See* Borgia, Lucrezia—incest legend and
Index (papal), 70
Infessura (Roman chronicler), 53, 89
Innocent VIII, Pope, 16, 17, 47, 53, 57, 73, 87, 88, 89, 90, 103, 114. *See also* Cibo, Battista
Isabella, Queen of Spain, 93, 108–109, 137, 144–146, 164, 176, 178, 243–244, 310, 311–312, 315–316; marriage of, 18–21. *See also* Spain
Isidore, Cardinal (Russia), 5

Islam, x, xvi, 119; leaders of *(see:* Bajacet; Mahomet II). *See also* Crusades

Italian city-states, ix–xvi; "warfare" between, 28, 183, 227, 244, 273. *See also:* Florence; Milan; Naples; Rome; Venice

Jacopo of Volterra, 32
Jews, papacy and, 66
Joan of Arc, 171
Juana the Mad, Queen of Spain, 178, 315, 316–317, 318–319, 320
Jubilees, 66–67
Julius II, Pope, 44, 87, 303–310, 312, 313, 317, 321, 327. *See also* Rovere, Giuliano della

Leo X, Pope, 330
Letterati (learned men), 26
Lorqua, Ramiro de, 235, 267–268, 284–285
Louis XII, King of France, 121, 125, 160, 161, 163–175 passim, 177, 179, 180, 181, 182–183, 184, 185, 218, 297, 299; and Cesare, 291–292, 321, 322–323, 326, 329; and Florence, 274, 278; and Naples, 240–243, 245, 247–248, 309; and Romagna, 191, 192, 193, 195, 204, 271, 276, 279–280, 281, 283. *See also* France

Machiavelli, Niccolo, 169–170, 199, 201, 227, 239–240, 241, 271, 273, 277, 278, 281, 282–283, 284, 286–288, 289, 295–296, 298, 300, 302, 304, 305–308, 327
Mahomet II, Sultan, xx
Malaria, 292–293, 298, 308
Malatesta family (Rimini), 28, 236–237, 280
Manfredi, Astorre, 237–240, 270, 296
Mangone, Garcia de, 318
Mantua. *See* Gonzaga family
Maximinius (Roman Emperor), 77–78
Medici, Giovanni de', 29, 190
Medici, Giuliano, 31
Medici, Lorenzo de', xiv, 29, 31, 45, 46
Medici family (Florence), xii, 68
Mila, Pedro de, 105. *See also* Orsini, Adriana da Mila

Milan (city-state), ix–x, xi, xvi, 119, 192; France vs., 182–183, 185, 218, 241, 246, 269, 280, 322; and Naples, 114–115; and Romagna, 190, 191, 193. *See also* Sforza family
Mirafonte, Gonzalo de, 313
Moles, Cardinal (Spain), 46
Monreale, Cardinal (Spain), 106
Montefeltro, Guidobaldo, 152, 233–234, 274–277, 281, 284, 288, 308
Montefeltro family (Urbino), 28
"Moro, Il." *See* Sforza, Ludovico
Mussolini, Benito, 13

Naples (city-state), xii–xiv, xvi, xvii, 47, 119; Cesare and, 242–246, 273, 309–313; France vs., 119–144 passim, 174, 177, 182–183, 204, 218, 228, 241–242, 247–248, 278, 290, 323 *(see also:* Charles VIII; Louis XII); papacy and, xvii, xxix, 55, 111–118; Spain and, 309, 316. *See also:* Alfonso II; Federigo; Ferrante; *and* Ferrantino
Nardini, Stefano, 24
Nation-states, xvi, xxi. *See also:* France; Spain
Navarre (kingdom), 320–322, 323
Nepotism, xxiii–xxv, 6, 9, 10, 37, 62
Nero (Roman Emperor), 23, 29, 58
New World, Portugal vs. Spain in, 70
Nicholas V, Pope, xviii, xix, xxii, 6, 29, 83
Nobility, xiv–xv; Alexander VI and, 143–145

Orsini, Adriana da Mila, 39, 40, 42, 98–99, 103, 105, 132–133, 263
Orsini, Clarice, xii
Orsini, Francesco, 272, 281, 286–289
Orsini, Niccolo, 57
Orsini, Orsina, 263
Orsini, Orsino, 39–42, 132, 135
Orsini, Paolo, 272, 281, 283, 286–289
Orsini, Virginio, 135
Orsini family (Rome), xxviii, xxix, 14, 39, 40, 45, 83, 135, 217–218, 299; Borgia vs., 143–144, 152, 154, 272, 275, 280, 300–301; Cardinals from, 6, 91, 281, 288

Oviedo, Pedro d', 309

Palazzo Venezia, 13
Pandolfini, Francesco, 312–313
Pantiselia (Lucrezia's maid), 215
Papacy: income of, 63–68; organization of (under Alexander VI), 59–68. *See also:* Castel Sant' Angelo; Cardinals, Sacred College of; Nepotism; Papal States; Popes; Schism; Simony; Vatican Palace
Papal States, papacy and, xxiii, xxvi, 13, 61, 65, 66, 101. *See also* Romagna
Paul II, Pope, 16, 17. *See also* Barbo, Pietro
Pesaro (Romagnol city-state), 234–236, 251, 283–284, 301, 328. *See also* Sforza, Giovanni
Petrucci, Pandolpho, 281, 289, 290
Piccolomini, Aeneas Silvius, 4–9, 30, 50, 52. *See also* Pius II, Pope
Piccolomini, Francesco (Pius III), 299–300
Pinturicchio (painter), 74–80, 83, 86, 87, 143
Pinzone, Sebastione, 267
Piombino (Romagnol city), 241, 243, 269
Pisa (city), Florence vs., xi, 232
Pius II, Pope, 9–14, 16, 17, 29, 30, 36, 64, 299. *See also* Piccolomini, Aeneas Silvius
Pius III, Pope (Francesco Piccolomini), 299–300
Podocatharo, Ludovico, 27
Poison, legend of, 268, 293, 294
Popes. *See:* Alexander VI; Calixtus III; Innocent VIII; Julius II; Leo X; Nicholas V; Paul II; Pius II; Pius III; Sixtus IV. *See also* Papacy
Portugal: and last Crusade, xxi; vs. Spain (New World), 70
Prisciano (Ferrarese pedant), 261
Pucci, Lorenzo, 99–100

Ramirez, Pedro, 328
Raphael (painter), 200
Renaissance, xviii; art of, 75, 77 (*see also* Pinturicchio); Cesare and, 268–269; and College of Cardinals, 29–30; in

Milan, 119, 120–121; palaces of (Rome), 12–15, 23–24; in Rome, 303; in Venice, x–xi; Urbino and, 277
Requesnez, Jaime de, 314, 322
Ressurection (Pinturicchio), 76
Riario, Caterina, 44–45
Riario, Girolamo, 30, 31, 43, 44–45, 128, 188–189
Riario, Piero, 23, 24, 30–31, 43
Rimini (Romagnol city), 301, 305. *See also* Malatesta family
Romagna: Cesare and, 184–185, 186–204, 226–246, 300, 301, 304–309, 311, 317, 323, 328. *See also* Papal States
Roman Empire, fall of, xiii, 273
Rome (city-state), xiii–xvi, 119, 192; barons of (*see* Nobility); Cardinals from, 12–13; Cesare in control of, 198–201; changes in (under Sixtus IV), 22–30; in French invasion, 132–138, 144, 176; and papacy, xiii, xv, 61–62; and Renaissance, 303 (*see also* Renaissance—palaces of); slavery in, 25–26
Rovere, Domenico della, 23
Rovere, Giuliano della, 43–44, 45, 46–47, 52, 60, 80, 126–131, 135, 167–168, 175, 276, 299, 301–303. *See also* Julius II, Pope

Sanazzaro, Jacopo, 205–206
San Gallo, Antonio, 83–86
Sanseverino, Robert, 89
Sanuto (Venetian observer), 221
Saraceni, Gerardo, 249–250, 251
Savelli family (Rome), 243, 246
Savonarola, Girolamo, 71–72
Schism, xiii, xv, xvii–xviii, 64
Seven Arts, The (Pinturicchio), 76
Seven Joyful Mysteries of the Virgin, The (Pinturicchio), 75–76
Sforza, Cardinal Ascanio, 14–15, 51, 52–53, 57, 61, 95, 106, 107, 108, 131, 137, 148, 152, 176–177, 178, 183, 204, 206, 218–219, 299, 302
Sforza, Caterina (of Forli), 31, 185, 187–197 passim, 199, 206, 237, 239–240

Sforza, Duke Galeazzo Maria (Milan), 188

Sforza, Gian Galeazzo, 112, 119, 120, 122, 123, 131

Sforza, Giovanni, viii, 100, 102, 104, 106, 124, 152, 196, 206–207, 211–214, 217, 234, 236, 249, 251–252, 284, 328

Sforza, Ludovico, 14, 102, 112, 114, 115, 119–124, 126, 127, 129, 131, 132, 134, 141, 178, 183, 206, 211–212, 213; fall of, 182, 188, 269; and Romagna, 194–195, 196, 204

Sforza family (Milan), x, 28, 100, 152, 182, 211

Sibylls, The (Pinturicchio), 76

Simony: Alexander VI and, 51–54, 63, 130–131, 137; Julius II and, 302

Sinigaglia (Romagnol city), 284–288, 290

Sistine Chapel, 73

Sixtus IV, Pope, 16, 17–18, 22, 23, 24, 30–31, 42–43, 44, 46, 73, 83, 95, 188

Slavery, revival of, 25–26

Soderini, Francesco, 277–278

Spain: Cesare's exile in, 313–320, 329; and Crusade (last), xxi; vs. France, 278–279, 309, 322; and Naples *(see* Naples); vs. Portugal (New World), 70; unification of, xvi, 18–21. *See also:* Cordoba, Gonzalo de; Ferdinand, King; Isabella, Queen

Sperulo, Francesco, 231

Strozzi, Ercole, 329–330

Syphilis, 201–203, 236, 257, 291, 298

Tolfa mines, discovery of, 64–65, 66

Torella, Caspare, 202

Urbino (Romagnol duchy), 274–277, 281, 283, 301, 308. *See also* Montefeltro family

Varano, Julius Cesare, 279–280

Vasari, Giorgio, 80

Vatican Library, xxii–xxiii, xviii

Vatican Palace, xviii, xxii, 73–80. *See also* Castel Sant' Angelo

Vega, Garcilaso de la, 144, 164, 176, 178

Venice (city-state), x–xi, xvi, 23, 26, 119; Cesare and, 246, 283, 292, 301; and Romagna, 191, 194, 301, 305–306, 317, 328

Veroba, Gaspare da, xxv

Vers, Stephen de, 126, 129

Vespucci (Florentine ambassador), 44, 45, 46

Vice-chancellorship, office of, 61–62

Villeneuve, Monsieur de, 164–165

Vinci, Leonardo da, 121, 269–270

Visconti dynasty (Milan), 183

Vitelli, Paolo, 232, 272, 290

Vitelli, Vitellozzo, 231–232, 233–234, 272, 273–274, 277–279, 281, 285–288, 290

Wars of the Roses (England), xvi

Xenophobia (Roman), vs. Spaniards, xxvi–xxvii

Zeno, Cardinal, 103